Distribution in the United States of America by
W.W. Norton & Company, Inc., 500 Fifth Avenue, New York, NY 10110, USA
Tel: 800-233-4830; Fax: 800-458-6515
World Wide Web: www.wwnorton.com

Library of Congress Catalog Card Number has been requested.
ISBN: 962-217-694-1

Grateful acknowledgment is made to the following authors and publishers:
Alfred A Knopf, Inc and Brook Hersey for *A Single Pebble* by John Hersey © 1989, 1984, 1956
First Vintage Books; Houghton Mifflin Co, Aitken, Stone & Wylie Ltd and Michael Russell Ltd for
Sailing Through China by Paul Theroux © 1984, 1983; Jonathan Cape Ltd for *Birdless Summer* by
Han Suyin © 1968; Penguin for *Poems of the Late T'ang* translated by A C Graham © 1985; Foreign
Language Press, Beijing for *Mao, Swimming in the Yangzi*.

Managing Editor: Helen Northey
Maps: Au Yeung Chui Kwai and Tom Le Bas
Cover Concept: Aubrey Tse
Pin Yin Translations: Luo Li Ju

Front and back cover photography: Wong How Man
Photography/illustrations courtesy of Magnus Bartlett 20; Kevin Bishop 105, 118, 130–131, 134,
139, 150, 151, 177; Hong Kong China Tourism Photo Library 36, 68, 73, 180; William Lindesay
13 (bottom); Tom Nebbia 76–77, 126–127; R Wada 45; Wattis Fine Art 167; Wong How Man 1,
8–9, 13 (top), 17, 28, 57, 61, 64, 101, 114 ; Sydney Wong 37; sketches by Bobby Chan 27; Teresa
Coleman Fine Arts Ltd. 97, 109; La Grande Artère de La Chine: Le Yangtseu, Joseph Dautremer 79;
GEOPIC™ images © Earth Satellite Corporation 52–53, 184–185; GEOCARTO™ image © 2001
Geocarto/Airphoto International Ltd. 80–81

Production by Twin Age Ltd, Hong Kong
Manufactured in China

(Previous page) *Near the source of the Yangzi River at over 5,000 metres (16,400 feet), high on the*
Qinghai-Tibetan plateau

THE
YANGZI RIVER
AND THE THREE GORGES

Judy Bonavia
Revised by William Hurst and Eric N. Danielson

4

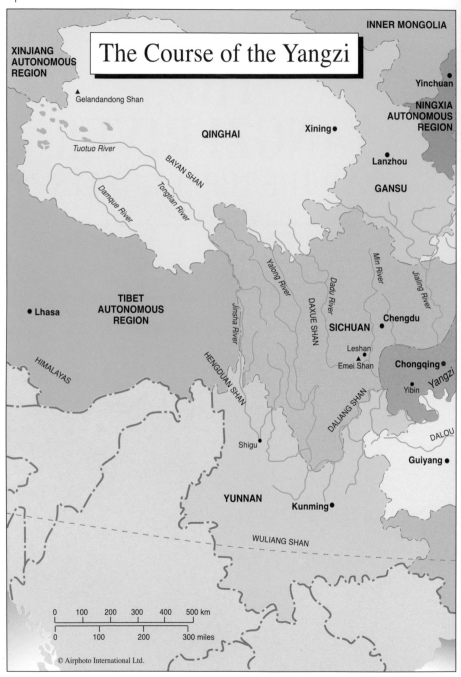

The Course of the Yangzi

INNER MONGOLIA

XINJIANG AUTONOMOUS REGION

Yinchuan

▲ Gelandandong Shan

NINGXIA AUTONOMOUS REGION

QINGHAI

Xining

Tuotuo River

Lanzhou

GANSU

BAYAN SHAN

Damque River

Tongtian River

Yalong River

Dadu River

Min River

Jialing River

TIBET AUTONOMOUS REGION

Lhasa

Jinsha River

DAXUE SHAN

SICHUAN

Chengdu

Leshan

HIMALAYAS

HENGDUAN SHAN

Emei Shan ▲

Chongqing

Yibin

Yangzi

DALIANG SHAN

DALOU

Shigu

Guiyang

YUNNAN

Kunming

WULIANG SHAN

| 0 | 100 | 200 | 300 | 400 | 500 km |

| 0 | 100 | 200 | 300 miles |

© Airphoto International Ltd.

5

Contents

The River's Source

From the bitter cold and treeless alps of Upper Qinghai, around the source of the Yangzi, the snow that gradually melts in the summer sun trickles down the beds of ancient glaciers, and finally reaches the pastures where man and beast can survive. The snowmelt forms small streams which sing through the tilted plateaus and nourish the grassroots and the hardy little flowers and plants that the local Tibetan people use as medicine for a variety of ills.

The streams flow more swiftly down the lower Qinghai mountains, which give an impression of Central Europe. On successive steps of mountain and plateau, the people of the Yushu Tibetan Autonomous District cultivate barley and shelter the herds in winter, sending them up to the high pastures only in spring. Their diet consists of meat, milk (fresh and fermented), and barley-meal, which is the staple. Sometimes they add sugar brought from distant parts of China. And in the forest belts they cut timber for the construction of new towns.

The ubiquitous yak is the most useful beast, but sheep are reared for meat and wool and there are some goats. The tough, shaggy little ponies of the mountains are used as a means of transport, and mares' milk is a treasured delicacy and cure-all.

Animal husbandry is the main occupation of these Tibetans and they continue to lead a semi-nomadic life, living in thick black yak-hair tents lined with bags of precious barley, and surrounded by their grazing flocks. For several days each spring the people gather together to sing, dance, hold horse races and tugs of war, before again returning to their lives of isolation.

The streams turn to sizeable rivers as they come down to the 3,000-metre (10,000-foot) level or thereabouts. Typically they flow blue and wide across valley floors where the barley is now fairly abundant and small villages—decorated with the inevitable Buddhist prayer flags—take the place of tent encampments. Despite their deep poverty, the women dress gaily in black and a rainbow of decorative colours, plaiting their hair almost like Africans, and wearing it in braids, sometimes interwoven with red cord. To commemorate special religious festivals, pilgrimages are made to monasteries (often many days' riding away) for they are social as well as religious occasions.

The wildlife is abundant—Tibetan antelopes, Mongolian gazelles, snow leopards, otters, martens, lynxes and deer, as well as dozens of species of birds. Carp throng the cold waters of the lakes. Nature reserves are being established to protect the beautiful and threatened snow leopard and the primeval forests in which the wild ass and the snow cock still roam.

(previous pages) At over 5,000 metres (16,400 feet) sheep graze near the tongue of one of the glaciers whose meltwaters feed the upper Tuotuohe in western Qinghai Province on the border with Tibet. For several years this river was considered to be the source of the Yangzi

Getting There

The Three Gorges, which lie between Chongqing and Yichang, are the most popular destination for tourists.

Chongqing, one of the Muncipalities directly answerable to Beijing, is the normal starting point for the downriver Yangzi cruises. Boat departures are normally early in the morning so it is usually necessary to spend the night in Chongqing. The journey through the Three Gorges to Yichang and on downstream to Wuhan takes three-and-a-half days, while the upriver journey, from Wuhan to Chongqing, takes four-and-a-half days. Following the completion of the *San Xia Ba* (Three Gorges Dam), and as a portion of the river becomes more lake-like up to 2009, upstream speeds are likely to increase, and downstream ones to slow slightly. Night navigation will become possible in formerly dangerous reaches, and may lead to the re-scheduling of boats other than those specifically for tourists. Check timings carefully to make sure you pass through the Three Gorges in daylight hours.

SCHEDULED PASSENGER BOATS

Regular passenger boats (*ban chuan*) travel all the way to Shanghai. However, it should be noted that most of these boats terminate at either Yichang or Wuhan, and it is therefore necessary to book onward passages at these stops. There are ticket offices at the piers. Depending on the type of boat and its schedule, the 1,125-kilometre (700-mile) journey between Wuhan and Shanghai may take up to four days upstream and three days downstream.

There are daily sailings of these scheduled passenger boats in both directions from Wuhan, Nanjing and Shanghai. They serve all the Yangzi towns and indeed, for many of these towns, the boats are the only viable means of long-distance transport, since the ports are not all connected by motorable roads. Fares vary with the distance travelled.

■ SCHEDULED SERVICES, WUHAN–CHONGQING–WUHAN

Going upstream from Wuhan, not only are there more ports of call, but the journey takes about 100 hours (four nights on board) compared with 57 hours (two nights on board) going downstream. Not every sailing makes the same stops, but the timetable includes a regular daily service on this run. Additional daily sailings make scheduled stops at towns not included in the regular downstream schedule.

Conditions on different steamers also vary; the East is Red Shipping Company may have updated its name to Golden Line, but it has scarcely modernized the rustier vessels in its fleet. Most of them, though, have four classes of accommodation starting with second class (there is no first class). Second class consists of two-berth cabins furnished with bedding, a desk, two chairs and a wash basin. On some boats there is also a communal sitting room for viewing. Third class provides ten-person accommodation in two-tiered bunks; fourth class is similar, with bunks for twelve or more persons; in fifth class passengers are packed into masses of three-tiered bunks.

At mealtimes an insistent loudspeaker system announces sittings in the steamer's huge and chaotic dining room. You need to buy a meal ticket in advance. Bottled soft drinks and snacks (biscuits, nuts and so on) are sold in the vicinity of the dining room. On some ships a separate dining room for second-class passengers makes feeding less of a fight, but it is always a good idea to bring some of your own food. There is an unceasing supply of hot boiled water, trickling in a mud-laden stream, from a tap somewhere on board.

Tickets for this portion may be bought through branches of China International Travel Service and China Travel Service in Chongqing and Wuhan (for addresses, see pages 187 and 197) or direct from Chaotianmen docks (opposite Wharf 2) in Chongqing and the Yangzi Passenger Terminal (80 Yanjiang Dadao) in Hankou, Wuhan. They are sold up to four days in advance of the sailing.

CRUISE BOATS

A more luxurious way of seeing the Three Gorges is to book on one of the many cruise ships catering mainly to foreign tour groups. Most sail the stretch to and from Chongqing–Yichang, or as far as Wuhan. Several de luxe cruise lines offer longer trips, some as long as nine nights, sailing from Shanghai to Chongqing, for instance. The boats operate from the beginning of April to October or November. Fitted out with private bathrooms for each cabin, air-conditioning, observation decks, gift shops and bars, these ships offer arranged excursions on shore and other entertainments during the cruise.

Many international travel companies run China tours which include a Yangzi River cruise on one of these de luxe ships, including Abercrombie and Kent and Victoria Cruises, who have long been famous for de luxe cruises on the river. China Travel Service runs a week-long tour from Chongqing to Wuhan, which begins and ends in Hong Kong (for addresses see pages 186–7). Bookings for all Yangzi cruises should be made well in advance, particularly for September and October, which is the peak tourist season. Although most people take these cruises as part of a group tour, it is also possible to buy individual tickets for the cruise only.

GETTING TO CHONGQING

■ BY AIR

Chongqing has an international airport. Charter services operate from Germany. It is usually cheaper to fly from Shenzhen, Guangzhou or Zhuhai than to fly from Hong Kong directly. There are domestic flights from all major cities in China.

■ BY RAIL

The rapid expansion and modernization of the Chinese railway network has yet to make much difference to services to Chongqing. Trains south and west to Kunming,

(above) *The Yangzi is navigable from Shanghai to Xinshezhen in Sichuan—a distance of over 3,000 kilometres (1,860 miles). Yangzi captains must keep a constant vigil and consider the Great River far more hazardous than mere ocean navigation*
(below) *Sailing junk in Sichuan (see Special Topic and sketches on pages 24–27)*

or south and east to Guangzhou pass on a single track line which is a miracle of engineering through spectacular mountain scenery and remote and impoverished areas. From Beijing's West Station it's a double overnight journey, and from Guangzhou about 11 hours.

■ BY ROAD

With China's rapidly explanding network of highways, travel by road must seriously be considered as an alternative to air and rail. In the past journeys of short distance took many hours of uncomfortable travel and they can now take one-third of that time in an excellent AC vehicle.

GETTING TO YICHANG

■ BY AIR

Yichang has air services an average of three times a week from Beijing, Changsha, Chengdu, Chongqing, Enshi, Guangzhou, Huangshan (daily), Kunming, Nanjing, Qingdao, Shanghai, Shenzhen, Xi'an, Zhangjiajie and Zhengzhou.

■ BY RAIL

There are direct trains from various cities, including Wuhan, Xi'an, and Beijing, but many services require a change at the nearby junction of Yaqueling. From Wuhan long-distance buses and overnight sleeper buses may be more convenient.

GETTING TO WUHAN

■ BY AIR

China Southern Airlines flies three times a week from Fukuoka, and Air Macau has flights from Macau. There are scheduled services direct from Hong Kong, but there may be charter flights run by China Travel Air Service Hong Kong. There are domestic flights from major cities in China.

■ BY RAIL

Wuhan is on a fast north-south route between Kowloon and Beijing West Railway Station, with comfortable expresses leaving Hong Kong daily and arriving at Wuhan the next day. You may not use the Kowloon service when coming south from Beijing, but there are several other services each day, and there are direct trains to Wuhan from other major Chinese cities such as Chengdu, Xi'an, Tianjin, and Guilin.

Facts for the Traveller

Climate

The three large cities along the Yangzi River—Chongqing, Wuhan and Nanjing—are known traditionally as the 'three furnaces of China'. Between April and September, the temperature in the Yangzi River valley reaches 36°C (97°F) and above. Spring and autumn are therefore the best seasons for making the river cruises. However, with the tall mountains and gorges through which the river threads its path, precipitation is very high and the peaks are often shrouded in cloud and mist, although a light haze can enhance the beauty of the scenery. Summer rains are torrential; you may find thunderstorms dramatic if you are on board your boat but a nuisance should you be trying to sightsee ashore. The winters are short, cold and crisp. Late-summer travels will coincide with the high-water periods, when the river rises swiftly, almost perceptibly.

CHONGQING
AVERAGE TEMPERATURES

	Jan	Feb	Mar	Apr	May	Jun	Jul	Aug	Sep	Oct	Nov	Dec
°C	7	10	14.5	19.5	23	25.5	29	30	25	19	14	10.5
°F	44.6	50	58.1	67.1	73.4	77.9	84.2	86	77	66.2	57.2	50.9

AVERAGE RAINFALL

	Jan	Feb	Mar	Apr	May	Jun	Jul	Aug	Sep	Oct	Nov	Dec
mm.	15	20	38	99	142	180	142	122	150	112	48	20
in.	0.6	0.8	1.5	3.9	5.6	7.1	5.6	4.8	5.9	4.4	1.9	0.8

WUHAN
AVERAGE TEMPERATURES

	Jan	Feb	Mar	Apr	May	Jun	Jul	Aug	Sep	Oct	Nov	Dec
°C	2.7	5.2	10	16.2	21.1	26.1	29.1	28.4	23.9	17.6	11.4	5.5
°F	36.8	41.3	50	61.1	69.9	79.8	84.3	83.1	75	63.6	52.5	41.9

AVERAGE RAINFALL

	Jan	Feb	Mar	Apr	May	Jun	Jul	Aug	Sep	Oct	Nov	Dec
mm.	152	152	203	279	305	381	254	203	178	178	152	127
in.	6	6	8	11	12	15	10	8	7	7	6	5

Clothing

Light summer clothing is all that is required between April and September, with a woollen cardigan or warm jacket for the cool evenings on board. To combat the summer mugginess, travellers should wear cotton rather than synthetic fibres. Those who rise at dawn to watch the passage through the gorges may imitate the Chinese passengers who huddle in blankets supplied by the ship.

The Yangzi River towns are very informal indeed; wear comfortable everyday clothes when you visit them. Steep steps from the jetties to the towns require walking shoes, and since the streets turn to mud within minutes of a heavy rainfall, you may need an extra pair. Umbrellas can be bought cheaply almost anywhere. On board the more deluxe ships, however, many like to dress a little more formally for the last night of the cruise; therefore women may want to bring a smart outfit and men a jacket and tie.

Warm clothes are essential for the river journeys during seasons other than summer. The boats can be draughty and the wind piercing. However, clothing is one of the best bargains in China, with excellent down or quilt jackets available in many of the big towns and cities. Bring a pair of light hiking boots as the terrain can be hilly, rocky and muddy.

Visas

Everyone must get a visa to go to China, but this is usually a trouble-free process. Tourists travelling in a group are listed on a single group visa issued in advance to the travel agent involved. Their passports will not be individually stamped with the visa or on arrival and departure unless specifically requested.

Tourist visas for individual travellers can be obtained at Chinese embassies and consulates as well as from certain travel agents in your respective countries; from the Chinese Ministry of Foreign Affairs visa office in Hong Kong or through several Hong Kong travel agents including branches of CTS. The application procedure is quite routine; you simply fill in a form, supply one photograph and hand in a fee with your passport.

Visa fees vary considerably depending on the source of the visa and on the time taken to get it. In Hong Kong, for instance, you can get a single-entry or double-entry, three-month tourist visa within one working day if the application is handed in before 9 am. Multi-entry business visas are also available.

Money

CHINESE CURRENCY

Chinese currency is called Renminbi (meaning 'people's currency') and this is abbreviated to Rmb. It is denominated in *yuan*, referred to as *kuai* in everyday speech. The *yuan* is divided into 10 *jiao* (colloquially called *mao*). Each *jiao* is divided into 10 *fen*. There are large notes for 100, 50, 5, 2 and 1 *yuan*, small notes for 5, 2, and 1 *jiao*, and coins and notes for 5, 2, 1 *fen* and 1 *yuan*.

FOREIGN CURRENCY, TRAVELLER'S CHEQUES AND CREDIT CARDS

There is no limit to the amount of foreign currency you can take into China. Traveller's cheques are changed at a slighter better rate than cash. All major European, American and Japanese traveller's cheques are accepted by the Bank of China. International credit cards may be used to draw cash at larger branches (1200 *yuan* minimum, 4 per cent commission) and for payment in international hotels. In most other cases only cards issued in China are acceptable.

Leshan Buddha, Sichuan—the world's largest stone sculpture cut in the eighth century during the Tang dynasty

Tipping

The accepted standard for tipping in the West is rapidly becoming the norm in modern China. While it is not normally practised in local establishments, tipping would certainly be expected by local guides, drivers and waiters in places frequented by foreigners.

Bargaining

With the exception of stores with marked prices, always bargain in markets and shops. Even state-run stores will often give discounts on expensive items like carpets intended for tourists. Bargaining in China can be good-humoured or it can be infuriating; it is a game won by technique and strategy, not by anger or threats. Thus, it should be leisurely and friendly, and not be seen as a one-way process at all, since the Chinese enjoy it. Finally, it is bad manners to continue to bargain after a deal has been struck.

Communications

China's post-office system is rather slow but reliable. Every post office counter has a pot of glue, as low-denomination stamps do not have glue on the back.

International Direct Dialling is available everywhere, and even by satellite phone from the more luxurious cruise ships (although at huge expense). Long-distance calls within China are often clearer than local ones, and even fairly modest hotels have business centres with fax and (slow) Internet connections.

Local Time

Amazingly for a country measuring 3,220 kilometres (over 2,000 miles) from east to west, most of China operates from one time zone 8 hours ahead of GMT and 13 hours ahead of EST. From Urumqi to Kashgar, local people work to a 'local time' which is two hours behind Beijing. This time difference is 'unofficial' but determines transport timetables and other services in the region.

Packing Checklist

As well as bringing along any prescription medicines you may need, it is a good idea to pack a supply of common cold and stomach trouble remedies. While it is not necessary to pack toilet paper these days, it is advisable to take some with you when going out sightseeing, as public toilets do not provide it. Bring plenty of film and camera accessories, such as batteries and flashes. Although film is widely available, the right type may not always be obtainable at the right time. Comfortable, non-slip shoes are a must.

Health

There are no mandatory vaccination requirements, although there is a nominal health form to fill out on arrival. Make sure your basic immunisations are up to date: polio, diphtheria and tetanus. To check on the latest recommendations contact your nearest specialist travel clinic or tropical medicine hospital—family doctors are sometimes not entirely up to date. The need for the following vaccinations may vary according to time of year and part of China to be visited: meningococcal meningitis, cholera, hepatitis A and B, and Japanese B encephalitis. Malarial protection must be begun one week before entering the affected area, and continued for four weeks afterwards. Plan well ahead: it's unwise to take some of these inoculations together, and some require multiple shots spread over a three-month period or more. They can also be very expensive.

The Yangzi River: An Introduction

The mighty Yangzi, or *Changjiang*, is the third largest river in the world. (The Nile is the longest, followed by the Amazon.) At 6,300 kilometres (3,900 miles), the Yangzi is closest in length to the Mississippi. Among the Chinese, the name Yangzi is rarely used. They prefer *Changjiang*—simply, Long River.

This extensive waterway cuts through the heart of China, and is regarded by the Chinese as marking the division of their country into north and south, both geographically and culturally. The river rises in the far western part of China and flows through eight provinces before disgorging its waters into the Yellow Sea. Over 700 tributaries draining a further six provinces join the Yangzi along its course.

The Yangzi is divided into three parts:

The Upper Reaches from the source in Qinghai Province to Yichang in Hubei Province, a distance of some 4,400 kilometres (2,700 miles). This stretch is one of great beauty, with wild mountain ranges, unbroken ravines, unnavigable rapids and rushing torrents. The Three Gorges are included in this section, as is the Sichuan Basin.

The Middle Reaches from Yichang to Hukou at the mouth of Poyang Lake in Jiangxi Province, a distance of about 1,000 kilometres (620 miles). Here, the river widens and flows through flat, low-lying land and and is fed by waters from two huge lakes, the Dongting and the Poyang. This is the region where the battle against flooding has been carried on for centuries; earthen dykes and paved embankments tell of past and present heroic struggles.

The Lower Reaches from Hukou to the estuary, a distance of some 900 kilometres (560 miles). The landscape in the river's lower course is typified by a flat delta plain crisscrossed by canals and waterways, with soil so rich and water so abundant that the region has been known for centuries as the 'Land of Fish and Rice'.

The wet season begins in April, bringing heavy rain in the middle and lower reaches. By July and August the wet weather reaches the Sichuan Basin where the prevalence of mountainous terrain causes widespread rainfall. Then, as the water level starts to subside, the 'Sichuan waters' begin to threaten again.

The rich Yangzi River Basin, according to current statistics, produces 40 per cent of the national grain (including 70 per cent of all paddy rice), one-third of the country's cotton, 48 per cent of its freshwater fish and 40 per cent of the total industrial output value. Its hydroelectric energy potential is almost boundless: Gezhou Dam at Yichang is one of the biggest low-water dams in the world and the Three Gorges Dam will be the world's largest hydroelectric project. One-third of China's 1.2 billion people live in this prosperous basin, which also boasts a rich cultural heritage.

Tiger Leaping Gorge on the upper reaches of the Yangzi River in Yunnan Province

One would imagine from the impressive statistics that the river would be choked with vessels of all descriptions, but this is not the case. Ocean-going ships do frequent the river from Wuhan down, but the traffic consists mainly of ferry boats, lighters, barges, tugs and logging rafts. Over the years, political instability had taken its toll on economic development, but it was the building of railways in the hinterland that really changed the life of the river. When rail freight proved to be cheaper than transportation along the Yangzi and its tributaries, the heyday of river transport was over.

Attempts are being made to revitalize the river transport system. Studies point out that it is cheaper to dredge than to build branch railways. Over three billion *yuan* of state investment has been fed into the Yangzi shipping industry over the last 40 years. When the Three Gorges Dam is completed in 2009, the watercourse through the Gorges will be deeper and safer, allowing larger vessels to sail to and from Chongqing.

Table of Distances Between Main Yangzi River Ports

Distances in kilometres (miles)

Chongqing	Chongqing										
Wanxian	327 (203)	Wanxian									
Fengjie	446 (277)	119 (74)	Fengjie								
Yichang	648 (403)	321 (200)	202 (126)	Yichang							
Shashi	815 (506)	488 (303)	369 (229)	167 (104)	Shashi						
Wuhan	1354 (841)	1027 (638)	908 (564)	706 (439)	539 (335)	Wuhan					
Jiujiang	1623 (1008)	1296 (805)	1177 (731)	975 (606)	806 (502)	269 (167)	Jiujiang				
Wuhu	1991 (1237)	1664 (1034)	1545 (960)	1343 (835)	1176 (731)	637 (396)	368 (229)	Wuhu			
Nanjing	2087 (1297)	1760 (1094)	1641 (1020)	1439 (894)	1272 (790)	733 (455)	464 (288)	96 (60)	Nanjing		
Zhenjiang	2174 (1351)	1847 (1148)	1728 (1074)	1526 (948)	1359 (844)	820 (510)	551 (342)	183 (114)	87 (54)	Zhenjiang	
Shanghai	2479 (1540)	2152 (1337)	2023 (1263)	1831 (1138)	1664 (1034)	1125 (699)	856 (532)	488 (303)	392 (244)	305 (190)	Shanghai

The Upper Reaches:
The Source to Yichang

The melting glaciers and snowfields of the rugged Tanggula Mountains in Qinghai Province form the headwaters of the Yangzi. It is only since 1976 that the river's true source, the 6,621-metre (21,700-foot) high Mount Geladandong, on the Qinghai-Tibet Plateau, has been conclusively explored and surveyed.

The source of this greatest of China's rivers had long been a geographical conundrum. The area is largely in permafrost, moraine-pitted and windswept; an inhospitable and discouraging environment for explorers. A treatise written in the Warring States period (480–221 BC) by geographer Yu Gong stated the source to be in the Mingshan Mountains of Sichuan Province. By the 16th century, explorers had named Jinsha River in Qinghai as the head stream. In the first half of the 18th century, an official Qing government expedition found its way to the Qinghai–Tibet Plateau; their reports were an impetus for further explorations. But it was only when the Changjiang Valley Planning Office sent forth a scientific investigative team in the mid-1970s that the source was finally ascertained.

As the snows melt in the short summer months, waters quietly trickle down to the foothills and flow through the marshes and lakes that form the plateau with its freshly verdant grassland. Among the many rivulets in this region, the Tuotuo River emerges as the main body of water, winding its way towards the Qinghai–Tibet Highway and eastwards, for a further 60 kilometres (37 miles), where it is joined by the Damqu River. At this point it becomes the broad upper reaches of the Tongtian River. This plateau abounds in wildlife: Tibetan antelope, wild yaks and asses, lynxes and geese.

The 813-kilometre (505-mile) Tongtian River, descending sharply, flows through the Yushu Tibetan Autonomous Region of Qinghai, where the flat lands are cultivated for highland barley or *qingke*—the Tibetan staple diet—and hill slopes provide grazing for the yak, sheep and white-lipped deer owned by Tibetan herdsmen whose dwellings are black, yak-wool tents. Below the Yushu region the river, navigable here only for short distances by skin coracle boats, becomes known as the Jinsha (Golden Sand) River and flows southwards, forming the border between Tibet and Sichuan on a 2,308-kilometre (1,434-mile) journey sweeping down into Yunnan Province and looping back up into Sichuan. On this southward sweep the Yangzi runs parallel to the upper reaches of the Mekong and Salween Rivers (both of which also rise in the high plateau of Tibet) and the eastern branch of the Irrawaddy. At Shigu (Stone Drum) in Yunnan, the river curves sharply north, actually flowing parallel to itself, separated by only 24 kilometres (15 miles). Here the river is wide in summer, but in winter, when the water level is low, the currents

Boats Great and Small   —by Judy Bonavia

The traditional Chinese boats that navigated the Yangzi were *sanpan* (meaning three planks), the larger-sized *wupan* (five planks) and junks. Their sails were tall to capture any welcome breeze, and stiffened by bamboo battens. The sculling oar, or *yulo*, was extremely long with normally four men working it. Mats overhead provided shelter for passengers; decks were covered with coils of bamboo rope. Local pilots were hired to negotiate the most difficult rapids. Their instructions were relayed to the harnessed trackers pulling the long hauling ropes—often far ahead of the boat—by a drum beaten at different rhythms. Large freight junks often required 300 or 400 trackers as well as groups of strong swimmers who would loosen the ropes should they snag on rocks along the way.

An eighth-century poem gives a compelling picture of the gruelling drudgery of a boat puller's life:

A Boatman's Song
Oh, it's hard to grow up at the way-station side!
The officials've set me to pullin' station boats;
Painful days are more, happy days are few,
Slippin' on water, walkin' on sand, lake birds of the sea;
Against the wind, upstream, a load of ten thousand bushels—
Ahead, the station's far away; behind, it's water everywhere!
Midnight on the dikes, there's snow and there's rain,
From up top our orders: you still have to go again!
Our clothes are wet and cold beneath our short rain cloaks,
Our hearts're broke, our feet're split, how can we stand the pain?
Till break of dawn we suffer, there's no one we can tell,
With one voice we trudge along, singing as we pull;
A thatch-roofed house, what's it worth,
When we can't get back to the place of our birth!
I would that this river turn to farm plots,
And long may we boatmen stop cursing our lots.
                     Wang Qian (768–833)

They were truly beasts of burden, as observed by an American, William L Hall, and his wife, who spent several weeks on a small Chinese cargo-boat in 1922:

If the boat happens to turn about when it is struck by a cross-current, a call from the pilot brings all the trackers to their knees or makes them dig their toes into the dirt. Another call makes them either claw the earth or catch their fingers over projecting stones. Then they stand perfectly still to hold the boat. When it is righted, another call makes them let up gradually and then begin again their hard pull.

Passengers usually took *kuaize*—large *wupan*—and paid for the Yichang–Chongqing trip 185 cash for every 100 *li* (18 cents for every 50 kilometres, or 30 miles). They would also supply wine for the crew, and incense and fireworks for a propitious journey. Going upriver, this journey used to take as long as 40–50 days in the high-water period and 30 days in low water, depending on the size of the boat, while the downriver trip could be completed in 5–12 days. At the end of the journey the passengers might buy some pork as a feast for the crew.

River life was varied along the Yangzi and its tributaries. Big junks, fitted out as theatres, sailed between the towns to give performances of Chinese opera or juggling. Some boats were built as hotels, offering accommodation to travellers arriving too late at night to enter the city gates. Others were floating restaurants and tea-houses, not to mention boats which were a source of livelihood as well as home to the numerous fisherfolk and their families.

Peasants along the lower and middle Yangzi first set eyes on foreign men-of-war and steamers when Britain's Lord Elgin journeyed as far as Wuhan (Han-kow) in 1842. Although the Chinese had in fact invented the paddle wheel (worked probably by the treadmill system) for driving their battleships as early as the eighth century, paddle boats were not widely used. In an incident on Dongting Lake in 1135, they were proved positively useless when the enemy threw straw matting on the water and brought the paddle wheels to a stop. They seem not to have been used since.

With the opening up of the Yangzi ports to foreign trade in the latter half of the 19th century, foreign shallow draught paddle steamers and Chinese junks worked side by side. But the traditional forms of river transport slowly became obsolete, and were confined to the Yangzi tributaries for transporting goods to the distribution centres.

Early Western shipping on the Shanghai–Wuhan stretch of the river was dominated by Americans, whose experience of paddle steamers on the Mississippi and other rivers had put them to the fore. The American firm of Russell and Company was the leading shipping and trading concern in those years. A fifth of the foreign trade was in opium shipped up to Wuhan. By the late 1860s, British companies such as Jardine & Matheson and Butterfield & Swire had successfully challenged the American supremacy. Accommodation on the companies' river boats was luxurious, and trade was brisk.

The Wuhan–Yichang stretch was pioneered by an English trader, Archibald Little, who established a regular passenger service in 1884 with his small steamer *Y-Ling*. In his book *Through the Yang-tse Gorges*, he described the bustling scene on the river:

The lively cry of the trackers rings in my ears, and will always be associated in my mind with the rapids of the Upper Yang-tse. This cry is 'Chor-Chor', said to mean 'Shang-chia', or 'Put your shoulder to it', 'it' being the line which is slung over the shoulder of each tracker, and attached to the quarter-mile-long tow-rope of plaited bamboo by a hitch, which can be instantaneously cast off and rehitched. The trackers mark time with this cry, swinging their arms to and fro at each short step, their bodies bent forward, so that their fingers almost touch the ground. . . Eighty or a hundred men make a tremendous noise at this work, almost drowning the roar of the rapids, and often half a dozen junks' crews are towing like this, one behind the other. From the solemn stillness of the gorge to the lively commotion of a rapid, the contrast is most striking.

Other companies soon followed, but none dared travel this route at night. Again, it was Archibald Little's perseverance that brought about steamship navigation through the gorges above Yichang to Chongqing. Acting as captain and engineer, he successfully navigated his 17-metre (55-foot) *Leechuan* up to Chongqing in 1898, though he still needed trackers to pull him over the worst rapids.

During the heyday of the Yangzi in the 1920s and 1930s, travel by steamer from Shanghai all the way up to Chongqing was luxurious though not entirely safe. Halfway, at Wuhan, passengers had to change to smaller boats for the rest of the journey.

After the establishment of the People's Republic of China, emphasis was placed on making the Yangzi safe for navigation all year round, and all the major obstructions were blown up. The Yangzi today is still a vital artery. Many river towns are almost entirely dependent on it for connecting them to each other. The regular ferries and boats, offering a range of accommodation, always overflow with passengers. There are also luxury cruise boats which normally ply the route from Chongqing to Wuhan or Yichang,. There are now more than 30 of these cruise boats, carrying from about 60 to over 200 passengers.

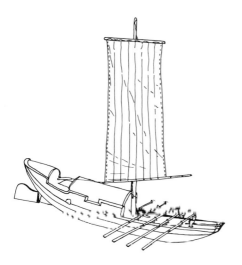

Laohuaqiu, *Sichuan's largest type of junk*

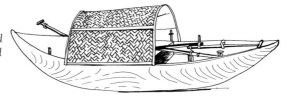

Type of crooked-stern junk (wai pigu), specially designed to negotiate sudden twists and turns in the river

Badong Xiao He huazi (*little river small boat*) *used on the shallow waters of the Little River, a Yangzi tributary upstream from Badong*

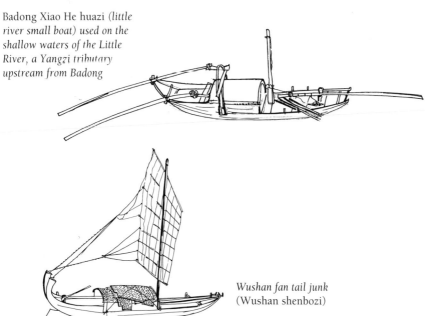

Wushan fan tail junk (Wushan shenbozi)

form sandbars that become the breeding grounds for many varieties of waterbirds. Further on the river again plunges south and east and eventually flows northwards towards Chongqing.

This southern region of the river is an area few Westerners have ever penetrated. In the second half of the 19th century, the British and French sought to establish back-door trade routes from their colonial possessions in Burma, Laos and Vietnam, through Yunnan and up to the navigable stretches of the Yangzi in Sichuan. Secret missions were sent into southwest China, as the British were anxious to study the feasibility of a railway link between Burma and Chongqing. It was these intrepid travellers (some of whom never lived to tell their tale) who recorded their encounters with the many tribal minority peoples inhabiting this area.

Western missionaries were a second source of information on customs and attitudes. But the first Westerner to explore and photograph the area extensively was an American, Joseph F Rock, leader of the National Geographic Society's Yunnan Province Expedition. His amazing black and white photographs, taken in the 1920s and developed by himself under the most difficult conditions, are, even today, outstanding.

Among the sloping forests of pine and spruce are alpine meadows of moss, blue gentians and white edelweiss bordered by hemlock and flowering rhododendron bushes. In the narrow valley floors live tribes of the Tibeto-Burmese ethnic group—the Lisu, Naxi, Lolo (also known as the Yi), Nu, Lahu, Xifan and Jing peoples. They have inhabited western Sichuan and northeast Yunnan since earliest times, cultivating barley, wheat, vegetables and indigo and keeping sheep or pigs. For the most part these people are Tibetan Buddhists, but some, like the Naxi, are animists whose priests, or *tombas*, practise exorcism in the pre-Buddhist tradition of the Bon sect of Tibet, others are simply shamanistic. They are brave hunters and warriors, who fought among themselves and against the Han Chinese for centuries. Until 1949, Buddhist kingdoms, such as the tiny kingdom of Muli, were ruled by reincarnated monk kings.

The Black Yi of Daliang Shan were landowners who kept their fellow tribesmen, the White Yi, as slaves. This practice was proscribed in 1956. The Yi—in their striking long thick black capes—were a constant headache to the Chinese administration, as they kidnapped officials and fomented rebellions. Their exploits were recorded as early as the first century BC by the great Chinese historian Sima Qian (*c.* 145–85 BC). Kublai Khan (1215–94), in an attempt to bring Burma under his sway, lost half his 500,000-man army to disease, exhaustion and tribal harassment in these mountains.

Though the great gorges of the Yangzi near Yichang are the most famous, there are even more spectacular gorges in the vicinity of Lijiang, where mountains rise more than 5,700 metres (18,700 feet) and canyons plunge 3,900 metres (12,800 feet), through which the water flows deeply, turbulently and treacherously. Access in this

Upper Yangzi River near Lijiang in Yunnan Province, just below Tiger Leaping Gorge.
The only access to this valley is via the narrow trackers' path cut into the cliff face on the right

region is still only by mountain pathways and cliff-hugging tracks. Single-rope bridges slung high above the water's surface are not uncommon; the rider is conveyed in a sling attached to a pulley which must be well greased with yak butter to avoid any build-up of friction.

The area is rich in mineral resources and timber. The 1,085-kilometre (675-mile) Chengdu–Kunming railway, which was constructed in the 1970s, has brought profound changes to this remote region.

From about the 27 degrees north parallel, the Yangzi, flowing north–northeast for some 800 kilometres (500 miles) and forming the borders of Sichuan and Yunnan, finally reaches the Sichuan or Red Basin. After Yibin, the river, now called the Changjiang, is joined by the Minjiang and Jialing Rivers from the north and the Wujiang from the south. Thus originates the name of Sichuan Province—'Four Rivers'. The 500-metre (1,640-foot) high Sichuan Basin, with its mild winters and long rainy season, has long been agriculturally rich; in the late Han dynasty, Chengdu (today's capital of Sichuan) was even bigger than the then capital of Luoyang. Sichuan has remained one of China's most important 'bread-baskets', producing cotton, hemp and silk as well as grain. On the large, flat Chengdu plain, the Minjiang was harnessed for irrigation as early as 250 BC by the Dujiangyan irrigation system, which has been the basis of the region's prosperity ever since.

Near the confluence of the Dadu and Min Rivers is the great sacred Buddhist mountain of Emei, studded with ancient temples. Not far distant, at **Leshan**, the river actually laps the stone feet of one of the world's largest carved Buddhas. The 70-metre (230-foot) high Tang-dynasty (618–907) statue took 90 years to complete.

The huge city of Chongqing stands at the confluence of the Jialing and the Yangzi. Below this city the river continues its progress through Sichuan, and on through the famous Yangzi Gorges into Hubei Province where, at Yichang, sharply checked by the Gezhou Ba (Dam), it enters the flat lands of its middle reaches.

Chongqing

The "Mountain City" of Chongqing clings to steep cliffs at the confluence of the Yangzi and a major tributary, the Jialing River. This bustling city rises high above docks held in the rushing currents by cables lashed to anchor holes cut into the rocky shore. Cable cars glide across to opposite banks and giant bridges carry creeping waves of trucks loaded with the city's varied industrial output. Caves perforate the steep hills, once built as bomb shelters and now busy as garages or naturally cool restaurants and hair salons.

For centuries the main commercial and transportation centre for Sichuan Province, Chongqing is now under rapid transformation due to the construction of the Three Gorges Dam. The city was granted national status in 1996 as a municipal region similar to Beijing, Shanghai and Tianjin with an administrative region that includes the eastern Sichuan counties downriver for a total population of some 30 million people. Chongqing is now proud to be the world's largest metropolitan region.

This area will bear the brunt and possible benefits of inundation by the world's largest dam that will displace over 1.3 million people. Chongqing is in the midst of vast reconstruction, demolishing many old neighbourhoods that had previously been bombed by the Japanese and reconstructed into the traditional ramshackle warrens laced with sandstone staircases. These squalid conditions gave close quarters to the city residents, who are known for their cheerful pleasure in sitting outside on cool summer nights. The folk cuisine of outdoor sidewalk dining is from *huo guo* or hot pots. These are basins filled with bubbling chili oil and *hua jiao*—flower pepper that causes the mouth to tingle, into which are dipped all kinds of meats and vegetables. Once the river boatmen's campfire meal of leftovers from the day's market, *huo guo* is now the local favourite, sometimes because opium pods are placed in the brew.

The traditional lifestyle of Chongqing is being transformed by giant shopping and residential construction complexes that all but eliminate the spicy street life into glitzy boutiques for the parade of newly flush consumers. The centre of town is the Jie Fang Bei—a modern tower built to memorialize the martyrs of the civil war—now covered with gaudy advertising. The city is plagued by the worst air pollution in China as industry and traffic jams spew toxins into the humid still air of this landlocked port. The dam project has initiated construction of massive new walls along the river shores with express highways on top to alleviate the thick crawl of traffic through town.

Hundreds of ships line the muddy banks below the remaining old city wall at Chao Tian Men—rusty ferries packed with commuters and barges heaped with goods plying the Three Gorges to the rest of China. Chongqing is the destination for most of the bulk transport that passes through the Gorges, which has been likened to an eyedropper that feeds the elephant of the most populous region of Sichuan. The port bustle is impressive and sweat-soaked. Thousands of porters known as the *bang bang jun*—the help army—line up with their bamboo poles and ropes to carry supplies up the staircases. These cheerful troops, some 200,000 on any given day, are farmers on leave from the season in the fields to earn cash in the city. Many also work on the construction sites, camping in the muddy disarray of the crowded city. Compared to the relatively clean and urbane cities of China's capital and coast, Chongqing is quite *tu*—earthy and real.

HISTORY OF CHONGQING

In the fourth century BC, Chongqing (then called Yuzhou) was the capital of the State of Ba, whose men were renowned for their prowess in battle and their military successes. In the Southern Song dynasty (1127–1279) the city's name was changed

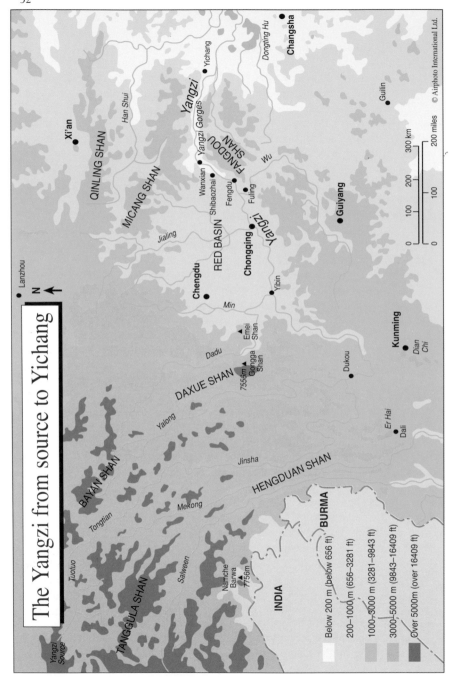

The Yangzi from source to Yichang

N

© Airphoto International Ltd.

	0 100 200 300 km
	0 100 200 miles

Below 200 m (below 656 ft)

200–1000 m (656–3281 ft)

1000–3000 m (3281–9843 ft)

3000–5000 m (9843–16409 ft)

Over 5000m (over 16409 ft)

Lanzhou

Xi'an

QINLING SHAN

MICANG SHAN

Han Shui

Yichang

Yangzi

Yangzi Gorges

FANGDOU SHAN

Wu

Dongting Hu

Changsha

Guilin

Wanxian

Shibaozhai

Fengdu

Fuling

Jialing

RED BASIN

Chongqing

Yangzi

Guiyang

Chengdu

Min

Yibin

Emei Shan

Dadu

7556m Gongga Shan

DAXUE SHAN

Yalong

Dukou

Kunming

Dian Chi

Er Hai

Dali

Jinsha

HENGDUAN SHAN

BAYAN SHAN

Mekong

Tongtian

BURMA

INDIA

Salween

Namche Barwa 756m

TANGGULA SHAN

Tuotuo

Yangzi Source

to Chongqing—meaning 'double celebration'—to mark the princedom and enthronement of Emperor Zhaodun in 1189. He was himself a native of the city.

Chongqing had always been an important port, bustling with junks from Sichuan's hinterlands and neighbouring provinces, and acting as the collection point for the abundant produce of the region, including hides and furs from Tibet, hemp, salt, silk, rhubarb, copper and iron. Under the Qifu Agreement of 1890, Chongqing was opened to foreign trade. This marked the beginning of the exciting history of steamboat navigation from Yichang through the treacherous gorges to Chongqing, a development aimed at opening up the riches of Sichuan to trade with the outside world. By the early part of this century, a massive trade in opium grown in southwest China had sprung up, abetted by warlord factionalism and greed.

Visitors to the city in the 1920s and '30s commented on its 30-metre (100-foot) high city wall, and the rough steps from the river up to the city gates 'dripping with slime from the endless procession of water carriers'. At that time, Chongqing, with a population of over 600,000, had no other water supply. Between 10,000 and 20,000 coolies carried water daily to shops and houses through the steep and narrow lanes of the city. All porterage was done by coolies as there were no wheeled vehicles in the city, only sedan chairs. The staircase streets are still there, but all that remains of the city wall today is the odd outcrop of masonry that props up a house here, or abuts a path there.

In 1939, during the Sino-Japanese War, the Nationalist Guomindang government of China moved the capital from Nanjing to Chongqing, and on the south bank of the Yangzi foreign delegations built substantial quarters, which can be seen from the river. The airstrip used then can still be seen on the Pinghu Sandbar as one crosses the Yangzi River Bridge. The Guomindang government headquarters is now the People's City Government Offices (only the gateway is left of that period), situated just opposite the **Renmin Hotel**.

During the Sino-Japanese War (1937–45), Chongqing's notorious foggy weather conditions probably saved the city from complete devastation, for only on clear days could the Japanese bombers, which flew over in 20-minute waves, succeed in accurately dropping their thousands of bombs.

WHAT TO SEE IN CHONGQING

Chongqing, always a trading city, was never noted for its cultural heritage or architecture. However, unlike most northern Chinese cities, Chongqing and other Yangzi River towns are very lively at night. On summer evenings residents stroll about in the hope of a refreshing breeze. Street markets, sidewalk restaurant stalls, herbalists and calligraphers can be found on Wuyi Lu and Bayi Lu. Informal Sichuanese opera can be heard at the **Workers' Park** on Saturday evenings.

The narrow streets near **Chaotianmen Docks** , flanked by clothes and noodle stalls, narrow streets, thread their way down to the harbour. At the waterfront, a busy panorama unfolds—steamers, tugboats, rows of pontoons, even a cable tramway to ease the ascent from shore to street. The **Jialing cable car** starts its journey from Cangbai Lu to Jinsha Jie on the north bank (Jiangbei). The five-minute ride is fun on a clear day. Another cable car, at Wanglongmen, spans the Yangzi to the south. The **Chongqing Zoo** has several pandas, which are native to Sichuan Province.

■ CHONGQING MUSEUM
Located at 72 Pipashan Zhengjie, it houses a good collection of earthenware figurines and brick reliefs from the Eastern Han period (AD 25–220). They came from tombs, most likely of wealthy and important men. As was the custom, the deceased were buried with objects recalling the preoccupations of everyday life—farming, hunting and entertainment. While Han tombs were elaborate affairs, the people of Ba, who roamed the plains of Sichuan 2,000 years ago, disposed of their dead in an even more singular fashion, encasing corpses in canoe-shaped wooden coffins and suspending them from cliffs along the river. Two of these huge coffins and the artefacts found inside them are on display here.

■ THE LUOHAN TEMPLE
This 19th-century temple is glimpsed through an ornate passage whose walls are encrusted with rock carvings in the manner of Buddhist grottoes. *Luohan* are Buddhist saints; they traditionally number 500, although in this temple there are actually 524 statues of them. They are of recent vintage, the last of the originals having been destroyed in the Cultural Revolution (1966–76). The present statues were made by the Sichuan Fine Arts Institute in 1985.

■ PAINTERS' VILLAGE (HUAJIA ZHI CUN)
Both Painters' Village and the Sichuan Fine Arts Institute, located in Hualongqiao, are often on tour-group itineraries. However, they are some way out of the city and difficult to reach by public transport. Both establishments maintain galleries and offer pieces for sale.

Painters' Village was established in the 1950s to nurture artists who would create paintings and lithographs to glorify the Revolution. These state-sponsored artists came from all over China and included members of minority nationalities. They are mostly elderly now and enjoy what, for China, are excellent conditions. They have their own studios and produce an impressive range of work. Since China embarked on economic reforms, however, they have had to become commercial, since the government no longer buys all their work.

■ SICHUAN FINE ARTS INSTITUTE (SICHUAN MEISHU XUEYUAN)
This is the only residential undergraduate- and graduate-level fine arts college in southwest China, with a student enrolment of around 300 a year. Students come

The Bombing of Chongqing

The bombing by the Japanese which began in 1939 continued in 1940 and in 1941 with increasing ferocity. As soon as the winter fogs lifted the planes came, and through the gruelling hot summer, until late in autumn, being bombed was part of the normal process of living. Our daily activities were geared to this predictable occurrence. One rose early, and since the nights were an inferno of heat and sweat, the rock exuding its day-stored heat, it was easy to wake when the sun rose, for dawn did not mean coolness, but another raging hot day. Quickly the fire was lit with sticks of wood and a fan to spurt the flame, water boiled for morning rice, and by nine o'clock the day's first meal (the before-the-bombing meal) had been consumed. The first alert then started. One went to the dugout, with some luggage in hand, kettle and iron pan (irreplaceable after 1940, as metal became almost non-existent); and there one spent the day. Sometimes the bombs fell very near and we came to know the peculiar whistling sound they made. At other times the drone was further away, and the explosions faint. Sometimes the bombers came over five or six times, on occasion up to twenty times a day. And once, in 1941, they continued without let for seven days and nights, and many people died, both in the bombings and also in the air-raid shelters, especially babies, from heat and exhaustion and diarrhoea.

The shelters were scooped-out tunnels in the rock, and since Chung-king was all rock, with juttings and small hollows and hillocks almost everywhere, the bowels of these promontories could easily be utilized. But some of the common shelters had been dug in softer earth, and were unsafe. They caved in after a while. There was no ventilation in them, and the people who sat deep inside, away from the one and only outlet, the mouth of the tunnel, became anoxic if the raid was prolonged. They started to thresh about, or to faint. In between the explosions, there was respite. While awaiting the next batch of bombs, everyone would come out of the dugout, sit round the mouth of the cave, fan, gulp the hot air; but this was almost as gruelling as sitting inside the dugout because there was hardly any shade, and if there was a single bush, it was monopolized in its thin narrow coolness by some police squad or some self-important official and his family.

Han Suyin, Birdless Summer, 1968

Chongqing at night

from all over China as well as from abroad. The college was founded in 1950, and has departments of sculpture, painting, crafts (including lacquerware, textile design, packaging design and ceramics) and teacher training. The institute is particularly proud of its gallery which displays the best work of its students. Many of the items are for sale. The institute is located at Huangjiaoping, on the northern bank of the Yangzi, about half-an-hour's drive from the centre of the city.

■ RENMIN HOTEL

Built as the administrative offices for southwest China in the early 1950s, it is now used as a hotel and venue for performances and meetings as it has an auditorium with seating for 4000. The architectural style is a combination of the Temple of Heaven and the Forbidden City. It is certainly the most spectacular building in Chongqing.

■ STILWELL MUSEUM

The museum, which was established in conjunction with the Stilwell Foundation in the USA and the Foreign Affairs Bureau in Chongqing, is dedicated to General Joseph Stilwell and the time he served as Commander-in-Chief of the American forces in the 'China-Burma-India theatre', between 1941 and 1945 when the threat of the Japanese Imperial Army was finally overcome. General Stilwell was instrumental in ridding Asia of that threat.

The museum is located at 33 Sixin Road in the actual house occupied by General Stilwell during the war. The house is a tribute to his daughters, Alison and Nancy, who devoted so much time and effort in bringing this project to fruition in 1992.

■ RED CRAG VILLAGE (HONGYAN CUN) AND GUI YUAN

Both these are now memorial museums to the 1949 revolutionary activities in the city. In the 1930s and '40s, during the period of co-operation between the Guomindang government and the Chinese Communist Party against the aggression of the Japanese, these buildings were the offices of the Communist Party and the Red Army. Mao Zedong stayed in Gui Yuan House during his brief stay in Chongqing in 1945.

Sights Around Chongqing

■ SOUTH MOUNTAINS PARK (NANSHAN GONGYUAN)

Situated on the southern side of the Yangzi, this park comprises a scenic group of five mountain peaks of between 400 and 600 metres (1,300 and 2,000 feet) high. On one of these, Yellow Hill (Huangshan), General Chiang Kai-shek, head of the Guomindang government, built his wartime residence. American, British, French and other allied powers also built ambassadorial residences, which are now used as guesthouses. The wife of the legendary founder of the Xia dynasty (2200–1800 BC) Emperor Dayu, was said to have lived on another peak, Yu Mountain, in 2200 BC. Dayu, who gained eternal fame for his diligence in harnessing the rivers of China, laboured for 13 years without once returning home. During that time he was said to have 'passed his house three times and never entered', so dedicated was he to his task.

Thousand-armed Guanyin, Dazu Buddhist Caves (see page 38)

■ NORTHERN HOT SPRINGS (BEI WENQUAN)

The Northern Hot Springs are some 50 km north of Chongqing, by the bank of the Jialing on Wentang Gorge. Historical records reveal that the Warm Spring Temple existed on this site 1,500 years ago, but the present temple dates from the Ming and Qing dynasties. The four halls rise up the hillside on a central axis. The Guanyin Hall, with iron tiles and stone pillars, is flanked on either side by natural springs. Lotus and fish ponds, ancient trees, bath-houses, restaurants and a guesthouse complete this scenic spot. A day's visit to the Northern Hot Springs may also include a visit to the **Beipei Natural History Museum** in which fossil remains of three dinosaurs are exhibited.

■ JINYUN MOUNTAIN

Located near the Northern Hot Springs, the mountain is 1,030 metres (3,380 feet) high and is also known as Little Emei Mountain. Tourists should begin their ascent at Jinyun Temple and climb the 680 steps to Lion's Peak where they may view the nine peaks of Jinyun. The area is a natural botanical garden with 1,700 species of plants and trees.

■ DAZU BUDDHIST CAVES

For tourists staying more than two days in Chongqing, it is possible to make a trip to see the spectacular Buddhist cave carvings of Dazu County.

'Dazu' can be translated in two ways: as 'Great Plenty' or more mundanely as 'Big Foot'. Locals say that the Buddha himself left a huge footprint in a nearby pond, and hence the name. The remoteness of the location has protected the caves and the painted sculptures are in excellent condition. Forty sites have been discovered, with 50,000 carvings in 290 niches and grottoes. Seven sites are open to the public, but those at **Beishan** and **Baodingshan** are the most frequently visited. The earliest sculptures date from the Tang dynasty (618–907), when the emperors Xuanzong (reigned 712–56) and Xizong (reigned 873–88) fled to Sichuan as civil war broke out in the north. With them came many monks, painters, sculptors and literati, who transformed Sichuan into a centre of culture. Bas-relief carvings of extraordinary grace and detail continued to be created up to the Ming dynasty (1368–1644). Figures and stories from the Buddhist pantheon dominate—a giant reclining Buddha, 31 metres (100 feet) long; a statue of Avalokiteshvara seated on a lotus flower, her 1,000 hands spread out over 88 square metres (950 square feet) of rock. An unusual feature here is the carving of scenes from everyday life executed with tender vividness. The most comfortable way to get to the caves is obviously to hire a car. Provided there is no major delay on the busy road, the return journey can be done hurriedly in one day. Allow for an overnight stay in Dazu and take the bus from Kangfulai Bus Company on Renmin Lu, about a ten-minute walk west from the Renmin Guesthouse. The 160-kilometre (100-mile) ride over hilly country can take up to three hours, but the bus is reasonably comfortable and air-conditioned.

At Dazu make for the Dazu Guesthouse or the Beishan Hotel, which cater to foreigners. There are two trains a day, but these take twice as long as the bus.

Note

The following descriptions of towns and historical sites have been retained in this issue of the Yangzi Guide because of their historical interest. However, in preparation for the rising waters of the Three Gorges Dam, major changes have already taken place in all the cities above the dam—between Chongqing and Yichang. The planned closure of the river, for the second phase of the dam construction, is scheduled for the end of 2002. Thereafter there will be a rapid rise in the river levels submerging many of the towns described in this Guide.

Fuling

The river Wu rises in Guizhou, and at its confluence with the Yangzi, stands the ancient town of Fuling on the south bank. Some 2,000 years ago Fuling was the political centre of the Kingdom of Ba (fourth to second centuries BC) and the site of its ancestral graves. Fuling is the connecting link in water transportation between northern Guizhou and eastern Sichuan. The town and its surrounding area are rich in such produce as grain, lacquer and tung oil, and the local specialities are hot pickled mustard tuber, Hundred-Flower sweet wine and pressed radish seeds. In 1972 archaeologists excavated graves from the Kingdom of Ba, and among the finds were ancient musical instruments.

West of the town is the White Crane Ridge, on which are carved ancient water level marks in the form of 14 scaled fish, and many inscriptions referring to the hydrology of the river at this point. These stone fish—the oldest of which was carved in the Tang dynasty (618–907)—are visible only at the lowest water level, which occurs perhaps once every decade or so. Locals say that 'when the stone fish appear the harvests will be good'. These stone fish will disappear at the end of 2002 once the dam is completed, never to be seen again.

Fengdu

Fengdu, on the north bank of the river, was in the past more popularly known as the 'City of Ghosts'. There is a temple here dedicated to the God of Hades. A pilgrim to the temple used to be able to purchase, for the sum of one dollar, a 'Passport to Heaven', stamped by the local magistrate and the abbot. Landmarks in the temple complex bear horrific names—Ghost Torturing Pass, Last Glance at Home Tower,

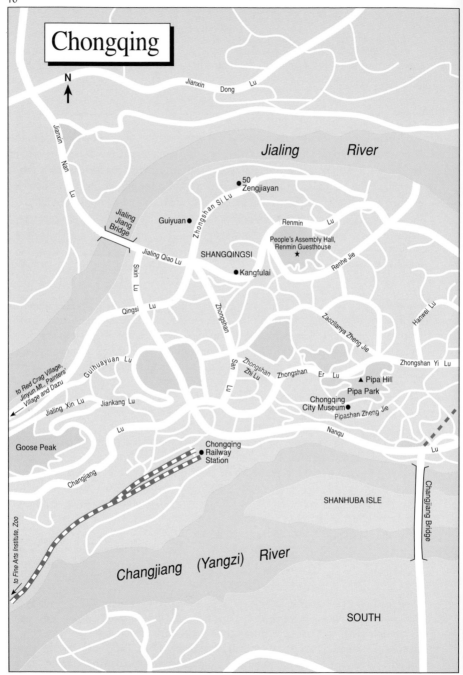

Chongqing

N

Jianxin Dong Lu

Jianxin Nan Lu

Jialing River

Jialing Jiang Bridge

Zhongshan Si Lu

● 50
Zengjiayan

Guiyuan ●

Renmin Lu

People's Assembly Hall,
Renmin Guesthouse
★

Jialing Qiao Lu

SHANGQINGSI

Renhe Jie

Sixin Lu

● Kangfulai

Qingsi Lu

Zhongshan

Zaozilanya Zheng Jie

Hanwei Lu

Guihuayuan Lu

Zhongshan San Lu

Zhongshan Zhi Lu

Zhongshan Er Lu

Zhongshan Yi Lu

▲ Pipa Hill
Pipa Park

to Red Crag Village,
Jinyun Mt., Painters'
Village and Dazu

Jialing Xin Lu

Jiankang Lu

Chongqing
City Museum ●

Pipashan Zheng Jie

Goose Peak

Lu

Nanqu Lu

Chongqing
Railway
Station

Changjiang

Changjiang Bridge

SHANHUBA ISLE

to Fine Arts Institute, Zoo

Changjiang (Yangzi) River

SOUTH

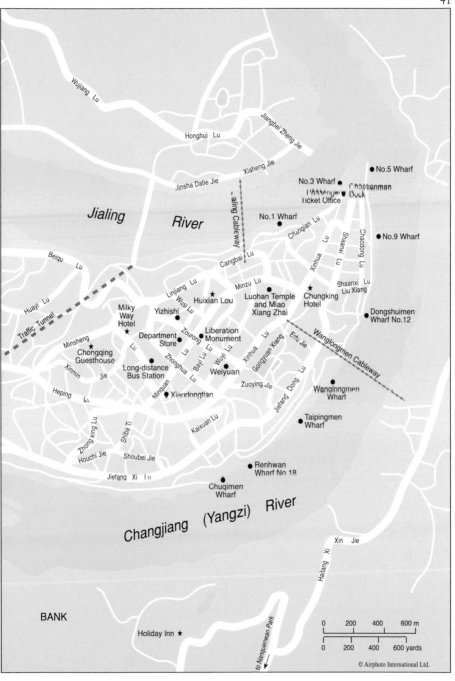

Wujiang Lu

Honghui Lu

Jiangbei Zheng Jie

Xiaheng Jie

Jinsha Datie Jie

No.3 Wharf
No.5 Wharf

Chaotianmen
Passenger Dock
Ticket Office

Jialing River

Jialing Cableway

No.1 Wharf

Chaoqian Lu

No.9 Wharf

Cangbai Lu

Beiqu Lu

Shaanxi Lu

Shaanxi Lu
Liu Xiang

Huayi Lu

Traffic Tunnel

Linjiang Lu

Minzu Lu

Wusi Lu

Huixian Lou

Luohan Temple
and Miao
Xiang Zhai

Chungking
Hotel

Xinhua Lu

Chaodong Lu

Dongshuimen
Wharf No.12

Milky
Way
Hotel

Yizhishi

Zourong Lu

Liberation
Monument

Minsheng

Chongqing
Guesthouse

Department
Store

Wuyi Lu

Bayi Lu

Xinhua Lu

Gongyuan Xiang

Erlu Jie

Wanglongmen Cableway

Xinmin

Jie

Long-distance
Bus Station

Zhonghua Lu

Weiyuan

Zuoying Jie

Jiefang Dong Lu

Wanglongmen
Wharf

Heping

Lu

Minquan

Xiaodongtian

Taipingmen
Wharf

Zhongxing Lu

Shiba Ti

Kaixuan Lu

Houchi Jie

Shoubei Jie

Jiefang Xi Lu

Renhwan
Wharf No 18

Chuqimen
Wharf

Changjiang (Yangzi) River

Xin Jie

Hailang Xi

BANK

Holiday Inn ★

to Nanquwan Park

| 0 | 200 | 400 | 600 m |

| 0 | 200 | 400 | 600 yards |

© Airphoto International Ltd.

THE STORY OF THE THREE KINGDOMS   —by Madeleine Lynn

If one wishes to understand China, one must have some familiarity with the history of
the Three Kingdoms and with the lore that surrounds it. Above all this is true on the
middle and upper Yangtse where it seems every bend in the river leads to another site
associated with this epoch and to the stories that have grown around it like the layers
of a pearl around its grain of historical fact. If the events seem complicated and the stage
crowded with unfamiliar actors, that too is part of China's reality. One might as well seek
to know the Greeks without the Trojan War or the English without Shakespeare.

Lyman P Van Slyke, *Yangtse: Nature, History and the River*, 1988.

By AD 150 the Han dynasty (206 BC–AD 220) was already rotting from within,
the result of a series of weak emperors. The uprising of peasant rebels known as the
Yellow Turbans (AD 184) gave three strong warlords (Cao Cao, Liu Bei and Sun
Quan) the opportunity to amass their own independent armies. They gradually
set up rival territories within the Empire and fought it out for the control of
China. The history of their struggle formed the basis for the 14th-century
popular novel *The Romance of the Three Kingdoms*, a compilation of fact and
fiction taken from the repertoires of 12 centuries of storytellers. It is a rambling
saga of heroism and treachery, of larger-than-life heroes and villains against the
backdrop of the dying dynasty. Tales from this era are also the subject of many
Chinese operas.

The three kingdoms were:

The Kingdom of Wei: North China, comprising the Yellow River basin; the
base of the Qin and Han dynasties. Its ruler was Cao Cao, Duke of Wei,
characterized in the novel as the archetypal Chinese villain, a brilliant but
ruthless general. 'Speak of Cao Cao and he is there' is the Chinese equivalent
of 'Talk of the devil'.

The Kingdom of Shu: the area that is now called Sichuan. It was established
by Liu Bei, pretender to the throne by virtue of being a distant relation of the
Han emperor. Although a rather weak and insignificant personality himself, his
royal blood attracted gifted followers, the most famous of whom are Zhuge
Liang and Liu's two sworn blood-brothers Zhang Fei and Guan Yu (*see* page 54).

Zhuge Liang was Liu's premier strategist and has been held up as an
example of military genius ever since. There are numerous stories of how he
defeated Cao Cao's larger armies by guile and bravado rather than strength. For
instance, there was the time he was staying in an unprotected city when Cao

Cao's army arrived unexpectedly. As the troops approached, they saw that the city gate was wide open and that Zhuge Liang, accompanied only by one young servant boy, was perched on top of the city wall calmly playing the harp. Convinced that they were about to walk into an ambush, the enemy withdrew.

Guan Yu was so revered for his loyalty that he was gradually turned into a god. Given the honorary title Guan Gong, and also known as Guan Di, God of War, Justice and Righteousness, until recently nearly every large town in China had a temple dedicated to him. His statue can be recognized by its distinctive red face, signifying bravery and goodness.

The Kingdom of Wu: The rich and fertile lower Yangzi region, as far as the sea. This was controlled by the treacherous Sun Quan, whose family was the most influential in the region.

Between Shu and Wu was the middle Yangzi basin, a no-man's land of marshes and lakes. From here one could threaten either Shu or Wu and it was here that some of the most crucial battles took place. On the run from Cao Cao's army, Liu Bei took refuge in this area and Zhuge Liang persuaded Sun Quan, the ruler of Wu, to ally with them against the powerful Cao Cao. Although their combined forces were still far less than Cao Cao's, together they routed him in the critical battle of Red Cliff (*see* page 89), at a site upriver from modern Wuhan.

Now it was Cao Cao's turn to flee for his life. Although Guan Yu actually cornered him and could have killed him he let him go, as Cao Cao had done the same for him in an earlier encounter.

But the alliance between Liu Bei and Sun Quan did not last long. Sun Quan tried to persuade Guan Yu to betray Liu Bei and join him. When Guan Yu refused, Sun had him beheaded and sent his head to Cao Cao, hoping for an alliance with him. The grief-stricken Liu Bei ignored Zhuge Liang's advice and launched a disastrous campaign against Sun. Before the fight even began, his other sworn brother Zhang Fei was murdered by two fellow officers who planned to surrender to Sun. Liu was ignominiously defeated and retreated to Baidi Cheng, where he died a few years later.

Cao Cao also died without achieving his ambitions. Although his son succeeded in conquering the other two Kingdoms, it was a short-lived triumph, as he was toppled in a *coup d'état*. So none of the three realized their dream of ruling over the whole of China.

Nothing-to-be-done Bridge. Fengdu's temples display instruments of torture and wild demon images. Shopkeepers kept a basin of water into which customers threw their coins: if they sank they were genuine, but if they floated the coins were ghost money and unacceptable. Boats would moor in midstream rather than by the bank in case of attack by ghosts. It seems that the origin of the town's extraordinary reputation dates back to the Han dynasty (206 BC–AD 220) when two officials, Yin and Wang, became Daoist (Taoist) recluses here and eventually Immortals. When combined, their names mean 'King of the Underworld'. Today, however, the town is thronged with tourists attracted by temples and shrines dedicated to the gods of the underworld. There is a ski lift to the original temple complex at Minshan. Otherwise it is a 30-minute hike starting at the Bridge to the Otherworld. This town will be completely submerged in 2003 but the historical temple located on Min shan will remain accessible.

Zhongxian

There are two moving stories about how Zhongxian (Loyal County) got its name. In the Warring States period (475–221 BC), Ba Manzi, a native of Zhongxian, became a general to the army of the Kingdom of Ba. Towards the end of the Zhou dynasty the Kingdom of Ba was in a state of civil war, and Ba Manzi was sent to the Kingdom of Chu to beg military assistance to put down the rebellion. The price demanded by Chu was the forfeit of three Ba cities. Once Chu's troops had helped restore stability to Ba, the King of Chu sent his minister to demand the payoff. Ba Manzi, however, said: 'Though I promised Chu the cities you will take my head in thanks to the King of Chu, for the cities of Ba cannot be given away', whereupon he cut off his own head. Receiving his minister's account, the King of Chu sighed: 'Cities would count as nothing had I loyal ministers like Ba Manzi'. He then ordered that Ba Manzi's head be buried with full honours.

The second tale is of another man of Zhongxian, the valiant general Yan Yan, who served the Minor Han dynasty (AD 221–63). Captured by the Shu general Zhang Fei, he refused to surrender, saying boldly: 'In my country we had a general who cut off his own head but we do not have a general who surrendered'. Enraged, Zhang Fei ordered Yan's beheading. The doomed general remained perfectly calm as he asked simply, 'Why are you so angry? If you want to cut off my head then give the order, but there is no point in getting angry and upsetting yourself.' Zhang Fei was so deeply moved by Yan's loyalty and bravery in the face of death that he personally unbound him, treating him as an honoured soldier.

Traditionally, the thick bamboo hawsers used to haul junks over the rapids were made in this area, as the local bamboo is especially tenacious. Today, bamboo handicrafts are a thriving industry, while the local food speciality is Zhongxian beancurd milk.

The red pavilion of Shibaozhai

Shibaozhai (Precious Stone Fortress)

Shibaozhai represents the first gem of Chinese architecture to be encountered on the downstream journey. From afar, the protruding 220-metre (720-foot) hill on the north bank can appear to resemble a jade seal, and is so named. The creation of the hill is attributed to the goddess Nuwo, who caused a rock slide while she was redecorating the sky after a fierce battle between two warring dukes.

A red pavilion hugs one side of this rock. Its tall yellow entrance gate is decorated with lions and dragons and etched with an inscription inviting the visitor to climb the ladder and ascend into a 'Little Fairyland'. The temple at the top was built during the reign of Emperor Qianlong (1736–96) and access to it was by an iron chain attached to the cliff. A nine-storeyed wooden pavilion was added in 1819 so that monks and visitors to the temple would not have to suffer the discomforts of the chain ascent. In 1956 three more storeys were added. Each floor is dedicated to famous generals of the Three Kingdoms period (AD 220–65), local scholars and renowned Chinese poets. The rising waters of the river will eventually surround the pagoda, which will be preserved with a tiny dam of its own, but left on an island.

In front of Ganyu Palace at the top of Jade Seal Hill is the Duck Hole. It is said that as spring turns to summer, if you take a live duck and drop it through the hole, it will quickly reappear swimming in the Yangzi. In the past the monks apparently drew their drinking water from this hole by using a pipe made of bamboo.

The spirit wall in the temple's main hall is constructed of excavated Han-dynasty (206 BC–AD 220) bricks. The hall behind is dedicated on the right to Generals Zhang Fei and Yan Yan (*see* above and page 42) of the Three Kingdoms, and on the left to General Qin Liangyu (1576–1648) who fought bravely against the Manchu forces. A mural shows the goddess Nuwo repairing the sky.

In the rear hall are the remains of the Rice Flowing Hole. Legend has it that long ago just enough husked rice would flow up from the small hole each day for the needs of the monks and their guests. One day a greedy monk, thinking he could become rich, chiselled a bigger hole, and the rice flow ceased forever.

Many of the tourist cruise ships dock at **Shibaozhai** for a few hours' visit. For those on scheduled passenger boats, you should disembark at **Xituozhen** on the south bank and transfer to local ferries to cross the river.

The new village of Shibaozhai is located above the present town which will be submerged by the end of 2002.

Wanxian

About two hours below Shibaozhai the boat reaches Wanxian, which is guarded by two nine-storeyed pagodas for good fortune. The city spreads out on both sides of the river and is known as the 'Gateway to East Sichuan'. It is situated high above the river and the foundations of the buildings are many metres high. Porters vie with each other to carry passengers' luggage up the steep stairways to the city. The winding streets vary in level from 29 to 206 metres (95 to 675 feet), so bicycles are a rare sight. Wanxian has a number of silk-weaving and spinning factories supported by intense silkworm cultivation—operated on a family basis—which continues year round in Wanxian County. Other light industries include tea, bamboo and cane goods, cotton clothing, leather and Chinese medicines. Paper mills utilizing wheat and rice straw from the countryside disgorge milky waste into the Yangzi, adding to the pollution.

Of the three major regions affected by the proposed Three Gorges Dam, Yichang, Wanxian and Chongqing, Wanxian will lose the most. Two-thirds of the total of 1.2 million people to be relocated live in the Wanxian prefecture and the reservoir will inundate two-thirds of the city. Over 900 factories are located below the new waterline, and many have already been replaced on higher ground.

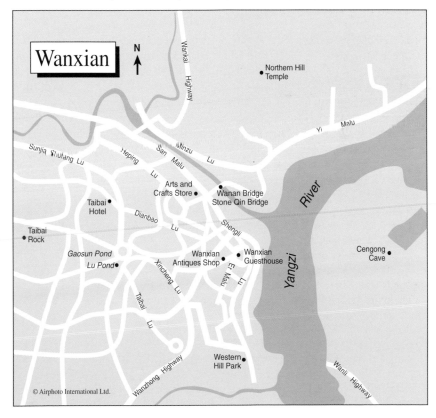

HISTORY OF WANXIAN

The city received its present name during the Ming dynasty (1368–1644), and became a foreign treaty port in 1902. In 1926 two British gunboats bombarded the city, causing massive fires, when the local warlord took to commandeering foreign vessels for the transport of his troops. Following this incident, a boycott on the loading and unloading of British vessels was enforced for several years. This became known as the Wanxian Incident.

As the halfway city between Yichang and Chongqing, Wanxian was a main port for East Sichuan merchandise (including large quantities of tung oil, used in treating wooden junks). Early travellers commented on the huge number of junks anchored at Wanxian. Junks also used to be built here from cypress wood found in the nearby hills.

WHAT TO SEE IN WANXIAN

The downriver boats from Chongqing usually reach Wanxian in the early evening, and depart in the small hours of the following morning although timings will change as the river rises.

This enables the passage of the Three Gorges to be made in daylight. Upstream boats also make a long stop. Passengers rush off the boats, hurrying up the hundreds of steps to the town where every night of the year the famous Wanxian rattan and cane market is held on **Shengli Lu**. Buyers and sellers mingle in a frenzy of bargaining for handmade summer bed mats, fans, hats, straw shoes, furniture and basketry. Small, round, red-trimmed baskets with lids are the most popular item and are well known throughout China. Roadside stalls trade in spicy noodles and cooling, opaque soyabean jelly and fresh fruit. In the mornings, just a little further west of the night market area, one of the city's ten free markets sells local produce and seasonal delicacies such as mountain mushrooms or live eels. **Second Street** (Er Malu) is the main shopping thoroughfare.

There was a community of foreign missionaries in this region (formerly Sichuan Province) before 1949, and two churches—Catholic and Protestant—continue to draw sizeable congregations of country folk.

In 1983 a small workshop was set up, employing two teenage boys and a few part-time workers to paint and varnish river stones from the Three Gorges and from the Daning River's Three Little Gorges. These make attractive mementoes and can be bought at the **Arts and Crafts Store**, 1 Third Street (San Malu). Visitors may also visit silk-weaving and cane-furniture factories.

■ LU POND AND XISHANPAI PAVILION

This small pool, originally dug by a locally revered Song-dynasty official, Lu Youkai, was once a very large lotus pond surrounded by decorative pavilions. Now it is not much more than a traffic roundabout. Nearby stands an ancient two-storey, yellow-tiled pavilion which houses a huge rock carved by the calligrapher Huang Tingzhen. Around the Xishanpai Pavilion once flowed a winding freshwater channel. Local literati would spend their evenings here, floating full wine cups along the channel. When a wine cup stopped in front of one of them his forfeit would be to compose a poem.

■ WESTERN HILL PARK
A clock tower, which dominates the town's skyline from the river, was built in this large park in 1924. The upper part was damaged by Japanese bombs in 1939. There is a memorial to a Russian volunteer pilot whose plane crashed in the river in the same year. During the summer, people relax in bamboo deck-chairs under the leafy trees, sipping tea and listening to Sichuan-style opera.

■ STONE QIN BRIDGE
A natural bridge in the shape of a Chinese zither crosses Chu River, which divides the town. It is said that Lu Ban, the patron saint of carpenters, spent a whole night building it.

■ TAIBAI ROCK
The poet Li Bai (701–62) lived here for a time; in the Ming dynasty a memorial hall was built to commemorate him. Stone inscriptions dating back to the Tang dynasty are still to be seen.

■ THE THREE GORGES MUSEUM, WANGZHONG HIGHWAY
This small museum, on the Wanzhong Highway, is a repository of some of the artefacts collected in advance of the flooding of the area by the new dam. Han tomb effigies and a Ba period 'hanging' coffin are featured. The museum's exhibits are rudimentary, but the shop is extensive—the usual tourist trap with no local products.

Yunyang

The county town of Yunyang (Clouded Sun) is situated on the north bank, 64 kilometres (40 miles) below Wanxian. On the south bank is Zhang Fei Temple.

The Tang-dynasty poet, Du Fu (712–70), banished to a minor position in Sichuan, fell ill while travelling through Yunyang and stayed for many months, recuperating and writing poetry.

■ ZHANG FEI TEMPLE
Zhang Fei, the 'Tiger General' of the Kingdom of Shu during the Three Kingdoms period (AD 220–65), is revered as a man who kept his word (*see* page 42). In 221, Guan Yu, Zhang Fei's sworn brother, was killed by the armies of the Kingdom of Wu. The Tiger General, then an official in Langzhong County, swore revenge and prepared to attack Wu with his army arrayed in white armour and pennants—white being the

colour of mourning. He ordered Commanders Zhang Da and Fan Jiang to lead the attack and avenge his brother, under pain of death.

The two pusillanimous officers got Zhang Fei drunk and cut off his head. They then fled by boat to Yunyang, intending to surrender to Wu. Here, however, they heard of a peace settlement between Wu and Shu, and threw Zhang Fei's head into the river, where it circled a fisherman's boat. Zhang Fei appealed to the fisherman in a dream to rescue his head and bury it in Shu. The fisherman obeyed, and the head was interred on Flying Phoenix Hill. A temple was built to commemorate the bold warrior. It is said that, before internment, the head was placed in a vat of oil, and when copper cash was thrown into the vat, the head would float up to give advice to the lovelorn and childless.

The temple was partly damaged in the flood of 1870, so most of the present ensemble of buildings dates from the late 19th century. It has been extensively restored. Sixty per cent of the temple's rich collections of paintings, tablets and inscriptions were lost during the Cultural Revolution. In front of the main hall are giant statues of the three famous sworn blood brothers—Liu Bei, Guan Yu and Zhang Fei. Inside the hall sits the wild-eyed, red-faced Guan Yu; on either side are scenes from his life. The Helpful Wind Pavilion contains steles and huge portraits of the general and his wife. It is said that his spirit, in the form of a helpful wind, frequently assisted passing boats. Junkmen used to stop at the temple to light firecrackers and burn incense in appreciation.The temple stands amid tranquil gardens, waterfalls and pools. At present, the fate of the temple is unknown after 2002.

Fengjie

Fengjie stands on the north bank, just above the western entrance to Qutang, the first of the three great Yangzi gorges. Fengjie town, the county seat for the area, has a population of 50,000. It is an attractive town, with part of its Ming-dynasty city wall intact. The stairways from the ferry pontoons lead up through three old city gates. The town is very lively, thronged with Chinese tourists who have come to visit the famous historical site of Baidi Cheng nearby.

Tourist boats normally stop here for about 20 minutes, which is long enough to enable ongoing passengers to take a brief stroll about the town. Some of the tourist cruise boats make a few hours' stop to allow a visit to **Baidi Cheng** (*see* page 54); but those on scheduled passenger ships who wish to see Baidi Cheng will have to spend a night at Fengjie.

History of Fengjie

The ancient town was called Kuifu in the Spring and Autumn period (722–481 BC), but became known as Fengjie after the Tang dynasty (AD618–907). It has long been famous as a poets' city, as many of China's greatest poets commemorated their visits here with verses. The Tang-dynasty poet Du Fu (AD712–70) wrote some 430 poems while serving as an official here for two years.

Liu Bei, the King of Shu during the Three Kingdoms period (AD 220–65, *see* page 42), died of despair in the Eternal Peace Palace after he was defeated by the armies of Wu. According to two ancient tablets unearthed in recent years, the Fengjie Teacher Training Institute now stands on the site of the palace. On his deathbed, Liu Bei entrusted his sons to the care of his loyal adviser, Zhuge Liang, entreating him to educate them in wisdom and to choose the most talented one to succeed him as king.

It was here that Zhuge Liang trained the troops of Shu in military strategy. He constructed the Eight Battle Arrays, 64 piles of stones 1.5 metres (5 feet) high erected in a grid pattern, 24 of which represented the surrounding troops. The principles of Zhuge Liang's manoeuvres have long been studied by China's military strategists and continue to be relevant to present-day concepts of Chinese warfare.

Nearby is the village of **Yufu**, which means 'the fish turns back' and relates to the legend of Qu Yuan, China's famous poet and statesman of the third century BC. During his service at court, the country was riven by factions and discord. His political enemies had him exiled; eventually, in despair, he drowned himself in Dongting Lake. His body was allegedly swallowed by a sacred fish which then swam up the gorges to Qu Yuan's birthplace, near Zigui (*see* page 69), where the fish intended to give Qu Yuan an honourable burial. However, so great were the lamentations and weeping of the mourners along the shore that the fish also became tearful and swam past Zigui. It was not until it reached Yufu that the fish realized its mistake and turned back.

WHAT TO SEE IN FENGJIE

Fengjie is typical of many of the Yangzi River towns. Its markets on **Zhonghua Lu**, **Heping Lu** and **Fandi Lu** are filled with local produce, clothing and Chinese mountain herbs. Its fruits—especially peaches, pomelos and snow-pears—are famous. Yellow-poplar combs were a speciality, but are now rare. **Dadongmen Jie** is lined with leafy trees and traditional whitewashed two-storeyed houses—the upper storey frequently in wood—and was once called Zhuge Liang Jie (*see* page 42), for it is said he passed this way. Outside the city wall, above the river, are makeshift mat-shed teahouses where the local men and travellers relax in bamboo deck-chairs, drinking tea and eating sunflower seeds or eggs boiled in tea, a tradition likely gradually to disappear as the waters rise, reaching their peak in 2009.

(following pages) *GEOPIC™ image of the Yangzi, taken in 1975 near Wanxian in eastern Sichuan, just upriver from the Three Gorges*

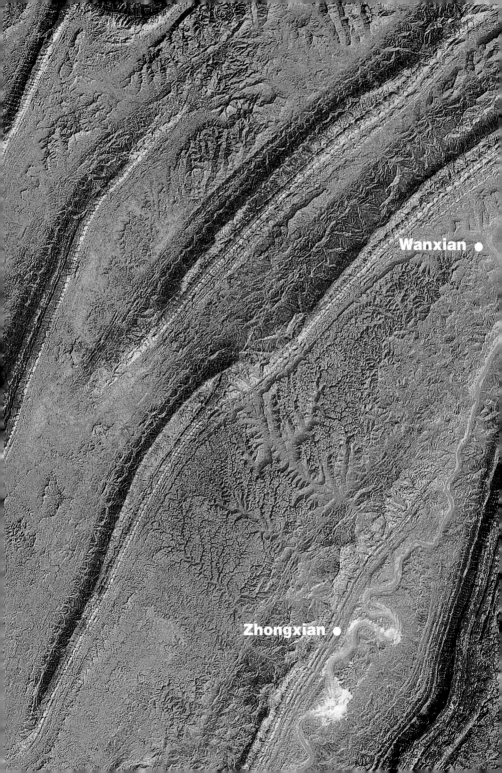

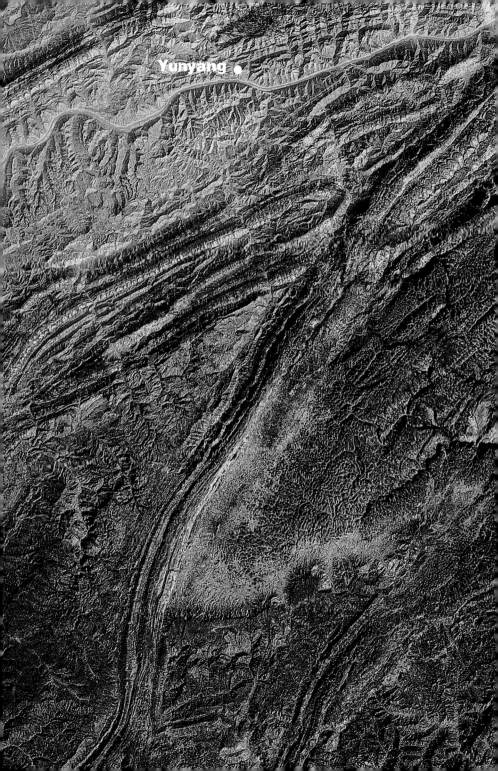
Yunyang

Baidi Cheng (White Emperor City)

The local ferry from Fengjie takes about 20 minutes to reach Baidi Cheng on the north bank of the river, passing several pagodas on the surrounding peaks (the return trip takes an hour). Sadly the approach to this historic site is quite spoilt by a factory and workers' housing built in the 1970s.

Because of its strategic position the town was chosen in the first century AD by Gong Sunshu, an official turned soldier, as the site of his headquarters. The legend goes that in AD 25 white vapour in the shape of a dragon was seen rising from a nearby well. Taking this as an auspicious omen, Gong declared himself the 'White Emperor' and the town 'White Emperor City'. Remains of the city wall can still be seen on the hill behind Baidi Mountain. The 12-year reign of the White Emperor was regarded as a time of peace and harmony, so after his death a temple was built to commemorate his reign. This temple dates back over 1,950 years.

Several hundred steps lead up the wooded Baidi Mountain. The **Western Pavilion** (at one time known as Guanyin Dong) on the slope is believed to have been occupied by the great poet Du Fu, who wrote numerous poems at this site. The pavilion overlooks what Du Fu described as 'the limitless Yangzi'. Further up the hill is a *stupa*, marking the grave of a much-loved literary monk who served at the temple during the Qing dynasty (1644–1911).

A red wall with an imposing yellow dragon-head gateway surrounds the temple complex. Though the temple was originally dedicated to Gong Sunshu, the White Emperor, his statue was removed in the Ming dynasty (1368–1644) and replaced with images of Liu Bei, Zhuge Liang, Guan Yu and Zhang Fei, heroes of the Shu Kingdom during the Three Kingdoms period. The present halls date from the Ming dynasty.

The front hall contains large modern statues which depict Liu Bei on his deathbed entrusting his sons to the care of Zhuge Liang. To the left is the handsome, winged **Observing the Stars Pavilion (Guanxing Ting)**, where a large bronze bell can be seen hanging in the upper storey. From this pavilion Zhuge Liang observed the stars and made accurate weather forecasts which helped him plan his victorious battles. The two Forest of Tablets halls contain several rare engraved stelae, some of which are over 1,300 years old. The Phoenix Tablet is particularly finely engraved. The Bamboo Leaf Poem Tablet is one of only three in China. It is considered a fine work of art, combining as it does poetry and calligraphy, for the tablet is engraved with three branches of bamboo, each leaf forming the Chinese characters of a poem.

The **Wuhou Hall** is dedicated to Zhuge Liang, his son and grandson. The bodies of the statues are of the Ming dynasty (1368–1644), but the heads, smashed in the Cultural Revolution (1966–76), are new. **Mingliang Hall** is dedicated to Liu Bei, who is shown surrounded by four attendants, as well as the black-faced Zhang Fei and the red-faced Guan Yu on one side, and Zhuge Liang on the other. Adjoining rooms display furniture, scrolls, porcelain and other cultural relics.

In 1987, several buildings were converted to form a museum displaying the many cultural relics found within the area, including two coffins from the Ba culture. One of these dates back to the Western Han dynasty (206 BC–AD 8).

Fine views of the entrance to **Qutang Gorge** can be seen from the temple. As the Three Gorges Dam begins to take effect, the water level will rise and Baidi Mountain will become an island.

At the foot of Baidi Mountain, **Yanyu Rock**—over 30 metres (100 feet) long, 20 metres (66 feet) wide and 40 metres (130 feet) high—used to be a constant hazard to boats riding the swift current and heading into the narrow entrance of Qutang Gorge. Over the ages, countless vessels perished. In 1959 it took a work team seven days to blow up this gigantic rock.

Qutang Gorge

Immediately below Baidi City is **Kui Men**, the entrance to the first of the three gorges of the Yangzi River—the eight-kilometre (five-mile) long Qutang Gorge (also known by early Western travellers as the Wind Box Gorge). The shortest but grandest of them all, the gorge's widest point is only 150 metres (500 feet). Mists frequently swirl around the mysterious limestone peaks, some nearly 1,200 metres (4,000 feet) high, and the river rushes swift as an arrow through the narrow entrance, pounding the perpendicular cliff faces on either side of the gorge.

This gorge was a particularly dangerous stretch during high-water seasons and has been known to rise to 50 metres (165 feet). An upper Yangzi steamboat captain recalled how in September 1929 the level of water was 75 metres (246 feet), and likened the passage to a trough, with the water banked up on both sides. His ship became quite unmanageable, and was carried down, broadside on, only coming under control again at the lower end. He would never, he vowed, try to negotiate it again at such a level.

Two mountains—**Red Passage Mountain (Chijia Shan)** to the north, once compared to a celestial peach, and **White Salt Mountain (Baiyan Shan)** to the south—form the Kui Men entrance, their steep precipices like the wings of a giant door guarding the tumultuous waters.

In the Tang dynasty (618–907) chains were strung across the river as an 'iron lock' to prevent passage of enemy boats. In the Song dynasty (960–1279) two iron pillars nearly two metres (six feet) tall were erected on the north side, and seven chains, some 250 metres (820 feet) long, were used to block the river passage. Although the original purpose was defensive, the chain locks were later used to enable local authorities to gather taxes from all boats travelling downriver. This system continued until the middle Qing dynasty (1644–1911). The iron pillars are only visible at low water.

On the precipice of **Bai Yan Shan** (south side) are a series of holes nearly a metre (three feet) apart and about one-third of a metre (one foot) deep, forming a 'Z' shape. These are known as the **Meng Liang Stairway**. According to legend, Yang Jiye, a Song-dynasty general, was buried on a terrace high up on the mountain. His loyal comrade-in-arms, Meng Liang, decided secretly to take the bones back for burial in Yang's home town. In the dead of night he took a small boat into the gorge and began to hack out a pathway to the terrace. Halfway up the rock face he was discovered by a monk who began crowing like a cock. Meng Liang, thinking that dawn was breaking and fearing discovery, abandoned his task. When he later discovered the monk's mischief, he was so provoked that he hung the monk upside down over a precipice. The rock below Meng Liang Stairway is known as **Hanging Monk Rock** (**Daodiao Heshangshi**). History records, however, that General Yang was not buried here and the steps are probably the remains of an ancient river pathway. Sections of a city wall, 1,400 years old, have been found on top of Bai Yan Shan so it is possible that the pathway led to this early settlement. Another theory about the stairway suggests that it was built to provide access to the rare medicinal herbs which grow high on the cliff faces.

At the highest point above Hanging Monk Rock one can see **Armour Cave** (**Kuangjia Dong**) where it is said a Song-dynasty woman general hid her weapons. In 1958 the cave was explored and found to contain three 2,000-year-old wooden coffins from the Kingdom of Ba, in which were bronze swords and lacquered wooden combs.

Near the Meng Liang Stairway is the **Drinking Phoenix Spring**, a stalagmite in the shape of a phoenix drinking the sweet spring-water. Nearby is the **Chalk Wall** (**Fengbi Tang**) where 900 characters, dating from the Song dynasty, have been carved by famous calligraphers on the rock face. The site derives its name from the limestone powder which was used to smooth rock surfaces before being carved.

On the north side of the river, opposite Meng Liang Stairway, is a coffee-coloured precipice called **Bellows Gorge** (**Fengxiang Xia**). The name refers to some square configurations in the rock face, which were supposed to be bellows used by Lu Ban, the god of carpenters. In 1971 the secret of Bellows Gorge was revealed, when ancient suspended wooden coffins, similar to those found in the Armour Cave, were discovered in the caves of the precipice. Some of these have been moved to museums, but three remain and can be seen from the river.

Wise Grandmother's Spring (**Shenglao Quan**) in a rock crevice on the southern bank was, according to legend, created by an immortal grandmother from heaven for thirsty travellers. They had only to call out to the spring 'Worthy Grandmother, a drink!' and water would gush for a moment from the rock.

East of Armour Cave (on the south side), on the top of a black rock, is a huge stone which the Chinese say resembles the body of a rhinoceros looking westwards as if forever enjoying 'the autumn moon over the gorge gate'. They call this rock **Rhinoceros Looking at the Moon**.

Hanging coffins in the Three Gorges

From Baidi Cheng to Daixi through the whole length of Qutang Gorge, visitors may see, high up on the northern face, the old towpath, hand-hewn in 1889 by the local people. Prior to this there existed a smaller towpath which was often submerged at high water. Remnants of this path can still be seen below Bellows Gorge. Travellers had to abandon their boats and climb over the peaks, a dangerous and time-wasting detour. Boats going upstream had to wait for a favourable east wind; if the wind was in the wrong quarter, boats could be stranded in the water for ten days or more.

The sandstone walls of the gorges have become pitted by natural erosion, causing lines of holes, some of which are several metres deep. The town of **Daixi**, at the mouth of a stream bearing the same name, marks the eastern end of Qutang Gorge. Over 200 burial sites have been found here, and excavations have revealed a rich collection of bone, stone and jade artefacts and pottery, as well as various burial forms of the middle and late New Stone Age period.

Below Daixi the river widens out. About five kilometres (three miles) downstream, on the south bank, are two sharp, black peaks which form the **Unlocked Gates Gorge** (**Suokai Xia**). On the west side of the gorge, midway up the mountain, is a semi-circular stone shaped roughly like a drum—this is the **Beheading Dragon Platform** (**Zhanglong Tai**). Facing this on the opposite side of the gorge is a thick, round stone

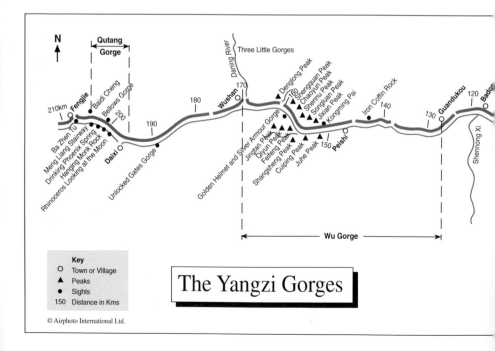

The Yangzi Gorges

pillar, the **Binding Dragon Pillar (Suolong Zhu)**. Once upon a time, the Jade Dragon, a son of the Dragon of the Eastern Sea, lived in a cave on the upper reaches of the Daixi Stream. One season he decided to visit his family by way of the Yangzi, but shortly afterwards found himself lost. Changing into the form of an old man, he asked his way of a herds boy. The boy pointed north with his sickle. The dragon rushed off in that direction but again got lost, whereupon he flew into a mighty rage and rushed at the mountains, causing them to crumble and dam up the river; farmlands were flooded, earthquakes toppled houses, and men and animals perished. At this moment the Goddess Yao Ji rushed to the spot on a cloud. She rebuked Jade Dragon, but he was unrepentant. She flung a string of pearls into the air; it changed into a rope that bound the dragon to the stone pillar. Yao Ji then ordered the great Da Yu, controller of rivers, to behead the murderous dragon on the nearby platform. He then diverted the river by cutting the gorge. The people of this valley have lived happily ever since.

Two kilometres (1.2 miles) further, the Baozi Tan (a triple rapid) and the Xiama Tan used to be serious dangers to shipping at low-water level. A traveller on one of the Yangzi steamships in the 1930s remarked:

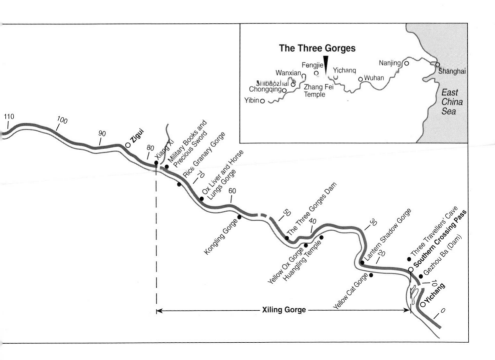

Only the throbbing of the engines as the bow entered the most turbulent part of the rapid, and buried its nose deep in the boiling water, revealed its presence to the uninitiated. But on looking back one could see that there had been a drop of two or three feet in the water where the rapid was most violent. Above it was a series of whirlpools and races.

Wushan

Wushan County is situated above the Yangzi on the north bank and embraced by lovely mountain peaks where flourishes the tung tree, whose oil was used for the caulking, oiling and varnishing of junks and sampans. The small town of Wuxia, with 15,000 residents, is the county seat. Wuxia is the starting point for boat trips up the Daning River through the Three Little Gorges—the main reason for making a stop at Wushan.

HISTORY OF WUSHAN

The town has existed since the latter part of the Shang dynasty (c. 1600–1027 BC). In the Warring States period (475–221 BC), the King of Chu established a palace west of the city. During the first century, the faith of the Buddha had reached China and many temples were built here; almost all the temples have been destroyed over the years. The name of the town originates with Wu Xian, a successful Tang-dynasty doctor to the imperial court, who was buried on Nanling Mountain, on the south bank opposite Wushan. A winding path—with 108 bends—leads from the foot of the mountain to the summit where there is a small temple. This path was an official road through to Hubei Province in ancient times.

WHAT TO SEE IN WUSHAN

The streets of this long and narrow town are named after the 12 peaks of the Wu Gorge. The old houses are mostly two-storeyed, with central courtyards on whose walls hang baskets of dried medicinal herbs. The markets supply the essentials for mountain living—back-baskets, broad-brimmed woven hats with plastic or waxed paper crowns to keep off the frequent summer rains, plastic and straw sandals (best for coping with the slippery mud after rain) and agricultural tools. Several street dentists with pedal-driven drills await customers. Some householders still use traditional stone grinders and pounders to make their wheat- and rice-flour. Although there is little left of the many temples here, one may visit, weather permitting, **Gaoqiu Mountain**, to the northwest of the town. This was the site of the King of Chu's palace and of Gaotang Temple, built to commemorate the fairy goddess Yao Ji and Emperor Da Yu, Controller of Rivers. According to the Daoist (Taoist) legend, it was on this site that Da Yu camped while cutting the three Yangzi River Gorges.

Steep field cultivation by the upper Yangzi, a major cause of erosion and river slit

*The village of Meirendao in the Three Gorges—its population has been relocated
by the government due to the new dam project*

THE DAM   —by Peter Neville-Hadley

THE THREE GORGES DAM

Monumental works of civil engineering undertaken by Chinese emperors, often at the cost of tens of thousands of lives, are strewn across China's landscape and history alike. The Qin organized the Great Wall and the Ming re-routed it and clad thousands of kilometres with stone; the Sui built the great canal network of the Imperial Highway, and various emperors constructed labyrinthine palaces and vast mausoleums, principal tourist attractions today.

China's modern leaders have not been slow to conceive super-projects of their own, although cement has replaced stone, and the raw muscle power of the surplus agricultural labourers known as the 'army of sticks' has been partly supplemented by machines. The greatest of these projects is undoubtedly the new San Xia (Three Gorges) Dam, a 17-year, US$70 billion operation involving the transportation of more than ten billion cubic metres (350 billion cubic feet) of rock and earth and the displacement of over 1 million people from the 60,000 hectares of land which will gradually be flooded by the resulting 640-kilometre (397-mile) long reservoir.

The dam is located near the mouth of the lowest of the Three Gorges, where the current was divided in two by an island. In November 1997, the first stage was completed with the blocking of two-thirds of the river's width. The water level had risen 18 metres (59 feet) by the end of 1998, will rise a further 52 metres (171 feet) by 2003, 30 metres (98 feet) more up to 2009, and a final ten metres (33 feet) that year, when the dam will come into operation. Smaller ships will use a single stage lift, and larger ones a stair of five locks. The waters in the Three Gorges will rise a total of 110 metres (361 feet), gradually changing the scenery forever.

The chief justifications offered for so much dislocation and destruction are twofold: the production of 18,200 megawatts of electricity, and the ending of frequently disastrous flooding of cities and farmland along the Yangzi. For centuries China's rivers have been a source both of immense fertility and massive destruction. Silt-laden, they can change course abruptly, and need ever higher levees to restrain them. In heavy rains they burst through, often with great loss of life. In restraining the river the Communists are again trying to take their place in history—figures who were even partially successful in flood control for the emperors are so revered as to have joined the Daoist (Taoist) pantheon.

THE IMPACT OF THE DAM

The final effect of the dam on river control is disputed. For more than 600 kilometres (372 miles) upstream the Yangzi will become more lake than river, but many experts argue that a slower flow rate will lead to an even more rapid build-up of silt, especially against the dam itself, causing floods to flow over the top of it. Some say more effective flood control would be provided by replacing the more than 800 lakes, vital for storing and dispersing flood waters, which have disappeared beneath unchecked urban expansion. Despite impressive forecasts for electricity generation, some argue that a series of smaller dams would have been more cost-effective, less dangerous and more productive.

The dam is only part of a larger project to alleviate poverty in rural areas, which until now have relied almost solely on the river for transport. Local governments have been working to attract fresh investment to soak up surplus agricultural labour, and new roads and railway lines are being built, with new bridges across the gorges of Yangzi tributaries.

Compensation of 40 billion *yuan* (about US$4.82 billion) has been allocated for those forced to move—as much as 3000 *yuan* per head in some small towns where average annual incomes are as little as 1500 *yuan* (US$180). Nevertheless the mass forced relocation has attracted widespread criticism. Relocation projects are running well behind schedule, and Chinese sociologists have criticized poor planning, falsified figures, corruption and inadequate resources.

THE FUTURE OF YANGZI CRUISES

Already the experience of passing through the gorges is changing. Gradually, the narrow ribbons of paths will disappear, and many temples and pagodas are reappearing on higher ground, some escaping from tactless development around them. In some ways the scenery will actually improve—several dark, Satanic concrete factories and mills will disappear below the waters as will brutally ugly accommodation blocks, their new modern counterparts on higher ground unlikely to win architectural awards, but still visually far more appealing. The colossal dam itself and the five-stage ride up or down it will be among the river's main attractions, and schedules will become more convenient as the deepening waters make night navigation possible on formerly dangerous reaches. Most travellers often feel the Three Gorges trip to be the perfect break from the clamour of China, and a cruise on the Yangzi is likely to remain one of the most pleasant memories of many China trips to come.

Sampans on the Daning River tributary,
the only access to the hinterland of the Three Gorges region

The energetic visitor may climb to the summit of Wushan (Witches Hill), a two-hour hike. Worshippers still come to a small shrine here, built within the ruins of an old Buddhist monastery. From the summit the views of Wu Gorge and the river are spectacular. A less strenuous outing may be made to the newly opened limestone cave complex in Wu Gorge high up on the cliff face above the north bank of the river. This involves a short boat ride from Wushan town, an easy scramble up the rocky slope and then a walk along the old towpath. Around the cave complex there are the usual teahouse and ornamental pavilions. The cave complex, **Luyou Dong**, is named after a Song-dynasty official who visited Wushan and left an appreciative record of his stay.

DANING RIVER EXCURSION: THE THREE LITTLE GORGES

To take a day trip up the crystal-clear Daning River through its magnificent Three Little Gorges (Xiao Sanxia)—whose total length is only 33 kilometres (20 miles)—is to experience the excitement and awe of bygone days of river travel in China.

The excursion is undertaken in air-conditioned boats, whose strong experienced boatmen pole with all their might when the river is too shallow for the engine to be used, heaving their bodies forward as they thrust long iron-tipped bamboo poles into the riverbed, and following through until they are almost lying on their backs in their struggle against the current. Some of the local boats encountered are not motorized and the boatmen must tow the boats— laden with local merchandise and coal— upriver, using a long bamboo rope and tracking in harness, along the water's edge or along cut pathways in the rock face. Negotiating a rapid may take several exhausting attempts before the boat is finally hauled over. Unfortunately, while the splendour of the scenery will remain, by 2003, the waters having risen about 50 metres (164 feet), the boatmen's poles will no longer touch bottom, the trackers' paths will have disappeared, and this description will be a souvenir of times gone by.

About 40 minutes from the mouth of the river, at its confluence with the Yangzi, the entrance to the first of the gorges is reached. This is the **Dragon Gate Gorge** (**Longmen Xia**), three kilometres (1.8 miles) long. On the cliff face to the right is the 1981 flood mark, over 40 metres (130 feet) above river level. The mouth of the gorge is like a massive gateway through which the river rushes like a green dragon, hence its name. The gateway appears to shut once one has passed through. On the east side is **Dragon Gate Spring (Longmen Quan)** and above it **Lingzhi Peak**, topped by the **Nine-Dragon Pillar**. On this peak, it is said, grow strange plants and the fungus of longevity (*lingzhi*), guarded by nine dragons. On the western bank, two rows of 15-centimetre (2-inch) square holes, continuing the entire length of the small gorges and numbering over 6,000 are all that remain of an astonishing plank walkway, which was first constructed in the Han period and recorded in the Annals of Wushan County in 246 BC. Wooden stakes inserted into these hand-hewn holes supported planks and large bamboo pipes, which stretched for 100 kilometres (62 miles) along the river. This pipeline conveyed brine, while the planks provided an access for maintenance. In the 17th century the pathway, used by the peasant leader Li Zicheng in his uprising against the Ming dynasty, was destroyed by the imperial army.

After leaving the gorge the boat passes the **Nest of Silver Rapid (Yinwo Tan)**. In the past, rich merchants trading in the hinterland often came to grief here; perhaps there are caches of silver under the bubbling surface still! In 1958 work began on clearing major obstacles from the river.

The Daning then meanders through terraced hillsides before entering the ten-kilometre (six-mile) **Misty Gorge (Bawu Xia)**, with its dramatic scenery of rocks, peaks and caves, including Fairy Maiden Cave, Fairy Throwing a Silk Ball, and Guanyin Seated on a Lotus Platform. A long, layered formation, like a scaly dragon, can be seen on the eastern cliff. Suspended upon the precipice is a relic of the ancient inhabitants of eastern Sichuan 2,000 years ago, an 'iron' coffin (which is actually made of wood that has turned black with age). This gorge is accordingly also known as **Iron Coffin Gorge**.

The village of **Twin Dragons** or **Shuanglong** (population 300), above Bawu Gorge, is the halfway point. Lunch can be provided at the reception centre, which also has some rooms for overnight accommodation.

Emerald Green Gorge (Dicui Xia), 20 kilometres (12.5 miles) long, is inhabited by wild ducks and covered with luxuriant bamboo groves from which rises a deafening cacophany of bird-song. There are also many types of monkey still to be seen if you are lucky. Once their shrill cries resounded throughout the Yangzi gorges, but today they can be heard only in Dicui Gorge. River stones of an extraordinary variety and colour can be gathered.

At the end of this gorge the tourist boat turns around and rushes downstream, arriving at Wushan in half the time it took to get here, aided by the skilful use of the long *yulo*, which is weighted by a stone to steady the boat. Groups may hire a boat for this trip at the mouth of the Daning River. Cheap local ferries also do this trip but it takes much longer and requires an overnight stop at Dachang (a town with fine farmhouse architecture and the remains of a Qing-dynasty city gate).

Wu Xia (Witches Gorge)

Below Wushan the river approaches the entrance to the 40-kilometre (25-mile) long Wu Gorge, the middle Yangzi gorge which straddles Sichuan and Hubei Provinces. So sheer are the cliffs that it is said the sun rarely penetrates. The boat passes, on the south side, the **Golden Helmet and Silver Armour Gorge (Jinkuang Yinjia Xia)** shaped, it is said, like an ancient warrior's silver coat of arms crowned by a round golden helmet. Ahead are the 12 peaks of Wu Gorge, famed for their dark and sombre grace. Poets have attempted to evoke both their bleakness and beauty:

Autumn Thoughts
Jade dews deeply wilt and wound the maple woods;
On Witch Mountain, in Witch Gorge, the air is sombre, desolate.
Billowy waves from the river roar and rush towards the sky
Over the frontier pass, wind and clouds sink to the darkening earth.
These clustered chrysanthemums, twice blooming, evoke the tears of yesteryear;
A lonely boat, as ever, is moored to the heart that yearns for home.
To cut winter clothes, women everywhere ply their scissors and foot-rulers
Below the White Emperor's tall city is heard the urgent pounding of the evening wash.

Six peaks line the north side:
Climbing Dragon Peak (Denglong Feng)
Sage Spring Peak (Shengquan Feng)

Facing Clouds Peak (Chaoyun Feng)
Goddess Peak (Shennu Feng)
Fir Tree Cone Peak (Songluan Feng)
Congregated Immortals Peak (Jixian Feng)

Three peaks flank the south side:
Assembled Cranes Peak (Juhe Feng)
Misty Screen Peak (Cuiping Feng)
Flying Phoenix Peak (Feifeng Feng)

Three more peaks may be glimpsed behind these:
Clean Altar Peak (Jingtan Feng)
Rising Cloud Peak (Qiyun Feng)
Mounting Aloft Peak (Shangsheng Feng)

More often than not these green-clad peaks are hidden by swirls of cloud and mist, and are difficult to distinguish, though each has its own characteristics and posture.

The most famous is the **Shennu Feng (Goddess Peak)**—also referred to as Observing the Clouds Peak—which resembles the figure of a maiden kneeling in front of a pillar. She is believed to be the embodiment of Yao Ji, the 23rd daughter of the Queen Mother of the West. Yao Ji, at the age of 18, was sent to oversee the Jade Pool of the Western Heaven, accompanied by 11 fairy handmaidens. But she found life there lonely and cold, and took to rambling among the mountains and rivers of the mortal world. Wushan became her favourite place, and there she established a small palace. Once, returning from a visit to the Eastern Sea on her floating cloud, she came upon 12 dragons playing havoc with the river and the mountains, and causing flooding and hardship in their wake. She summoned Da Yu the Great from his work on the Yellow River and, alighting from her cloud, presented him with a heavenly supernatural book. This endowed him with powers to call upon the wind, rain, thunder and lightning to move the earth, thus enabling his sacred ox to slash open the gorges (which is why all oxen have bent horns), and permit the waters to drain into the Eastern Sea. Yao Ji resolved to stay here with her 11 maidens to protect the boats from the dangerous rapids, the peasants' crops from damage, the woodcutters from wild animals, and to grow the fungus of longevity for the sick. Eventually these 12 maidens became the 12 sentinel peaks of Wu Gorge. There are, of course, many variations to this story.

As the river twists and turns, a mountain comes into view, appearing as if it will block the way. This is **Congregated Immortals Peak**, on whose grey-white rock face can just be made out a carved inscription, known as the **Kongming Pai**, which legend attributed to the great third-century politician and strategist Zhuge Liang (*see* page 42). However, it seems that the inscription was in fact carved during the Ming Dynasty by the local people to show their eternal respect and regard for this hero.

Five kilometres (three miles) below Kongming Pai on the south bank is the small trading town of **Peishi**, which marks the provincial border between Sichuan and Hubei. Whitewashed villages cling to the mountain terraces which produce grain crops and fruits—apples, persimmons, peaches, apricots and Chinese chestnuts.

Just above the north-bank town of **Guandukou**—marking the end of Wu Gorge—was the site of the Flint Rapid (Huoyan Shi), which was very violent at high water, with limestone rocks jutting into the river like huge stone gates beckoning helpless craft. These, along with all the dangerous rocks in the shipping channel, were blown up in the 1950s. Besides rapids, other dangers to navigators included whirlpools, quicksand and currents which varied from hour to hour

Badong

Badong, the county seat, has developed around one main street, extending from a power station at the eastern end to factories spreading along three or four hill slopes to the west. It is the westernmost county town of Hubei Province. Labourers, pitch black from coal-dust, with staff in hand, negotiate the steep slopes above the river, humping baskets of coal as they load and unload river lighters. Houses with wooden balconies huddle together on pillars embedded in solid concrete foundations above the bank of the river.

In ancient times, Badong was situated on the other side of the Yangzi and belonged to the State of Ba; in the Song dynasty (960–1279) the town was moved to the southern bank. The new city will be relocated again on the north bank, five km upstream from the present city.

Badong has two pavilions of architectural interest—the **Autumn Wind Pavilion (Qiufeng Ting)** and the **White Cloud Pavilion (Baiyun Ting)**. Local products include tung oil, lacquer, tea, medicinal herbs and animal skins.

The **Shennong Xi** (stream) is a small tributary of the Yangzi boasting gorges that rival those of the Daning River and is visited by many tourist ships. A team of trackers push and haul wooden sampans over the shallow rapids.

Zigui

Qu Yuan, one of China's greatly loved patriotic poets, was born in 340 BC in the Qu family village very near Zigui. The fame of the walled town on the north bank dates from this period long ago.

Qu Yuan's Memorial Hall, with its distinctive white gateway and walls edged in

One of the Three Little Gorges

How Much for a Life?

In 1854, a rich merchant living near Xin Tan, one of the most dangerous of all the rapids in the Three Gorges, raised subscriptions to build three life-boats. Painted red to distinguish them from regular craft, they soon became known as the Red Boats. More money was raised over the years to increase the fleet and in the 1880s the running of the service was taken over by the government, although funds still came from public subscription. By the early 1900s there were almost 50 boats stationed along the river. In 1899 alone they saved 1,473 lives from 49 wrecked junks.

A Red Boat would accompany each vessel on the most perilous parts of the journey—being dragged upstream by the trackers over the different sets of rapids. Downstream voyages were not as dangerous, so a special escort was not deemed necessary. When a wreck occurred a gun was fired as the summons for all Red Boats to come and help.

The life-boats were not allowed to salvage cargo from the wrecks. However, there was a reward system for the salvaging of human beings. W E Geil, who travelled along the Yangzi in 1904 on his way to Burma, describes how it worked:

On life-saving the Chinese have curious notions. While eating cakes cooked in lamp oil in a tea house in Chintan village, the skipper of the Red Boat came in and I asked him certain questions about the pagoda for destitute souls. He told me that for the recovery of a dead body from the water, a reward of eight hundred cash is given by the Emperor. It used to be eight hundred cash for saving a live man and four hundred for a dead one. But it was soon discovered that this did not pay, so it was reversed, and now four hundred cash are given to save a live man and eight hundred to recover a dead one. This allows four hundred cash to bury the man if he dies after being taken out of the water. This interesting fact was further explained to me by another of the Red Boat men—that the dead man involves funeral expenses and the live man none! This is good Celestial reasoning. It would be more profitable to drown a man before pulling him out. I found out afterwards that the reward of four hundred cash is given provided the rescuer gets his clothes wet; otherwise he gets but two hundred.

W E Geil, A Yankee on the Yangtse, 1904

red, is visible on the hillside east of the town. It contains a Ming-dynasty (1368–1644) statue of the poet, as well as stone inscriptions.

The great poet served as a chancellor to King Huai of the Kingdom of Chu, with special responsibility for the royal clans. The king had complete trust in him until discord developed among the clans and Qu was falsely slandered. Banished from the capital, he wandered about in Hubei Province, deeply sad and bitter. His poetry and essays reveal his romanticism, loyalty and patriotism. Qu had vigorously advocated that the State of Chu stand firm against attack by the Qin state, but his advice had gone unheeded, and in May of the year 278 BC, he drowned himself in Dongting Lake at the age of 62.

According to historical records, the local people scoured Dongting Lake for his body, beating drums and racing their boats in the course of their search. This event came to be commemorated each May, and to this day the **Dragon Boat Festival** (Duanwu Jie) is held in the river towns up and down the Yangzi and in many other parts of China. *Zongzi*—packets of sweetened rice steamed in leaves and tied with reeds—were thrown into the water as a sacrifice to Qu Yuan. The tradition of eating *zongzi* at this festival continues in Chinese communities the world over.

There are many fairy tales about Qu Yuan. East of Zigui is a bay named after him. It is said that when he died, a huge fish swallowed him up and swam all the way from Dongting Lake past Zigui to Yufu and back again, where it disgorged the body, amazingly still intact (*see also* page 51). In his home village is the Qu Field which he allegedly tilled. It is said that he never forgot his ancestral home; to the farmers there he introduced a jade-white rice which was soft and fragrant. Locals remember him at each new rice harvest.

■ XIANG XI (FRAGRANT STREAM)

A small stream just below Zigui and above the entrance to Xiling Gorge is well known to all Chinese as the home of the beautiful Han-dynasty (206 BC–AD 220) heroine Wang Zhaojun. Her story is the quintessence of virtuous patriotism.

Zhaojun, a maid of honour to the emperor, refused to bribe the painter from whose portraits of court ladies the emperor traditionally chose his concubines. In revenge, the painter portrayed her as quite hideous, and so imperial favour was denied her. In 22 BC the emperor, wishing to make a marriage alliance with the northern Xiongnu king, chose Wang Zhaojun. Only then did he set eyes on her; he was captivated but it was too late. Married to the Xiongnu king, Zhaojun was able to exert a good influence on relations between the Xiongnu and Han peoples, which gained her great respect. The emperor, in his rage at having lost her, decreed the beheading of the corrupt court painter. Local people say that before her marriage, Wang Zhaojun returned to her home town and, when washing in the stream, dropped a precious pearl which caused the stream to become crystal-clear and fragrant. Tradition names a pavilion-topped mound to the south of Hohhot in Inner Mongolia as her burial site.

Xiling Gorge

Xiling Gorge starts at Xiang Xi and zigzags for 76 kilometres (47 miles) down to Yichang (see photograph on pages 76–77). It is the longest and historically the most dangerous of the Yangzi gorges. Before the passage was made safe in the 1950s, 'the whole surface of the water was a swirling mass of whirlpools sucking the froth they created into their centres'. Xiling comprises seven small gorges and two of the fiercest rapids in the stretch of the Yangzi between Chongqing and Yichang.

On entering the western entrance the boat passes through the four-kilometre (2.4-mile) long **Military Books and Precious Sword Gorge (Bingshu Baojian Xia)**. The name of the gorge refers to a stratified layer of rock resembling a stack of books, and a perpendicular rock shaft below it, at a small cave on the north bank. There are two stories told of these formations, both concerning heroes from the classical novel *Romance of the Three Kingdoms (see page 42)*.

One legend has it that Zhuge Liang (181–234), military adviser to the King of Shu, became seriously ill while passing this way. Unwilling to entrust his valuable military treatises to any member of his entourage, he placed them up here on this inaccessible ledge, to be kept safe for later generations. The second tale is also about Zhuge Liang. It was he who devised the stratagems which enabled Liu Bei, the king, to defeat the Kingdom of Chu and establish the Minor Han dynasty (AD 221–63). Afraid that he would eventually fall out of favour, Zhuge Liang retired from official life and went into seclusion, hiding his military writings and sword here.

A large cleft rock stands at the mouth of a ravine—**Rice Granary Gorge (Micang Xia)**—on the south side. Fine sand, blown by river winds, piles up on this rock, and slowly sifts through a hole underneath. People call this Zhuge Liang's Granary.

Further on, the perilous **Xin Tan** (new rapid) rushes over submerged rocks, the oily surface of the water churned by whirlpools. In 1524, rock slides from the northern mountainside created this 3.2-kilometre (1.9-mile) long, triple-headed rapid. The fall of the riverbed had been estimated at about 6 metres (20 feet), but today it has a drop of only 2 metres (6.5 feet).

When the water level was low, junks would unload their cargo and be hauled over by 100 or more trackers. Passengers would join their boat beyond the rapid after walking along a winding mountain track and passing through the village of **Xintan**, once the site of the White Bone Pagoda—a giant pile of bleached bones, which was all that survived of the many thousands who had lost their lives at this frightening place. In 1941 the steamboat *Minxi* came to grief and several hundred people perished. The swift current carried boats downriver through Xin Tan at the rate of 7 metres (30 feet) per second.

Mr Hu Zhenhao, one of the last of the Xiling Gorge trackers, famous for his performances of old boat songs, with his troupe based in Zigui, Hubei, original home of dragon boat races

In 1854 a local merchant collected subscriptions from river traders and built three life-saving craft to patrol this rapid, and to salvage boats and survivors. This was the beginning of the Yangzi River Lifeboat Office, which eventually maintained its Red Boats on all the danger spots along the Chongqing–Yichang stretch until the 1940s.

The channel winds east and then south, towards **Ox Liver and Horse Lungs Gorge**, apparently named after the yellow stalactite formations on the north side. One of the 'Horse's Lungs' is missing, blown up by British gunboats during the reign of Guangxu (1875–1908).

In the middle stretch of **Xiling Gorge**, the strangely lovely **Kongling Gorge** towers above the iron-green rocks of the 2.5-kilometre (1.5-mile) long **Kongling Tan**, the worst of all the Yangzi rapids. Seventeen catastrophes involving steamships occurred here between 1900 and 1945. The larger boulders choking the channel had names such as 'Big Pearl', 'Monk's Rock' and 'Chickens' Wings', but the deadliest of all was known as 'Come to Me'.

As the boat enters **Yellow Ox Gorge (Huangniu Xia)**—said to look like a man riding an ox—the passage widens out and sweeps under the ancient **Huangling Temple (Huangling Miao)** on the south face, nestling amid orange and pomelo trees. The great poet Du Fu wrote of his journey through this gorge:

Three dawns shine upon the Yellow Ox.
Three sunsets—and we go so slowly.
Three dawns—again three sunsets—
And we do not notice that our hair is white as silk.

Huangling Temple, said to have been first built during the Spring and Autumn period (770–476 BC), is dedicated to the great Dayu who, with his yellow ox, controlled the flood waters and dug the gorges (*see* page 37). The present hall was built in the Ming dynasty (1368–1644) and houses a statue of Da Yu, as well as stone inscriptions. Zhuge Liang is also said to have dug the Yellow Ox Spring (or Toad Rock, as it is sometimes called) nearby. Its clear water, according to the Tang-dynasty *Book of Teas*, was excellent for the brewing of tea, and Yellow Ox was classified as the Fourth Spring under Heaven.

After one passes below Huangling Temple, the **Bright Moon Gorge (Mingyue Xia)** and the **Lantern Shadow Gorge (Dengying Xia)** loom ahead. The latter is overlooked on the south side by peaks in the shape of four figures from the 16th-century Chinese novel, *Pilgrimage to the West* (also known as *Monkey*). When the evening sun's rays fall upon these peaks, the figures do appear lifelike—Xuan Zang standing on the precipice edge; Monkey (Sun Wukong) peering into the distance; Sandy (Sha Heshang) carrying the luggage; and Pigsy (Zhu Bajie) riding a horse, all silhouetted against the fading light like characters in a shadow play.

The last of the smaller gorges is **Yellow Cat Gorge (Huangmao Xia)**, so named from the yellow cat-shaped rock on the riverside. **Qi Taigong Fishing** is the name given to a rock beside a cave on the south face, because of its fancied resemblance to a bearded old man wearing yellow trousers.

The vast construction site of the world's largest hydro-electric project, the Three Gorges Dam, offers the possibility of side trips to view the lock and ship lift mechanisms and an exhibition about the dam. Smaller ships descend via the single stage lift, and larger ones via a series of locks—a total of five when the waters have risen the full 110 metres (351 feet) above their previous levels (*see* pages 62–63.)

Now the boat reaches the strategic **Southern Crossing Pass (Nanjin Guan)**, with Three Travellers' Cave above (*see* page 84), marking the end of Xiling Gorge and the three great Yangzi gorges. The river widens dramatically and ahead lies Gezhou Dam and Yichang.

The Gezhou Dam, impressive if first seen coming up-river, is now an anticlimax for those coming down. Nevertheless, it was China's largest before the construction of the Three Gorges Dam and a similar project on the Yellow River, and still produces 2.715 million kilowatts of electricity per hour. A single stage lock allows ships to descend to the level of Yichang.

Tracking through the Rapids

Though the junk was now apparently safe, for it breasted the smooth, swift water of the second sluice and was no longer being thrown from side to side, the heaviest work still remained to be done. I turned to watch the trackers, for theirs was now the heavy work of making many tons of cypress go uphill on a fiercely resisting roadway of water. It was a moving sight—horribly depressing, to see more than three hundred human beings reduced to the level of work animals, blind-folded asses and oxen; yet thrilling too, to see the irresistible force of their co-operation, for the three hundred and fifty cloth shoes of their each step up the slope were planted in the same moment, and the sad trackers' cries, 'Ayah! . . . Ayah!,' were sung in a great unison choir of agony and joy, and the junk did move.

It moved, however, more and more slowly, as the last and hardest test of the trackers' labor began—heaving the junk over the head of the rapid, over the round, swift crest of the sluice. The bow of the junk seemed to dig into the water there. The rope grew taut. The great crowd of towing men hung for a long time unable to move. I saw the cook look down toward the junk, obviously at a loss what to do.

Then suddenly from midstream, from the very center of danger, came a lovely, clear, high-pitched line of song.

It was Old Pebble. I looked out and saw him standing on the deck, himself leaning as if to pull, hurling a beautiful song at the crowd on the bank.

On the proper beat the many trackers gave out a kind of growl and moved their feet forward a few inches, and the bow of the junk dug deeper into the head of the sluice. They took a second, firmer step. And a third, and a fourth.

I had never heard Old Pebble sing such a haunting melody. I saw that he was in a kind of ecstasy. His face shone in a grimace of hard work and happiness. I remembered my doubts about his credo of 'simplicity', which he had recited to me in our first evening on the river, and I remembered my distress that such a sturdy young man did not avow personal goals of wealth, love, honor, and fame. Now I saw from his face that this was his life's goal; this instant of work, this moment's line of song, this accord with his poor fellow men, this brief spurt of useful loyalty to the cranky, skinny, half-mad owner of the junk on which he had shipped, and above all this fleeting triumph over the Great River.

At last the junk raised its head, shivered, and shot suddenly forward into the still water of the pond above the rapids.

When it was over, and the junk was pulled up to the loading platform, Old Pebble was streaming sweat, but he looked very happy.

I walked down to the river's edge to see what he would say. He jumped ashore and bent down to the river and scooped up double handfuls of the brown water and washed his face, sloshing and snorting like a small boy. I moved near him. He looked up. All he said was, 'Ayah, this river is a turtle.'

John Hersey, A Single Pebble, 1914

Satellite image showing the Yangzi River in western Hubei Province downstream of the Wu Gorge. The river flows from left to right. The Three Gorges Dam site can be seen at the top of the photograph, and further downstream the existing Gezhou Dam is located immediately above Yichang. These can also be seen in the close up inset. The tributary of the Qing Jiang can be seen running across the middle of the photograph and joining the Yangzi at Zhicheng.

Landsat-7 satellite data acquired by USGS. This fusion image was processed and supplied by Geocarto International Centre, Hong Kong. Copyright © 2001 Geocarto and Airphoto International Ltd.

The Middle Reaches: Yichang to Hukou

From Yichang the Yangzi enters its middle basin, flowing for 1,010 kilometres (630 miles) to the mouth of Poyang Lake in Jiangxi Province. The river, widening out abruptly from the narrow confines of Xiling Gorge and with a pent-up force out of Gezhou Dam, rolls through broad floodplains, fed by tributaries and lakes that become serious flood points during heavy summer rains.

Networks of dykes and embankments—obscuring the view—stretch the length of the river, which can be as wide as 1.5 to 2 kilometres (1 to 1.3 miles), and can even today cause widespread flooding during normal rainy seasons. In abnormal summer deluges the many lakes in the area, joining forces with the Yangzi and its tributaries, inundate the land, forming great expanses of water. This must have been the situation observed by two great foreign travellers in China: Marco Polo in the 13th century and the French Lazarist priest, Abbé Huc, in the 18th century, both of whom recorded the Yangzi as being more than 15 kilometres (nine miles) wide. However, Polo may not even have visited China, and although Huc did he has often been accused of exaggeration.

Up to the Sui dynasty (581–618) the middle reaches were sparsely inhabited, but from the Tang dynasty (618–907) on, waves of people migrated from the north, fleeing from civil wars, famines, heavy taxation and harassment from marauding Tibetans and Turks. With the sharp rise in population, dyke construction became more intense. But it was during the Ming and Qing dynasties (1368–1644 and 1644–1911) that treasury funds were allocated to the construction of dykes—mainly along the north bank of the Yangzi—which were built as high as 10–16 metres (33–52 feet) in places. Once built, the burden of maintenance fell to local landowners and peasants, and upkeep was often neglected.

The meandering, looping course of the river creates severe silting so that the raised riverbed requires constant dredging, and as large boats crisscross the channel, their wash churns into the embankment causing mini-landslides. The rich alluvial Jianghan Plain, between the north bank of the Yangzi and the Han River, is a major cotton- and grain-growing area very vulnerable to flooding. In 1952 the Jingjiang Flood Diversion Project was launched. Flood prevention measures included the strengthening of the 180-kilometre (110-mile) stretch of dyke along the Yangzi's northern bank (in the Shashi region), and the construction of flood-intake sluices, regulating dams and retention basins on the south side to divert the waters. On the Han River, the Danjiangkou Water Conservancy Project and dam draw the flood waters from this tributary to irrigate the more arid regions of northwest Hubei. The Shashi retention basin, covering an area of 920 square kilometres (355 square miles), took 300,000 workers some 75 days to construct in 1954.

Above **Dongting Lake**, the Yangzi forms the border between the provinces of Hubei and Hunan. The lake is the second largest in China. Fed by four rivers and emptying its waters into the Yangzi, it abounds in aquatic products. At Dongting Lake the river streaks northeastwards, beside hinterland dotted with numerous lakes, towards Wuhan, the largest city along its middle reaches. Here it is joined by the 1,532-kilometre (952-mile) long Han River.

During the dry winters, shifting sandbars and low water levels pose serious hazards to shipping. At Wuhan, the navigation channel can be as shallow as 2 metres (6.5 feet). Estimates put the volume of silt passing Wuhan each year at more than 140 million cubic metres (183 million cubic yards).

Freshwater fish abound—silver and big-head carp, Yangzi sturgeon and Wuchang fish, to name a few. Native to the river are dolphins and a species of alligator, though both of these are extremely rare today.

Having crossed the entire width of Hubei Province, the river enters Jiangxi, forming its border with Anhui. Immediately below the city of Jiujiang and the cherished, beautiful mountain of Lushan, it is joined by the blue freshwaters of Poyang Lake, the biggest in all of China. From here on, the Yangzi enters its lower reaches.

The river traffic is light, mostly convoys of barges or boats linked to a single tugboat, dredgers excavating the navigational channels, and fishing *sampans* with patched sails. Steamer ferries stop briefly at the coal-mining town of **Zhicheng** and pass under one of the many bridges that span the Yangzi.

Yichang

Situated at the eastern mouth of the gorges, Yichang is the administrative centre of nine surrounding counties. Its population is engaged in light industry, chemical and steel production. The construction of the **Gezhou Dam** helped Yichang to grow from a small town of 30,000 into a city. The Three Gorges Dam is only 44 kilometres (27 miles) upstream. Thus although some houses and factories will be submerged, a plethora of new buildings has been built higher up, in anticipation of the economic boom in the Yichang administrative region.

HISTORY OF YICHANG

History records that as early as 278 BC the town was razed to the ground in a battle between the armies of Chu and Qin. In the Three Kingdoms period (*see* page 42) 50, 000 Wu troops set fire to the encampments of the Shu army, utterly routing Liu Bei, who retreated upriver to Baidi Cheng (*see* page 54).

Yichang became a treaty port in April 1877, in accordance with the Chefoo (Yantai) Convention of 1876 signed with Britain and continued to be the furthest inland treaty port for many years, as large merchant and passenger vessels were not yet able to navigate the gorges upsteam to Chongqing. Here, cargo was unloaded from the larger boats plying the stretch of river between Yichang and Wuhan, and reloaded onto smaller ones running between Yichang and Chongqing.

An American traveller in 1921 described the port as 'crowded, incessantly busy, a perfect maelstrom of sampans, junks, lighters with cargo, steamers and gunboats. 'Eventually technology enabled ships to continue the journey upstream and Chongqing itself became a treaty port in 1891.

The English trader Archibald Little, noting his expenses for a night's stay in the treaty port, showed how far four English pennies went in late 19th-century Yichang, and incidentally his solicitude for his servant:

> Supper for self and coolie, 4 bowls of rice at 10 cash (copper cash),
>
> 'fixings' of cabbage and bean curd free 40
> Use of straw-plaited mattress for ditto, 2 at 10 20
> Breakfast, same as supper 40
> Supper and breakfast for 'Nigger', my dog 20
> Pair of straw sandals for coolie (his old ones being worn out) 12
> Total 132 copper cash, or, in English money, 4d 132

During the warlord years of the early part of this century, Yichang's revenue was greatly boosted by taxes imposed on boats carrying homegrown opium from Yunnan and Guizhou Provinces by its Opium Suppression Bureau.

During the war with Japan, the gorges above Yichang again acted as a barrier. When Wuhan fell to the Japanese in 1938, Yichang became the centre for shipping essential personnel, machinery, libraries and museum collections up the Yangzi to Chongqing. After the Battle of Yichang in 1940 the Japanese capture of Yichang marked their furthest westward advance. The Japanese also used Yichang as a staging area for bombing raids over Chongqing.

WHAT TO SEE IN YICHANG

The streets of the old town centre are lined with trees. Though the city wall was pulled down in 1929, the street names still indicate where it once stood (Eastern Ring Road, Southern Ring Road and so on). The main market is found just off Jiefang Lu. Along the waterfront a few old foreign buildings of the treaty port days can be seen.

Apart from the Gezhou Dam (*see* page 75), tourists may also visit the **Three Travellers' Cave**, ten kilometres (six miles) northwest of the city. In 819, three Tang-dynasty poets, Bai Zhuyi, his brother Bai Xingjian and Yuan Zhen, met up in Yichang and made an excursion to this site. While enjoying the spectacular scenery, they inscribed some poems on the cave walls. Afterwards they were dubbed the 'First Three Travellers'. In the Song dynasty (960–1279) the famous literary family of Su—the father and two sons—on their way to the capital to take the imperial examinations, visited the cave and added poems as well. All three passed the imperial examinations at the same time. People call these gentlemen the 'Second Three Travellers'. Throughout the ages, other visiting literati and officials have left their contributions on the cave walls.

A small spring trickles through the rock near the entrance; local superstition maintains that if women wash their hands in its pure water it will improve their

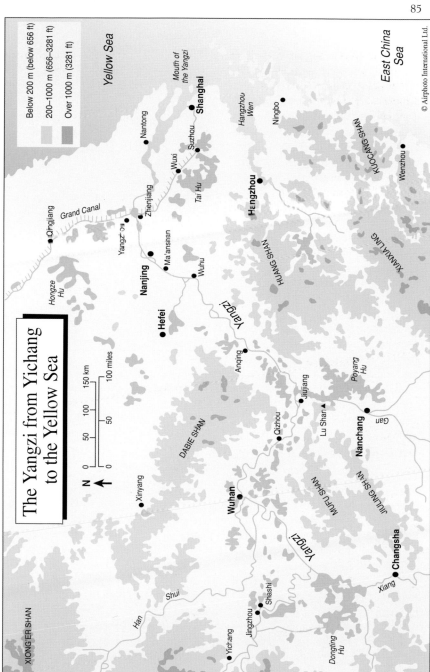

The Yangzi from Yichang to the Yellow Sea

Below 200 m (below 656 ft)
200–1000 m (656–3281 ft)
Over 1000 m (3281 ft)

© Airphoto International Ltd.

culinary skills. The hill above the cave presents a fine view of the entrance to Xiling Gorge: The Zixi Pavilion contains a memorial stone to the 11th-century philosopher Ouyang Xiu, who lived in Yichang for three years. Nearby is a drum platform said to be the site where Zhang Fei (*see* page 42), a general of the third-century Kingdom of Shu, beat his battle drums.

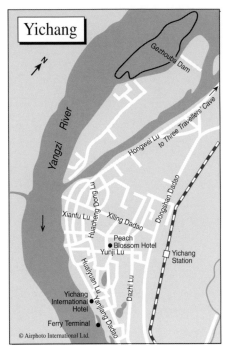

Visitors are usually taken on a short excursion along a mountain road offering stunning views of **Xiling Gorge**, and passing several peaks, including **Filial Mountain** and **Camel Mountain**. The road continues over a natural stone bridge, which was originally—so legend has it—a fairy's silken sash, thrown up to help her mortal husband ascend to heaven with her. The stone gateway and its steep stone steps delineate the ancient land route crossed by travellers to western Hubei and Sichuan.

Below Yichang lies the bluff known as **Tiger's Teeth Gorge** which, for travellers upriver, is the first glimpse of sights to come.

Jingzhou

Jingzhou, previously the famous city of **Jiangling**, has now been somewhat absorbed by the sprawling growth of Shashi, but it is still surrounded by its 16-kilometre (ten-mile) long and nine-metre (30-foot) high city wall. Jingzhou is visited from Shashi. Jingzhou was the capital of Jing, one of the nine great regions into which Emperor Yu, founder of the Xia dynasty (2200–1800 BC), divided China. From Jingzhou the emperor received as tribute exotic gifts of gold, ivory, cinnabar, silver and feathers.

In the Spring and Autumn period (722–481 BC) the city was the capital of the Kingdom of Chu. Its walls, according to tradition, were first built in the third century by Guan Yu, a hero of the Three Kingdoms era. Guan Yu was renowned for his strength, height and valour. A thousand years after his death he was deified as the god of war, and his fierce red-faced image appears in many Chinese temples throughout Asia. Stories of his exploits and battles over the city are vividly told in the novel, *Romance of the Three Kingdoms*.

What to See in Jingzhou

Since Jingzhou was the capital of 20 kingdoms during both the Spring and Autumn and Warring States periods, it is not surprising that valuable artefacts have been found buried in the many tombs on Phoenix Hill. These relics, in particular an important collection of lacquerware, 2,000-year-old silk garments and fabrics, and an almost perfectly preserved male corpse of a Han-dynasty official, are exhibited at the fine **Jingzhou Museum**, also an important research centre, and well worth a visit.

Shashi

Shashi is situated on the north bank of the Yangzi, and its cotton mills are supplied with raw cotton from the rich Jianghan Plain on which it stands. Shashi's population of 240,000 is principally employed in its many light-industrial enterprises—machinery, durable consumer goods, printing, dyeing and textiles. Tourist boats frequently stop in Shashi for a visit to the ancient walled city of Jingzhou nearby.

The city was the port for the ancient city of Jiangling and a distribution centre for produce from surrounding towns and Dongting Lake, which was trans-shipped mostly to Wuhan. This trade was in cotton, beans, grain and aquatic products. In the Tang dynasty (618–907) it already enjoyed a reputation as a prosperous city, but its peak was reached during the years of the Taiping Rebellion, in the mid-19th century (*see* page 112–113). After the rebels captured Nanjing in 1853, river trade on the Yangzi between Shashi and Shanghai more or less came to a standstill, so Shashi became vital to the distribution of products coming downriver from Sichuan.

The Sino-Japanese Treaty of 1895 opened the city to foreign trade; Japanese engaged in the cotton-seed trade formed the majority of the resident foreigners, though this community was never large.

There is a story that the army of Communist General He Long captured Swedish missionaries here in 1931. The women were released following negotiations with the Swedish Consul General, but the release of a doctor was delayed until a ransom was paid. The ransom demanded was: four dozen Parker fountain pens, four dozen watches and 60 or 70 cases of medical drugs!

West of the city, the seven-storeyed **Wanshoubao Pagoda**, built in the Ming dynasty (1368–1644), stands directly on the waterfront. Bas-relief figures of Buddha, set into niches, and inscriptions by the donors adorn its brick facade. A temple once adjoined it.

Below Shashi the river winds tortuously towards Dongting Lake for about 320 kilometres (200 miles). Villages dot the south bank of the river and water buffalo graze in the paddy fields. The north embankment is often too high for a view of the surrounding country.

DONGTING LAKE

The beautiful Dongting Lake is rich in fairy tales and legends. On its eastern shore stands the graceful three-storey **Yueyang Tower** of Yueyang City, one of the Three Great Towers south of the Yangzi (the other two being Yellow Crane Tower in Wuchang, and Prince Teng Pavilion in Nanchang). From its terraces and from pleasure boats on the lake, many famous Chinese poets have been moved to verse.

> The lake embraces distant hills and devours the Yangzi, its mighty
> waves rolling endlessly.
> From morning glow to evening light, the views change a thousand,
> ten thousand times.
> On top of the tower the mind relaxes, the heart delights.
> All honours and disgrace are forgotten.
> What pleasure, what joy to sit here and drink in the breeze.
>
> Fan Zhongyan (989–1052)

Said to have been constructed on the site of a reviewing platform for navy manoeuvres on the lake during the third century, the first tower was erected in 716. The present golden-tiled, square tower dates from 1985, but it has been rebuilt in the Song-dynasty style at great expense.

Legend has it that the tower was saved from collapse by the supernatural powers of Lu Dongbin, a Daoist (Taoist) Immortal, who also got drunk here three times. These occasions are remembered in the form of the Thrice Drunken Pavilion, which flanks the tower.

An excursion on to the lake can be made to **Junshan Island**, 15 kilometres (nine miles) away. Some 4,000 years ago, Emperor Shun, on an inspection tour, died at Mount Jiuyi on the south bank of the lake. Two of his devoted concubines, hurrying to his side, became stranded on Junshan Island. The story goes that in their distress, their copious tears blotted the local bamboo, henceforth known as the Spotted Bamboo of Junshan. They drowned themselves in the lake, and their graves remain. In 219 BC, Emperor Qin Shihuangdi, also on a tour of Dongting Lake, was delayed at Junshan Island by a sudden storm. When he consulted his geomancer as to whether spirits were impeding his progress, he was told of the concubines' graves. In a fury he ordered the burning of the island and had five stone seals placed there, forbidding its name to be used or anyone to visit it.

On the 100-hectare (250-acre) island, Junshan Silver Needle Tea is grown, so highly prized that it was once presented as a tribute to the imperial court.

Once China's largest freshwater lake, the Dongting now ranks second, due to sandbars and silt accumulation from the four rivers which feed it. As a result of flood prevention schemes—6,100 irrigation and drainage channels and 15,000 sluices—the surrounding land has become productive all year round and the lake acts as a reservoir for summer flood waters. The 3,000-square-kilometre (1,160-square-mile) lake abounds in fish.

Luxury goods from Canton—from pearls to kingfisher feathers—reached the ancient capitals by way of the Xiang River, through Dongting Lake, down the Yangzi to Yangzhou and then on up the Grand Canal.

THREE KINGDOMS' RED CLIFF

From the flat bank appears a sharp rock escarpment dotted with pavilions and paths. This is the site of the great Battle of the Red Cliff between the huge forces of Cao Cao of Wei and the combined, lesser armies of Shu and Wu in AD 208. Cao Cao had consolidated the power of the Kingdom of Wei in the north and sought to extend it to the Yangzi. His troops, all from the northern plains, were not accustomed to naval warfare. Nevertheless, he took his army of 200,000 men to launch his attack on the Kingdom of Shu, whose king, Liu Bei, called upon the King of Wu for assistance.

In urgent need of 100,000 arrows to repel the invaders, Zhuge Liang (adviser to Liu Bei) devised a brilliant stratagem. Twenty naval junks, beating war drums, but stacked high with only bundles of straw shrouded in black cloth, feigned an advance on the Wei encampment on a dark, foggy night. The Wei commanders responded by discharging their arrows into the indistinct hulks on the junks. By dawn, each junk bristled with thousands of arrows, more than enough for the army's requirements.

By another ruse, Cao Cao was persuaded by a spy in his camp to secure all his boats together for a forthcoming attack, so that his soldiers would feel as if they were on firm ground. The armies of Wu and Shu set fire to the boats in the midst of the battle and, with a favourable wind, the great conflagration brought about the defeat of Cao Cao, who fled northwards.

Red Cliff itself is said to have been forever scorched red by the flames of this day-long battle. In a victory celebration, General Zhou Yu of Wu, flourishing his writing brush, jubilantly inscribed the gigantic characters 'Red Cliff' (Chi Bi) on the cliff face, which can be seen to this day.

Pavilions on the hill commemorate specific incidents in the battle, and there is an exhibition of over 2,000 weapons, dating from the Three Kingdoms period, that were found in the area. The story of the battle is known to all Chinese, and this makes the site a very popular tourist spot.

HAN RIVER

The Han River, at 1,532 kilometres, or 952 miles, the Yangzi's longest tributary, rises in the Qingling Mountains of Shaanxi Province. In 1488 it changed its course, separating the city of Hanyang from the fishing village of Hankou, as it then was. Though dikes line much of its lower course, this stretch has a history of frequent flooding. The British consular officer, August R. Margary, who travelled all the way from Shanghai up the Yangzi and on to the Burmese border in 1876, only to be murdered by tribesmen as he crossed back into China, wrote of Hankou:

> This year they have had no inundation, but it is of almost annual occurrence. Even at Hankow the foreign settlement is frequently submerged. The river rises

six feet above the level of the fine stone bund they have made there, and quietly takes possession of all the lower rooms in the noble-looking mansions which the merchants occupy. All their dining-room furniture has to be removed above. Boats become the only means of locomotion, and ladies can be seen canoeing in and out of their houses, and over the bund where they are wont to promenade at other times.

Flooding occurred 11 times from 1931 to 1949; in 1931 and 1935 boats sailed down the streets of Wuhan. Though much has been done in recent years to control the Han's waters, the danger of flooding is still very real.

Wuhan

At the centre of the Long River's course to the sea and on the main rail line between north and south China sprawls the tripartite city of Wuhan. Wuhan is set in the vast Jianghan Plain, a region that is more water than land. Levees protect the city from the seasonal ravages of the Yangzi. Wuhan serves as the capital of Hubei Province. It is comprised of three formerly separate cities—Wuchang, Hankou and Hanyang.

On the north bank lies Hankou, the commercial centre and port complex, now gleaming with a new skyline sprouting along its broad avenues. Hankou has always been the most developed of the three cities, ever since treaty port days. It is still the business and shopping heart of the city and contains the sites of former foreign concessions and the waterfront Bund. One may dock in summer flood season to walk down gangways onto the dykes and then down to street level. The passenger ship terminal in Hankou is shaped like a cartoon image of a ship, from where stream thousands of travellers from the sharp-prowed transport ships from Shanghai and Chongqing. Deluxe cruise ships—Chinese style—tie up with their flashing karaoke club lights and "welcome" maidens wearing silk *qipao* on the gangway.

The former British Customs House clock tower remains at water's edge, now topped with a red star. Its prominence is today eclipsed by mirrored nightclubs. New hotels line the waterfront where clipper ships once loaded tea. The jumbled old neighbourhoods and alleyways where foreign sailors once entered at their own risk are being torn down for grander shopping malls. Many of the graceful European-style buildings of the early century are being replaced with glass-walled towers.

One can still hop on bicycle pedicabs to wind through the neighbourhood street markets, which are also being chased out by development. In the remaining old sections, the most interesting parts are too narrow for bikes, but good to walk. Watch your step! The local cuisine is rich in aquatic products including snails, frogs, eels and myriad pond and river fish. Rats are also trapped for culinary use.

Across the Han River flowing from the north is Hanyang, known for the Turtle Hill (Gui Shan) overlooking the Wuhan Chang Jiang Da Qiao (Bridge), the Qing

Chuan Pavilion with its superb river views and the Gi Yuan Si, an active Buddhist temple. Upriver in Hanyang are vast steel plants and factories.

On the south bank of the Yangzi are the administrative and educational campuses of Wuchang, the seat of the Hubei Provincial Government and Wuhan University. The Yellow Crane Tower (Huang He Lou), the famous symbol of Wuhan, rises above the Great River at Wuchang at the foot of the bridge. The Wuhan Chang Jiang Er Qiao (Bridge) links Hankou with Wuchang downriver. The calm reaches of Wuchang's East Lake (Dong Hu) with its bonsai gardens and excellent museums are the best antidote to the smoggy hubbub of the downtown districts.

Wuchang was the site of the 1911 uprising that led to the overthrow of the Qing Dynasty. Mao Ze Dong enjoyed staying in this city and had his own villa on the shore of the Dong Hu.

The Tian He International Airport is just north of the city via a direct expressway. As the city economy continues to grow, much of the old city is being lost to redevelopment, and as in much of China, the new construction lacks the social web of the old neighbourhoods, though many of the traditional fragrances remain.

HISTORY OF WUHAN

The area on which Wuhan stands was settled in the first century; in the third century it was part of the Kingdom of Wu. Wuchang is the oldest of the three cities. By the Yuan dynasty (1279–1368) it was the capital of the region and was enclosed by a city wall until the end of the 19th century.

Hanyang was founded in the Sui dynasty (581–618) and remained a small walled city until a farsighted official of the Qing dynasty (1644–1911), Zhang Zhidong, established factories and an arsenal there in the 1890s.

Hankou was only a fishing village until the 19th century. It is, however, the city of Hankou which is best known to foreigners, for after it was declared a treaty port in 1861 it became a major centre of the tea trade and the focal point of the annual China Tea Races.

There were five Foreign Concessions—British, Russian, French, German and Japanese—situated side by side along the north embankment of the Yangzi. Ocean-going steamers from New York, Odessa and London anchored at their docks. Until the foreign import of opium ceased in the first decade of this century, opium-laden ships sailed up the river as far as Hankou.

Life in the foreign concessions was similar to that in Shanghai. Horse-racing was popular, with Hankou boasting two racecourses, one for Chinese and one for foreigners. There was even a golf course, while the Recreation Club was considered by many to be the best in China at that time.

In the 1911 Revolution, much of Hankou was burnt to the ground during clashes between revolutionaries and imperial troops.

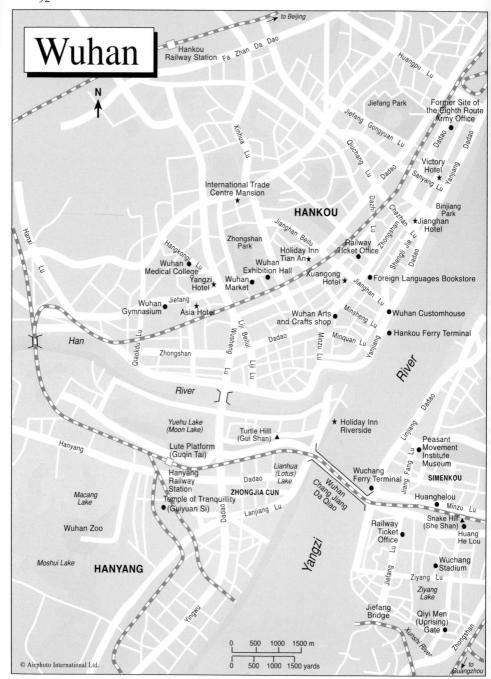

Wuhan

N

to Beijing

Hankou Railway Station

Fa Zhan Da Dao

Xinhua Lu

Huangpu Lu

Jiefang Park

Former Site of the Eighth Route Army Office

Jiefang Gongyuan Lu

Qiuchang Lu

Dadao

Dadao

Victory Hotel

Sanyang Lu

Yanjiang

Dadao

International Trade Centre Mansion

HANKOU

Dazhi Lu

Chezhan Lu

Zhongshan

Binjiang Park

Jianghan Hotel

Shengli Jie

Dadao

Hangkongi Lu

Zhongshan Park

Jianghan Beilu

Railway Ticket Office

Wuhan Medical College

Holiday Inn Tian An

Wuhan Exhibition Hall

Yangzi Hotel

Wuhan Market

Xuangong Hotel

Jianghan Lu

Foreign Languages Bookstore

Wuhan Gymnasium

Jiefang

Asia Hotel

Liji Beilu

Wusheng Lu

Liji Lu

Dadao

Wuhan Arts and Crafts shop

Minsheng Lu

Minzu Lu

Minquan Lu

Yanjiang

Wuhan Customhouse

Hankou Ferry Terminal

Hanxi Lu

Qiaokou Lu

Han

Zhongshan

River

Dadao

Linjiang Dadao

Yuehu Lake (Moon Lake)

Turtle Hilll (Gui Shan) ▲

Holiday Inn Riverside

Lute Platform (Guqin Tai)

Jiang Fang Lu

Peasant Movement Institute Museum

SIMENKOU

Hanyang

Hanyang Railway Station

Lianhua (Lotus) Lake

Dadao

ZHONGJIA CUN

Wuhan Chang Jiang Da Qiao

Wuchang Ferry Terminal

Linjiang Dadao

Huanghelou

Minzu Lu

Macang Lake

Temple of Tranquillity (Guiyuan Si)

Lanjiang Lu

Snake Hill (She Shan) ▲

Huang He Lou

Wuhan Zoo

Railway Ticket Office

Lu

Wuchang Stadium

Moshui Lake

HANYANG

Yangzi

Ziyang Lu

Jiefang

Ziyang Lake

Yingwu

Jiefang Bridge

Qiyi Men (Uprising) Gate

Zhongshan

Xunshi River

Zhongshan

to Guangzhou

0   500   1000   1500 m

0   500   1000   1500 yards

© Airphoto International Ltd.

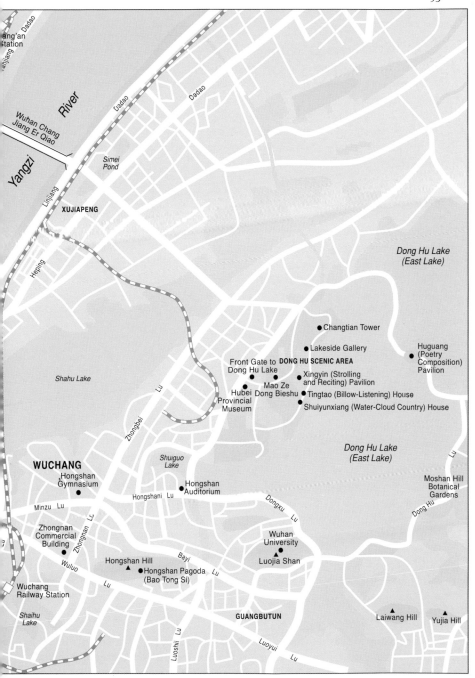

ang'an
Station

Dadao

Linjiang

River

Wuhan Chang
Jiang Er Qiao

Yangzi

Dadao

Dadao

Simei
Pond

Linjiang

Heping

XUJIAPENG

Dong Hu Lake
(East Lake)

Shahu Lake

Lu

Zhongbei

● Changtian Tower

● Lakeside Gallery

Front Gate to **DONG HU SCENIC AREA**
Dong Hu Lake ●
● Xingyin (Strolling
and Reciting) Pavilion
Mao Ze ●
Hubei Dong Bieshu ● Tingtao (Billow-Listening) House
Provincial
Museum ● Shuiyunxiang (Water-Cloud Country) House

Huguang
(Poetry
Composition)
Pavilion ●

Dong Hu Lake
(East Lake)

Lu

Shuiguo
Lake

WUCHANG

Hongshan
Gymnasium ●

● Hongshan
Auditorium

Hongshani *Lu*

Zhongnan Lu

Minzu *Lu*

Zhongnan
Commercial
Building ●

Wuluo

Bayi

Hongshan Hill ▲
● Hongshan Pagoda
(Bao Tong Si)

Lu

Lu

Dongxu
Lu

Wuhan
University
● ▲
Luojia Shan

Moshan Hill
Botanical
Gardens

Dong Hu *Lu*

Wuchang
Railway Station

Shaihu
Lake

Luoshi Lu

GUANGBUTUN

Luoyui
Lu

Laiwang Hill ▲

Yujia Hill ▲

After the fall of the capital, Nanjing, in 1937 to the Japanese during the Sino-Japanese War, the Guomindang government made Wuhan its capital for a year, before moving to Chongqing. In the 1938 assault on Wuhan, casualty figures were in the tens of thousands.

The Communist Party was very active in Wuhan before 1949, organizing railway strikes and peasant training programmes. It was here that Chairman Mao, at the age of 73, took his famous 15-kilometre (nine-mile) swim in the Yangzi during the Cultural Revolution days of 1966.

WHAT TO SEE IN WUHAN

■ HANKOU

Hankou is the main commercial area of Wuhan. Between its long main shopping street, Zhongshan Dadao, and the high embankment along the river are numerous street markets. The old foreign concessions line the embankment for three kilometres (two miles) and this area is still very much intact. The vicinity of Hankou Railway Station is always busy and interesting to walk around. The old Customs House on the waterfront is a distinctive landmark. Jiefang Park and Zhongshan Park, across the railway line, are the sites of the former racecourses.

■ HANYANG

LUTE PLATFORM (GUQIN TAI)

Opposite Turtle Hill (Gui Shan), which overlooks the Han River, is the Hanyang Workers Cultural Palace Gardens, encompassing the charming Lute Platform, a small complex of courtyards, pavilions and gardens enclosed by a tiled wall. It was built in commemoration of two musicians, Yu Baiya and Zhong Ziqi, who lived 2,000 years ago. While visiting Hanyang, Yu played his lute but only Zhong understood and appreciated his performance. They became fast friends and arranged to meet again at the same time the following year. Yu returned only to find that his friend had died. At Zhong's grave, Yu played a farewell song and, vowing never again to use the instrument, broke its strings.

The Lute Platform is now a haven for Chinese opera lovers (mostly men) who gather on Sunday mornings to sip tea and listen to the performers. In the gardens, *wushu* and *taijiquan* (martial arts and exercise) classes are held. Paintings by local artists are on exhibition and for sale in the main hall. Nearby is a Qing memorial stone dedicated to the lute player.

TEMPLE OF TRANQUILLITY (GUIYUAN SI)

This fine Zen Buddhist temple on Cuiwei Lu, where monks from the surrounding provinces gathered to study the scriptures, is 300 years old. The striking architectural complex includes Drum and Bell Towers, temple halls, the Luohan Hall and the

Lotus Pond. The Luohan Hall contains 500 gold-painted wooden statues of Buddhist monk-saints; no two are the same. It is said the two sculptors employed on this task took nine years to complete it. The main hall has a statue of Sakyamuni Buddha which was carved from a single block of jade—a gift from Burma in 1935. The scripture collection includes the rare 7000-volume Longcan Sutra. The temple runs a vegetarian restaurant, the Yunjizhai, for visitors.

QING CHUAN PAVILION (QING CHUAN TING)
The original pavilion was a 16th-century Ming-dynasty structure. The current pavilion is a 1983 reconstruction. The top floor of the pavilon offers a fine view of the Yangzi River and the Yellow Crane Tower, situated on the opposite bank.

■ WUCHANG
YELLOW CRANE TOWER (HUANG HE LOU)
On Snake Hill (She Shan) is the site of the ancient Yellow Crane Tower (Hung He Lou), widely celebrated by Chinese poets throughout the ages. Cranes are one of the traditional Chinese symbols of long life. The legend concerns a Daoist (Taoist) sage who flew away on a yellow crane to become an Immortal. The tower has been rebuilt many times. The tower has five levels covered with yellow tiles and supported by red columns. Being over 50 metres high, the top level offers a wonderful view of the entire Wuhan area. Beside the new Yellow Crane Tower (completed in 1986) is a white *stupa* that dates from the Yuan dynasty (1279–1368).

PROVINCIAL MUSEUM (HUBEI BOWUGUAN)
Off Donghu Lu, near East Lake, this small provincial museum has a rich collection of artefacts excavated in the province. Of special interest is a display of finds from the tomb of Marquis Yi of Zeng from the Warring States period (480–221 BC). Among them is a set of 64 bronze chime bells. Replicas of these have been made and concerts of ancient music are given by a special chime-bells orchestra under the auspices of the Hubei Provincial Museum and Art Institute of Wuhan. The second floor of the museum is devoted to the province's revolutionary history.

HEADQUARTERS OF THE 1911 REVOLUTION (HONG GE)
Known as the Red House, this building on Shouyi Lu was the headquarters of the 1911 Revolution against the Manchu Qing dynasty, led by Dr Sun Yatsen. Today, the building, in front of which stands a statue of Sun, is a museum to that revolution. It is located at the foot of She Shan on Wuluo Lu.

PEASANT MOVEMENT INSTITUTE MUSEUM
Mao Zedong directed this institute between 1926 and 1927. Its object was to train men to organize the peasants into associations to carry out underground activities.

THE HANKOW TEA RACES —Judy Bonavia

The handsome, full-sailed tea clippers which plied the high seas between China and Britain from the 18th to the 19th century were initially confined to the coastal ports—first Canton, then Shanghai and eventually Fuzhou. As the British East India Company lost its monopoly and the tea trade gathered momentum, so did the competition between shipping companies, particularly as the quality of the tea could deteriorate on a long sea journey. The fastest ships charged the highest freight rates in this lucrative trade. This was the origin of the annual China Tea Races, first in elegant clippers and later in the early steamships.

Following the opening of the Yangzi River cities to foreign trade after the 1858 Treaty of Tientsin (Tianjin), the first tea clipper, the *Challenger*, reached Hankou in 1861.

The introduction of the steamship in the middle of the 19th century saw an end to these romantic sailing ships, and the opening of the Suez Canal in 1869 greatly reduced the sailing time. Nevertheless, the Hankow (Hankou) Tea Races continued. Each May, tea buyers, known as *chazi*, came to Hankou as the ships began to arrive from England, Russia and America. The Hankow (Hankou) Club, sprang to life, with the Russian *chazi* drinking only champagne throughout the season. As many as 16 or 17 vessels would make up the British fleet, of which only two or three would be hot favourites and allowed to charge the highest freight rates.

Loaded with their cargo of black and green tea, the race began. The first leg from Hankou to the Red Buoy at Wusong (near Shanghai) could take as little as 36 hours if the ships did not run aground; then down the South China Sea to Singapore, where time was always lost in stockpiling coal for the last leg to London. In the 1877 race, two ships passed the Red Buoy together and reached Singapore with only 1 hour and 40 minutes between them. One ship lost six hours in port and arrived in London only 23 hours behind the winner after an exciting voyage of 31 days.

As the first ships were sighted in the English Channel, word was sent to the London brokers who would rush to the docks as the vessels berthed. In great excitement the tea chests were broken open for samples which were hurried off for inspection by the various buyers.

By the late 1880s India had moved into the lead of tea-exporting countries. The collapse of the China tea market brought about the end of a romantic era.

Picking tea leaves, gouache on pith paper, c. 1870

Tea manufacture, gouache on pith paper, c. 1870

A Hankow Flood

On the outskirts of Hankow, nearly all the so-called Chinese houses—
or, more correctly speaking, all the most miserable shanties, letting in
both wind and rain—on the bank of the river, are raised well up on
piles, thirty to forty feet above high-water mark; narrow wooden
pathways, running between the rows of houses, and small bridges
connecting these pathways where the houses are not continuous. In
these wretched dwellings live some hundreds of families, to all appearance without a care, and in the greatest state of contentment. Their
business, whatever it may be, is mostly connected with boats and junks,
for each house possesses either a sampan or a small, home-made, flat-
bottomed boat, mostly rotten and leaky, which is continually bringing
its occupants to grief, and when not in use is moored to the lower end
of the piles. The owners ascend and descend by means of some iron
spikes, driven in alternatively on either side of one of the piles.

There is in times of flood the greatest distress among the riverside
population. When the water rises twenty-five, thirty, or more feet above
its ordinary level, many of these piles are swept away, down come the
houses, bringing their occupants with them, who are carried away in
the current. Whatever becomes of the remains of these unfortunates, no
one seems to know or to care; not one in twenty is recovered, or ever seen
again. Of course there is great lamentation among the survivors for the
next week; crackers are let off by the thousand, small floating fires are
set adrift on the stream to pacify the river god, gongs are beaten, and
altogether the priests have a busy time.

So little value do the Chinese set upon human life in disasters of this
description, which are of yearly occurrence in one part of the Empire
or another, that the whole thing is soon forgotten, a fresh crowd
occupies the places of the former crowd, piles are re-driven, shanties
rebuilt, and so the new lot live their careless, contented lives till, history
repeating itself, these people follow the lead of their predecessors.

In the early summer of 1887, the Bothwell Castle, a large ocean-
going steamer of three thousand tons, was lying at anchor opposite
Hankow, waiting for a cargo of tea. She had already been there two or

three weeks, and was likely to remain two or three more; the weather being very bad, she made her holding secure with two anchors and a great length of cable. Before receiving her full cargo, one of these sudden floods occurred, and a week or two later I received from Captain Tod the following account of the disaster. He said:

One morning, shortly after breakfast, we heard a rumbling noise far away up the stream, and not long after an immense rush of water, like a large wave, came rolling down the river, carrying with it numbers of junks, boats, houses, trees, cattle, and I should be afraid to say how many human beings, all mixed up in the most inextricable confusion. We heard that the river Han had somewhere received an enormous and sudden flood of water, which, added to its already swollen state, had for many miles flooded the country, and was washing all before it into the Yangtze. Across our anchor-chains eight or ten junks had drifted, and were washed and piled up one over the other. It was impossible to reach them to set them adrift, and I was very much afraid the extra strain on the cables would be too much for them. Fortunately they held, thanks to the best of iron, without a flaw in any of the links.

Numbers of junks came sweeping down with the flood, all unmanageable, many coming broadside on across our bows, which went through them like a knife, the two parts of the junk floating past on either side of our ship. It was quite impossible to launch a boat, she would have been rolled over and swamped the moment she touched the water. With great difficulty and with much risk, we managed to save the lives of three or four dozen people; but, strange to say, some of them were very much displeased at being fished up out of the water. The Chinese said it was 'joss pidgeon', their fate, and as the river joss had taken away their all, he had much better take themselves also. Three or four afterwards tried to jump overboard. We put them ashore as soon as we could, and so relieved ourselves of any further responsibility.'

William Spencer Percival, The Land of the Dragon: My Boating and Shooting Excursions to the Gorges of the Upper Yangtse, *1889*

EAST LAKE (DONG HU)

A large scenic area, in the eastern suburbs of Wuchang, is centred on East Lake. Established in 1949, this enormous park covers 73 square kilometres of lake shore. The lake itself is six times the size of West Lake (Xi Hu) in Hangzhou. The park is full of natural beauty, containing over 372 plant varieties as well as more than 80 species of birds and fish. Around its shores are numerous pavilions, museums and halls, including a memorial to Qu Yuan, the third-century BC poet (*see* page 69), and a monument (Jiu Nudun) to nine heroines who died fighting the Manchu troops during the Taiping Rebellion in the 19th century (*see* page 112). A low causeway leads to Moshan Hill and its botanical gardens with views across the city and the beautiful countryside.

DONGPO RED CLIFF

On the north bank of the Yangzi, just west of Huangzhou city, is the Red Cliff of Su Dongpo. On its summit are pavilions and halls dedicated to one of China's great poets, Su Dongpo (1037–1101). Having passed the imperial examinations at the young age of 20, he held various important scholarly posts in the Northern Song capital of Kaifeng but fell from grace when he criticized new law reforms. After arrest and imprisonment, he was demoted to the status of assistant commissioner to the Huangzhou militia. He lived in considerable hardship with his household of 20 members, tilling a few acres of land himself. The Red Cliff became one of his favourite haunts, and he and his guests, boating beneath the cliff, would compose poetry, drink wine, admire the moon and carouse all night long. In the Qing dynasty (1644–1911) this cliff was named Dongpo Red Cliff to distinguish it from the other Red Cliff that was the scene of a battle in the Three Kingdoms period (*see* page 89). The Qing-dynasty halls contain examples of Su Dongpo's beautiful calligraphy, poems, essays and paintings carved on both stone and wooden tablets.

BAOTONG SI

A buddhist temple located on the slopes of Hong Shan. It features a Grand Hall, Meditation Hall and Abbots Hall. There are two gargantuan iron bells here, almost 900 years old, dating back to the Southern Song Dynasty. It is located inside Hongshan Park.

CHANG CHUN TAOIST TEMPLE (CHANG CHUN GUAN)

The largest and best-preserved Taoist temple in Wuhan. The temple consists of numerous corridors and stone staircases with grand eaves and arches. Decorating the halls are life-sized carvings and niches. Most of the religious relics were destroyed during the Cultural Revolution. Since restoration, the temple now displays a wide range of Taoist cultural relics. It is located in the Dadongmen area, near the intersection of Zhongshan Lu and Wuluo Lu.

Flood level marker from 1931 on Customs House, Wuhan

*The Wuhan steel mill, one of the country's largest, was constructed in 1957
and employs over 120,000 workers*

OLD MAN RIVER: CHAIRMAN MAO AND THE YANGZI
—by Madeleine Lynn

All his life Chairman Mao loved swimming and regarded it as the best of sports, the struggle of man against nature. The Yangzi had powerful associations for him. He grew up with the stories of the heroic battles of the Three Kingdoms period (AD 220–65) which took place along the Yangzi and often sailed the river. His luxurious boat, the *Kunlun*, later became a tourist vessel. A constant theme in his writings is the overcoming of natural and man-made obstacles through sheer determination and courage. As he once observed: 'The Yangzi is a big river, people say. It is big, but not frightening. Is imperialist America big? We challenged it; nothing happened. So, there are things in this world that are big but not frightening.'

Naturally the idea of taming the Yangzi greatly appealed to him. In his 1956 poem 'Swimming', written about the Yangzi, he dreams of a great bridge and a dam to reshape the river forever:

> Great plans are afoot:
> A bridge will fly to span the north and south,
> Turning a deep chasm into a thoroughfare;
> Walls of stone will stand upstream to the west
> To hold back Wushan's clouds and rain
> Till a smooth lake rises in the narrow gorges.
> The mountain goddess if she is still there
> Will marvel at a world so changed.

He was referring to the bridge at Wuhan linking Hanyang and Wuchang, whose opening he presided at a few months later in 1957, naming it 'Iron and Steel Rainbow'. Mao expected that the Three Gorges dam would soon follow, but fierce controversy over the project delayed his dream until 1993, when work was finally begun.

In 1956, 1958 and again most famously in 1966, Mao made a series of highly publicized long swims across the Yangzi at Wuhan (the above poem was written after the first of these). These were all years when Mao felt that his position was threatened by rumours of bad health and by the machinations of his enemies. Swimming the Yangzi was his way of showing the world that he was still healthy and in command; that he could keep his head above water, so to speak.

The celebrated 1966 swim, when Mao was 73, was part of the launch of the Cultural Revolution and the cult of Mao as a superhuman figure. Power struggles had been going on behind the scenes. Mao's whereabouts were kept secret and he had appeared in public only once all year. There were rumours that he was gravely ill or even dead. Then came the 16 July swim. Accompanying 5,000 young swimmers in the annual race across the river at Wuhan, he is reported to have swum almost 15 kilometres (nine miles) in 65 minutes, swimming along with the currents. Pictures of Mao's head bobbing above the water, surrounded by swimmers carrying huge banners celebrating his achievement, were seen not only throughout China but around the world. The message was clear; even in his 70s, Mao was a force to be reckoned with.

WUHAN UNIVERSITY (WUHAN DAXUE)
Founded in 1913, it is still considered one of the best universities in the country. Its campus displays many examples of pre-1949 Chinese architecture. It is located at the foot of Luo Jia Shan near Dong Hu.

Qizhou

About one hour's sailing east of **Huangshi**, the industrial and iron ore mining city below Wuhan, is the small town of Qizhou. Though it has a history of 1,000 years, it is famous as the home town of Li Shizhen (1518–93), a Ming-dynasty herbalist and physician. After practising Chinese medicine in his youth, Li spent 30 years rewriting and categorizing ancient Chinese medical books, travelling far and wide in search of specimens. His treatise formed 52 scrolls, with almost 2,000 entries. Sadly, he died before receiving recognition. However, his son presented a copy of Li's work to Emperor Wanli (1573–1620), a patron of scholarship. The emperor, much pleased with the work, ordered its wide distribution. Li Shizhen's classical works are the basis of traditional Chinese medical practice today and have been translated into a number of foreign languages.

The graves of Li Shizhen and his wife are situated at Rain Lake, north of the town, surrounded by gardens of medicinal herbs.

The local bamboo is used for making summer bed mats, and flutes made from this bamboo were widely praised as early as the Tang dynasty. Qizhou's White Flower Snake medicine is supposed to relieve rheumatic pains, while its Green Hairy-backed Turtles are used in medicines that allegedly cure tuberculosis and body fluid deficiencies.

About halfway between Qizhou and Jiujiang, the river leaves Hubei Province and thenceforth marks the provincial boundary between Hubei to the north and Jiangxi to the south as far as the mouth of Poyang Lake.

Jiujiang

Though the capital of Jiangxi Province is Nanchang, Jiujiang, with a population of 355,000, is the main port for distributing products from Poyang Lake and the surrounding counties as well as much of the chinaware produced at the porcelain capital of Jingdezhen. It has the reputation of being the hottest port on the Yangzi, with extremely oppressive summers. Though once an important tea-buying centre in its own right, it was gradually superseded by Wuhan, and tea grown in Jiangxi was shipped either upstream to Wuhan or downstream to Shanghai. Today, cotton textiles form Jiujiang's main industry.

Jiujiang is the main access city to one of China's most famous mountain beauty spots, Lushan, lying only a short distance to the south, which attracts 2.5 million tourists a year. Jiujiang no longer has an airport. The closest airport is Nanchang.

HISTORY OF JIUJIANG

In ancient times, nine rivers were said to have converged at this point, hence the name Jiujiang—'Nine Rivers'—though it was also called Jiangzhou and Xunyang. In its long history it has seen many upheavals; in the last century it was a Taiping stronghold from which the rebels held out against the imperial Qing armies for five years.

The area holds many memories for lovers of Chinese poetry. Tao Yuanming (365–429) lived at the foot of Lushan and was appointed magistrate of nearby Pengze County. This post was so poorly endowed that, rather than work 'for five pecks of grain to break one's back', he resigned after 83 days, preferring to eke out a living as a recluse in his home village. His essay *Peach Flower Garden* depicts his idea of a perfect society. Li Bai (701–62), implicated in the An Lushan Rebellion, was imprisoned briefly in Jiujiang in 757. Bai Juyi (772–846) also spent a period of official disgrace here as a middle-ranking official and is affectionately remembered. His poem *The Lute Song* tells of his sadness at his isolation in this small town. Su Dongpo was a frequent visitor to the area.

When Jiujiang was thrown open as a treaty port in 1862 it had suffered terribly as a consequence of the Taiping Rebellion (1850–64, *see* pages 112–113). A British member of Lord Elgin's mission noted in 1858:

> We found it to the last degree deplorable. A single dilapidated street, composed only of a few mean shops, was all that existed of this once thriving and populous city: the remainder of the vast area, composed within walls five or six miles in circumference, contained nothing but ruins, weeds, and kitchen gardens.

Jiujiang was once one of the three centres of the tea trade in China, along with Hankou and Fuzhou. There were two Russian factories producing brick-tea, but these ceased to operate after 1917. The British concession in Jiujiang was given up in 1927 after looting by mutineering garrisons and mobs.

With most of his 65 years spent on the barges of the Grand Canal in Jiangsu Province, Huang Bing Zhang retired a few years ago. But bored with life on dry land he returned to work on the water once more, his barges carrying cargo destined for the industrial area along the Yangzi River.

Economic recession set in by the 1880s with greater competition from tea producers in India and Ceylon. With the military advance downriver from Wuhan led by the Guomindang in 1927, the remaining foreign community fled on British and American warships to the safety of Shanghai, never to return. Jiujiang was surrendered officially by Britain in 1927.

What to See in Jiujiang

Sycamore trees line the streets of Jiujiang. The old downtown area is not large, sandwiched between Gantang Lake and the river bank. The old foreign concession area abuts the riversteamer dock and some old buildings remain—a church, the old French hospital and the Council House (now the Bank of China).

Crunchy, sweet Jiujiang tea biscuits made from tea oil, sesame and orange osmanthus flower originated in the Song dynasty; so did the potent, strange-tasting local wine, Fenggang Jiu, made from glutinous rice and fermented in sealed vats for five years.

■ GAN TANG LAKE (GAN TANG HU) AND YAN SHUI PAVILION (YAN SHUI TING)
Gantang Lake was divided into two by a dyke and bridge built in 821 during the Tang dynasty. Sixian Bridge, now enlarged, still stands on the causeway which one crosses to reach Yangyue Pavilion on the low hill overlooking the lake. It is well stocked with silver and grass carp, and seagulls skim its surface. It is said that in the Three Kingdoms period (220–265) the Eastern Wu general, Zhou Yu, inspected his warships from a reviewing platform on the lake, traces of which remain.

Linked to the shore by a zigzag bridge is the pretty **Yanshui (Misty Water) Pavilion**. A pavilion was first built here in the Tang dynasty (618–907) by the poet Bai Juyi during his unhappy posting in Jiujiang. It was named the Drenched Moon Pavilion after a line from one of his poems: 'Bidding farewell I saw the moon drenched by the river.'

In the Northern Song period (960–1127) a highly regarded Neo-Confucian philosopher, Zhou Dun, taught in Jiujiang and his son built a pavilion on the lake to his father's memory, calling it Yanshui Pavilion. The present island pavilion dates from the late Qing period (1644–1911). One small hall is dedicated to Bai Juyi, and other rooms display local archaeological discoveries. The city's antiques store is located here.

■ NENG REN TEMPLE (NENG REN SI)
The Qing halls here are the oldest buildings left in Jiujiang, although this Yuan-dynasty Buddhist temple was established earlier, in the sixth century. Three or four monks and several nuns tend the temple. The seven-storey **Great Victory Pagoda**, beside the temple, dates from the Song period (960–1279).

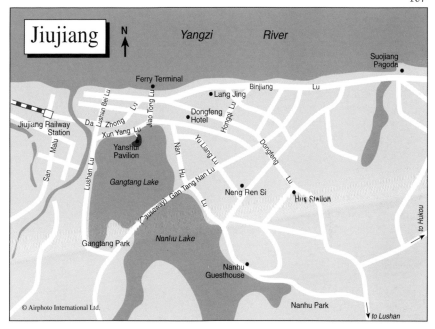

■ SUO JIANG PAGODA (SUO JIANG TA)

This hexagonal seven-storey pagoda, overlooking the Yangzi embankment to the north-east of the city, was built in 1585. Damage to the 35-metre (115-foot) high pagoda caused by shelling from Japanese gunboats in World War II is still visible.

■ WAVE WELL (LANG JING)

Near the waterfront is a small ancient well with a quaint history. Dug early in the Han dynasty (206 BC–AD 220), it connected with the Yangzi so that when a wind created waves on the river the surface of the well water would ripple too. The well became clogged and disused over the years until it was rediscovered in the third century, and the original inscription and date were uncovered. This was such a good omen that the well was renamed Auspicious Well. The poet Li Bai in the eighth century referred to it as the Wave Well in one of his poems, as did Su Dongpo. Waves no longer appear on its surface but the well is still in use.

■ DONG LIN TEMPLE (DONG LIN SI)

Twenty-two kilometres (13.5 miles) southwest of Jiujiang at the foot of Lushan is the Donglin (Eastern Forest) Temple, built in 386 for the monk Hui Yuan (334–416), founder of the Pure Land sect of Buddhism, whose overgrown grave is behind the temple. He spent many years translating Buddhist scriptures, and among his 123 disciples were an Indian and a Nepali. The temple reached its zenith in the Tang dynasty (618–907), with a vast library of scriptures and over 300 halls and residences. Seriously damaged during the Taiping Rebellion (1850–64), the temple was almost ruined in the Republican period (1911–49). Today there is a community of 20 monks who hold daily services in the temple halls. Behind the temple in a bamboo grove is the Well of Intelligence—from which every visitor is anxious for a sip. The Luohan Pine trees in the courtyard are said to have been planted by Hui Yuan himself. Hui Yuan is also said to have struck the ground with his staff, causing the Ancient Dragon Spring to gush forth, thus proving his right to establish himself here. Nearby is the Xi Lin Pagoda(Xi Lin Ta), all that remains of an earlier temple complex.

Lushan

Lushan, in the vicinity of Jiujiang, has always been appreciated by the Chinese as a mountain of great beauty and as a haven from the intense humid heat of the Yangzi valley summers. Its views eastwards to Poyang Lake and northward across the river are spectacular. Guesthouses and sanatoriums (over 1,000 of them) abound in the Guling valley.

Since passengers from the downstream steamers usually disembark in the small hours of the morning, it is possible to enjoy the sunrise as your vehicle negotiates the hairpin bends on the 29-kilometre (18-mile) trip to the top of Lushan.

April and May are the best times to visit, when the hills are covered with wild azalea and peach blossoms, and there are many waterfalls. In the enervating months of June, July and August, the average temperature on Lushan is a comfortable 23°C (73°F), and during this peak season 35,000 tourists visit each day. In autumn the numbers drop off markedly and one is able to enjoy the changing autumnal colours of the trees at leisure, though the waterfalls dry up.

The town of **Guling** was established at the end of the 19th century by foreign traders and missionaries as a summer retreat for their families from as far away as Shanghai. They built over 100 summer bungalows and an American hospital (now the Lushan Guesthouse). They would be carried by sedan chair along the narrow path up the mountainside. Today the town is almost perfectly preserved. Chiang Kai-shek's summer house—Meilu Villa—is still there near the lake Lu Lin Hu, as is his library which now houses the **Lushan Museum**. Beside this is **Lushan People's Theatre** where in 1959 the Communist Party of China held its eighth plenary session, known later as the Lushan Conference, which resulted in the dismissal of the People's Liberation Army Commander-in-Chief, Peng Dehuai. In December 1926, the Guomindang held an important party conference at the same place to mediate between the rival Wuhan and Nanjing factions. Two more important party conferences were held there in 1959 and 1970. The **Botanical Garden** (Zhi Wu Yuan) was established in 1934; it has more than 4,000 kinds of flowers, trees and other plants.

Strange rock shapes, sheer peaks (the highest, Dahanyang is 1,543 metres, or 5,060 feet), steep cliffs, overhangs and caves, as well as a wide variety of lovely trees, are some of the splendours of Lushan. Its mystery is captured by Su Dongpo, who wrote:

Economy of Time and Labour, *copper engraving, c. 1790*

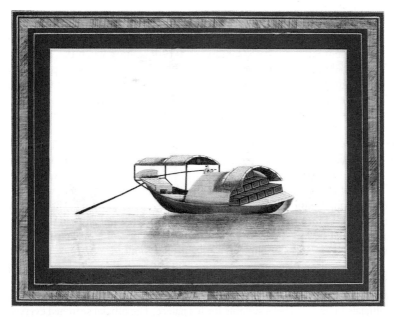

Chinese Junk, *gouache on pith paper, 19th century*

It's a ridge when looked at face to face,
It's a peak when looked at sidewise;
It's always not the same when looked at from afar or near, when looked at from above or below.
You don't know what Lushan is really like,
Merely because you yourself are living in it.

Special Lushan dishes are the small Stone Fish from the Xilin River (best eaten in spring and autumn), Stone Ear (a black fungus), and Stone Chicken (a black-skinned frog found in the damp caves on Lushan, tasting rather like chicken and best eaten between June and September), as well as fish from Poyang Lake.

Lushan's Misty Cloud Green Tea (Yunwu Lu Cha), once sent as tribute to the emperors, should be sampled. The tea leaves are processed seven times to obtain their special fragrance.

STONE BELL HILL (SHIZHONG SHAN)

After taking a small vehicular ferry across the mouth of Poyang Lake to Hukou, one may climb the small, 50-metre (165-foot) high Stone Bell Hill, to which visitors have been coming for centuries. The hill overlooks the lake and the Yangzi River, and the meeting of the waters is clearly defined by an abrupt colour change. Mystery surrounds the strange bell-like sound that can be heard at Stone Bell Hill. There are three theories: that the hill is shaped like a bell and is hollow inside; that the rock, when struck, rings like a bell; or that the water, lapping into the nooks and crannies around the base, causes a bell-like sound. Su Dongpo made three special trips to try to solve the mystery, and having eventually settled on the last explanation, wrote an essay on the subject.

The present buildings date from the mid-19th century when the Taiping rebel commander Shi Dakai, choosing the mouth of the lake as a defensive position, built a stronghold on the hill, occupying it between 1853 and 1857. The Qing armies, miscalculating their enemy's strength, entered the lake in their war-junks, where upon the Taipings stretched ropes across the lake mouth, dividing the Qing navy into two and routing them. The Qing general, Zeng Guofan, utterly humiliated, attempted to drown himself but was rescued by his retinue. The remains of the Taiping army stronghold can still be seen, and a pavilion on the hillside contains a stone tablet dedicated by Zeng Guofan to those who lost their lives in that battle (*see* page 112).

Peng Yulin, also a Qing general, later built a wonderful villa here with winding balconies, small ponds, carved pavilions and exquisite gardens. The lovely two-storeyed **Plum Flower Hall** (**Meihua Ting**) was erected in memory of the cultivated young woman he loved but could not marry. She died of a broken heart and he painted 11,000 pictures of plum flowers with her in mind.

This hill is also called the Lower Stone Bell Hill to distinguish it from the Upper Stone Bell Hill nearby. There is a delightful legend about the formation of these two small hills. The supreme Daoist (Taoist) deity, the Jade Emperor, instructed one of his officials to find two bells suitable for his palace. The official searched everywhere until he finally found two stone hills shaped like bells. He was delivering them to the palace when his carrying pole broke at the mouth of Poyang Lake; the stone hills fell to the ground and have remained there ever since.

DRAGON PALACE CAVE
Sixty-seven kilometres (42 miles) east of Jiujiang, this 1,700-metre (1,860-yard) long natural cave is in the scenic surroundings of **Dark Dragon Hill (Wulong Shan)**, in Pengze County, Jiangxi Province. This natural beauty spot comprises eight adjoining caverns with interior limestone formations resembling palace lanterns, dragon thrones, boats and other objects. One section is called the East Sea Dragon Palace after the classic 16th-century Chinese novel *Pilgrimage to the West* (sometimes known as *Monkey*). Coloured lighting heightens the effect.

POYANG LAKE
The surface area of China's largest freshwater lake is around 5,000 square kilometres (1,930 square miles), increasing in size during the flood season and shrinking in winter. Five rivers flow into the lake and eight counties border it. The Yangzi, Poyang Lake and the Gan River form a link, via the Meiling Pass on the border between Jiangxi and Guangdong provinces, as far south as Guangzhou. From ancient times, this fertile region has been one of the 'rice-bowls' of China. The Poyang teems with fish, such as mandarin, anchovy and whitebait. It continues to fulfil its age-old function as a transport link for local produce—grain, tea, silk, bamboo, and particularly the porcelain from the kaolin (white clay) potteries of Jingdezhen, which have been producing since the second century BC, and supplying the imperial court from the fifth century on.

A 22,000-hectare (54,000-acre) nature reserve has been established in the vicinity of Wucheng on the western side of the lake. It hosts Asia's greatest bird spectacle in winter, when over 4,000 cranes, 40,000 swan geese and around a quarter of a million ducks flock here. Over 90 per cent of the world's population of the Siberian Crane winter at the reserve. Numbers have increased dramatically since the area became a protected reserve, with 1,700 birds counted in 1988.

Owing to the lake's strategic importance, numerous naval encounters took place on its waters. Emperor Wudi (reigned 420–23) was embattled here. It was the site of a decisive battle in the overthrow of the Yuan dynasty in the 14th century. Another naval battle was fought between the Taiping rebels and the Qing imperial forces in 1855. Today, only graceful fishing boats in full sail occupy the lake.

Local fairy tales connect a small island in the lake, **Shoe Hill** or **Dagu Shan**, with the stories of Xiaogu Shan (*see* page 116) further downstream. It seems that Xiaogu Niang Niang and her betrothed escaped from her Emei Shan prison with the help of a precious umbrella. The pursuing Immortal, confronting them at Poyang Lake, threw his flying sword at the precious umbrella and, in her confusion, Xiaogu Niang Niang lost one of her embroidered slippers, which fell into the lake and was transformed into a shoe-shaped island.

THE TAIPING REBELLION   —by Madeleine Lynn

There were many violent peasant uprisings between 1840–1911. But the Taiping Rebellion (1850–64) was more than just another revolt; it was the most devastating civil war the world has ever known. It affected nearly two-thirds of China, destroying entire cities and causing an estimated 20 to 30 million deaths, more people than China lost in the war against Japan (1937–45). A 1950s government census found that the population of provinces near the mouth of the Yangzi was still a total of 20 million lower than it had been in 1850.

The rebellions of the period were prompted by a series of interlinked misfortunes. The unpopular Manchurian Qing dynasty (1644–1911) was growing weaker and Western incursions more far-reaching. Thousands lost their jobs as traditional industries such as weaving were wiped out by Western imports. Corrupt officials taxed the peasants ever more extortionately in order to pay for these imports, the chief of which was opium. To make matters worse, untold numbers died in famine after terrible famine. These were caused by natural disasters, a huge population increase during the early Qing, and neglect of the irrigation systems.

The Taiping leader Hong Xiuquan was a poor school teacher from a village near Guangzhou (Canton) who had had some contact with missionaries and their teachings. After failing the imperial examinations several times, he suffered a nervous breakdown, during which he saw visions. These revealed to him that he was the son of God, the younger brother of Jesus Christ. His earthly mission was to expel the Manchu demons from China and to create a Heavenly Kingdom of Peace on earth (Taiping Tianguo), where all men and women would be equal.

The Taipings formally declared rebellion in 1851 and thousands of peasants and dispossessed workers rose up to join them. In 1852 they took to the water on a motley collection of boats and rafts, sweeping through the waterways of Guangxi, along the Grand Canal and up the Yangzi, sacking cities and amassing loot, boats and followers as they went. Their numbers grew to over a million people and they easily defeated the demoralized imperial troops in their path. In 1853 they reached Nanjing, where they set up their capital. From here they ruled over their Heavenly Kingdom for the next 11 years. At their peak, almost half of China was under their control.

After establishing their government, the Taipings sent an army to attack the Manchu capital of Beijing. But they were turned back by imperial forces organized by the big Northern landlords. Returning to Nanjing, they consolidated their power, successfully repelling a Qing attack in 1860 and to many it seemed that they would become the next ruling Dynasty.

Although it is hard to know how far the Taiping reforms extended throughout their territory, in Nanjing and its environs at least, land was divided equally between all men and women over 16, half-shares going to those under 16. Footbinding, slavery and concubinage were abolished. Women served in their own battalions, which were commanded by female officers. Opium and infanticide were illegal.

Yet this supposedly egalitarian society was actually a totalitarian theocracy, run by the Heavenly King Hong Xiuquan himself and four assistant Kings. While ordinary Taipings were allowed only one wife and lived spartan, disciplined lives, the Kings lived in luxury surrounded by concubines. As time went on Hong became ever more paranoid and in 1856, suspecting the East King of treachery, he had him and about 20,000 of his followers killed in one bloody night. Later he also turned on the North King and had him assassinated.

Meanwhile after the defeat of 1860, the Manchus and Chinese gentry continued to fight the Taipings under the able leadership of Zeng Guofan. At first the Western powers remained neutral and many Westerners, particularly missionaries, were favourable towards the Taipings. But the devastation they wrought—some cities changed hands so many times in the fighting that there was little left to fight over—and a closer look at their version of Christianity, changed most people's minds. The final straw came when the Taipings closed in on Shanghai in 1862 and threatened the foreign community there. Thereafter the West supplied the Manchus with western weapons and lent them commanders to train their forces. One such was 'Chinese Gordon', who took part in the burning of the Summer Palace and later died at Khartoum.

The end came with the long siege of Nanjing in 1864. As the siege wore on, Hong grew more and more out of touch with reality. After praying for Manna from Heaven, he told his starving citizens to gather ten loads each of grass and leaves and eat that. A few days before the imperial forces finally dynamited the city walls, Hong died of a lingering illness probably compounded by following the diet he had imposed on the others. Many committed suicide, chanting hymns as they did so, some by throwing themselves in the moat, others by torching their houses. Many of Hong's concubines hanged themselves in the Palace garden. Over 7,000 people were massacred in three days. Lord Elgin on visiting Nanjing soon afterwards, said that the desertion of the streets and the universal stillness reminded him of Pompeii.

The Lower Reaches:
Hukou to the Yellow Sea

The region around the lower Yangzi and its delta, the most prosperous in the country, is known as China's 'Land of Fish and Rice'.

From Hukou at the mouth of the Poyang, the Yangzi widens on its final sweep to the Yellow Sea, skirting northern Jiangxi and traversing the provinces of Anhui and Jiangsu. Hundreds of shallow lakes and streams, rich in freshwater crabs, prawns and fish, feed the river From Nanjing downwards the river becomes tidal, and ocean-going vessels of 10,000 to 15,000 tons navigate its channels.

The deltaic plain of coastal Jiangsu—the most densely populated of China's provinces—is a veritable maze of natural waterways, man-made dykes and canals. Mulberry trees line their banks and humpbacked stone bridges link the picturesque towns and villages. These waterways serve as irrigation channels, drainage outlets and transport canals. Three staple grain crops—two of paddy rice and one of winter wheat—are harvested each year. Since earliest times, sericulture has been an important economic factor, and though cotton replaced silk in importance after the 1930s, silkworm breeding is still a major home industry and hard-cash earner for peasant families. Sericulture formed the basis on which the region's famous textile cities of Hangzhou, Suzhou, Wuxi, Nanjing and Shanghai were established.

Water conservation plans are underway to divert water from the Yangzi northwards, linking up with similar projects on the Huai River, which will eventually irrigate the large arid areas of north China.

Neolithic rice-growing cultures occupied this area as early as 5000 BC, domesticating pigs and dogs. By the fifth century BC much of the lower Yangzi formed one of nine huge provincial areas known as Yangzhou; its imperial tribute included silks, fruits and timber. During the Tang dynasty (618–907) the city of Yangzhou was the main port of call for Arabian traders.

The town of Jiangyin demarcates the estuary, and for the next 200 kilometres (125 miles) the Yangzi widens from 1,200 metres (1,300 yards) to 91 kilometres (56 miles) below the confluence with the Huangpu, the last of its tributaries. In ancient times the Yangzi was said to have had three mouths; down the centuries the river outlet was a source of much academic speculation in China, as silt deposits continually changed the shape and form of the river's mouth. Now its outlet to the Yellow Sea is divided into two by the intensely cultivated island of Chongming (1,083 square kilometres, or 420 square miles, in area) and by several smaller islands, whose farming produce supplies the massive Shanghai area (*see* satellite photograph on pages 4–5). In August 1983, when low-lying land in 30 Anhui counties that border

A large junk under full sail, a rare sight on the Yangzi River today

the Yangzi was inundated by flood waters, nearly a million peasants battled to drain the land and sow autumn crops. Ninety people were reported dead and hundreds injured as the flood crest swept by. In Jiangsu, 500,000 civilians and soldiers reinforced dykes and stood watch as floods threatened Nanjing and other cities along the banks. Luckily no further serious damage occurred, although similar flooding claimed hundreds more lives in 1998.

XIAOGU SHAN

About 35 kilometres (22 miles) below the mouth of the Poyang, the magical little island of Xiaogu Shan comes into view. It is situated by the north bank of the Yangzi in Anhui Province, while across the river is the county town of Pengze in Jiangxi.

The white walls and grey-tile roofs of **Qisu Temple** nestle into Xiaogu Shan's steep slope, and pavilions adorn its bamboo-groved peak. A handful of elderly monks inhabit the temple (first established in the Song dynasty, 907–1279), which is dedicated to Xiaogu Niang Niang, and visited by childless women offering incense to her.

As a result of silt accumulation, Xiaogu Shan now adjoins the riverbank. The characters 'First Pass of the Sea Gate' are painted on the rock face. Stairs lead up to the temple, but to reach the peak one must cling to chains fixed to the rock to negotiate the steep climb.

The island is named after the legendary Lin Xiaogu, later known as Xiaogu Niang Niang, who grew up in Fujian Province and became betrothed to a local village lad, Peng Liang. Unhappily, her parents died, and she was adopted by a Daoist (Taoist) Immortal at Mount Emei in Sichuan Province, where she studied Daoism for many years. One day, while gathering herbs on the mountain, she slipped and fell, and was saved by a wandering woodcutter who was none other than Peng Liang. Peng's mother, attending to the girl's injuries, noticed a small birthmark behind her ear and recognized her as the long-lost Lin Xiaogu. In renewing her betrothal to Peng Liang, Xiaogu broke her religious vows and was incarcerated by the Immortal.

With the help of a sympathetic monk she stole the Immortal's precious umbrella, and the lovers flew away. However, the pursuing Immortal cut off their escape at Poyang Lake with his flying sword, which tore the umbrella and caused Xiaogu to drop her slipper (*see* page 111). At Pengze the umbrella finally split in two. The lovers fell on different sides of the Yangzi, turning into two steep hills: Pengliang Ji on the south and Xiaogu Shan on the north. The temple on Pengliang Ji was destroyed in the Cultural Revolution (1966–76).

At the top of Xiaogu Shan is her 'Make-up and Dressing Terrace'. A stone tablet beside it describes her story, as well as a related anecdote concerning Zhu Yuan-zhong, founder of the Ming dynasty in 1368, who was saved by the appearance of Xiaogu Niang Niang while retreating downstream one night after a naval defeat.

About 32 kilometres (20 miles) below Pengze the river enters Anhui and winds its way northeast across the province until, just below Ma'anshan, it enters the province of Jiangsu. Bulk carriers, strings of barges and fishing *sampans*—their nets attached to long bamboo poles extending forward and aft—frequent the stretch of river between here and Anqing, about three hours' sailing downriver. The south bank is hilly while the north bank is flat, broken only by trees and bamboo groves. A number of shallow lakes feed into the river.

Anqing

The city of Anqing, on the north bank, is situated in that area of Anhui Province called Huainan, meaning south of the Huai River. It is built along the Dalong Hills amidst pretty surroundings. Historical records refer to the appointment of an official to the town as early as the Spring and Autumn period (770–476 BC). During the Qing dynasty (1644–1911) and the Republican period (1911–49) the city was the capital of the province, though today the capital is Hefei, further north. Anqing's main function is to gather and distribute local produce; it also has a petrochemical industry.

The handsome octagonal **Zhenfeng Pagoda**, the major landmark, was built in 1570 amidst the remains of the Song-dynasty Welcoming the River Temple (Yingjiang Si). A fine view of the city can be enjoyed from its top storey.

The pagoda was built by a Daoist (Taoist) architect, Zhang Wencai, who was brought to Anqing specially from Baiyun Temple in Beijing. Stone balconies surround six of its seven storeys. Inside, over 600 Buddha images cover the brick walls. Set into the lower half of the pagoda are images of the local prefect, Wang Erquan, who commissioned its construction, and other personages of the period.

The town was occupied by the Taiping rebels for six years, and one of its kings built a residence here. It seems that the imperial defences of Anqing left much to be desired, for when it fell to the rebels in 1853 Emperor Xianfeng wrote: 'Great has been my indignation on reading the memorial . . . how could that important provincial capital be captured by the bandits in one day?' The city, retaken in 1861, was ravaged. Travellers to the city 60 years later noted that large parts of it were still in ruins.

Riverboats stop at **Guichi** (at the mouth of the Qiupu River), which is the closest Yangzi port for those visiting the sacred Buddhist mountain of Jiuhua and the famous scenic area of Huangshan to the south. These can be reached by bus, although Wuhu, further downriver, offers more choice of transport.

Wuhu

Wuhu, on the south bank of the river, is in southeastern Anhui Province at the confluence of the Qingyi and Yangzi Rivers. Its population is only 440,000, not large by Chinese standards. In the last century, Wuhu was one of the four great rice-marketing centres (the others being Wuxi, Jiujiang and Changsha), but it is now principally a producer of light-industrial goods, such as thermos flasks, machine tools, cotton textiles, kitschy mantlepiece clocks and cement. It is specially known for its scissors, its variety of local twig and leaf brooms and its wrought-iron pictures.

As a good transportation system links Wuhu with other parts of the province, the city is a transfer stop for visitors to the famous scenic spots of Huangshan and Jiuhua. However, this is the farthest up the Yangzi River valley you can travel by train from Shanghai and Nanjing. From here the train line travels north to Hefei.

HISTORY OF WUHU
In the Spring and Autumn period (770–476 BC) the city was known as Jiuzi. Its present name was adopted in the Han dynasty (206 BC–AD 220). By the Three Kingdoms period (220–65 AD, *see page 42*) it had become a strategically important town in the Kingdom of Eastern Wu. In a fierce battle between the Kingdoms of Eastern Wu and Shu, the Wu general Zhou Yu was killed. The King of Wu, Sun Quan, donned white mourning clothes and made a special journey to Wuhu to receive Zhou Yu's coffin.

In the Tang dynasty (618–907) the poet Du Fu's many visits were recollected in his poem, *Thoughts on Staying Again at Wuhu*. When Wuhu became a Treaty Port under the Chefoo (Yan Tai) Convention of 1876 a small foreign community resided here. Trading principally in rice, wood and tea, it had become a flourishing commercial port by the end of the 19th century. Trade dropped off severely in the 1920s and 1930s due to bandit activity in the area. When the city was captured by the Guomindang army in March 1927, anti-foreign riots broke out. The foreign community had to be evacuated by warships patrolling the Yangzi.

WHAT TO SEE IN WUHU
There is little of historical interest to be found in Wuhu, but a stroll along the east embankment of the Qingyi River is worthwhile. Here barges and small boats load and discharge vegetables, fruit, sand and everyday items; boat families and their pets add to the cacophony of noise. Bamboo rafts, at intervals along the river's edge, serve as platforms for the local women to do their washing. In the narrow streets parallel to the river, such as Zhongchang Jie and Shangchang Jie, shops sell fishing tackle and nets, baskets, firecrackers, bamboo steamers, and Chinese weights and measures. In

The morning's fishing completed, a fisherman in Jiangsu Province wheels his small craft home. His trained cormorants perch obediently on the boat preening themselves. This fishing method is still practised in areas along the Yangzi River.

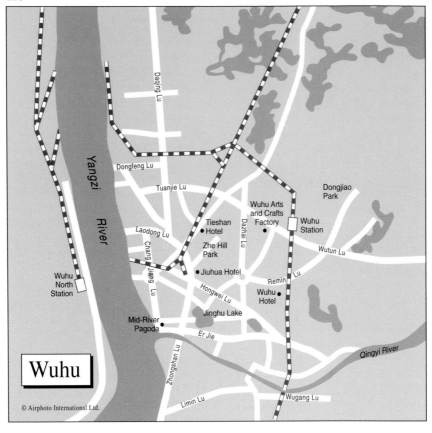

Daqing Lu

Yangzi

River

Dongfeng Lu

Tuanjie Lu

Laodong Lu

Chang Jiang Lu

Wuhu
North
Station

Tieshan
Hotel

Zhe Hill
Park

Jiuhua Hotel

Hongwei Lu

Jinghu Lake

Mid-River
Pagoda

Er Jie

Zhongshan Lu

Limin Lu

Dazhai Lu

Wuhu Arts
and Crafts
Factory

Wuhu
Station

Remin Lu

Wuhu
Hotel

Dongjiao
Park

Wutun Lu

Qingyi River

Wugang Lu

Wuhu

© Airphoto International Ltd.

the cobbled streets, bamboo chicken coops stand outside front doors that open into
dark, high-ceilinged old houses. Xinwu Jie running west off the main street,
Zhongshan Jie, is busy with restaurants and food stalls serving crispy rice cakes,
sweet dumpling soup and large dough fritters. Near the scruffy memorial to the 1949
Revolution is Jiuhe Jie, which is now a market area. At No 26 a huge, fanciful,
American-built Catholic Church, dating from the Treaty Port days, is open for
worship on Sundays. At **Jinghu Lake**, in the town centre, people gather to play cards
or chess and to sell their miniature potted plants.

■ ZHE HILL

The highest point in the city is only 86 metres (282 feet), but the view from the
pagoda at the top sweeps over the whole city and down the Yangzi. It seems that this
five-storey **Zheshan Pagoda** and the Mid-River Pagoda (*see* below) were built at the
same time, at the beginning of the Song dynasty (960–1279). A competition
apparently developed between the two teams of builders. The two brothers engaged
in the construction of Zheshan Pagoda, who were desperate to complete first and so

avoid losing face, finished off the very top with a cooking wok turned upside down. A small zoo is to be found in the public park.

■ GUANGJI TEMPLE
Of the four main temples which existed in Wuhu, three were destroyed in the Sino-Japanese War and only the Guangji Temple, at the foot of Zhe Hill, remains. The main hall is hung with ten scrolls depicting the Buddhist Hell. The temple was established in the Tang dynasty (618–907) and Emperor Dezong (reigned 780–5) came here as a monk. When omens indicated that this was an unsafe place for him to reside, he went to live on the famous Buddhist mountain of Jinhua, further south.

■ MID RIVER PAGODA
This six storey pagoda stands at the point where the Qingyi River enters the Yangzi, a danger spot for navigation. A local fisherman named Huang suggested that this octagonal pagoda be built to serve as a lighthouse. Its name derives from its position—it is exactly in the middle of the lower reaches of the Yangzi.

■ WUHU ARTS AND CRAFTS FACTORY
The art of wrought-iron picture-making originated in Wuhu and this factory in Jiuhua Lu continues the tradition, besides producing pictures made of feathers or golden wheat stalks, poker-burned wooden decorations and copies of old paintings.

Iron picture-making is very laborious and amazingly intricate. This art form was started by an itinerant blacksmith, Tang Tianchi, during the reign of Emperor Kangxi (1662–1723). Tang used to sit and watch a local painter, whose work he much admired. The artist chided Tang: 'I paint my pictures, you beat your iron, but you will never make pictures by beating iron.' Tang promptly went away and produced an iron picture, 'using a hammer as a brush and iron as ink'.

A huge 'Welcoming Pine' iron picture by the artists of Wuhu adorns the Anhui Room in the Great Hall of the People in Beijing.

Ma'anshan

Anhui's biggest industrial city, Ma'anshan, mines much of the pig iron used in the Shanghai steel industry. It also has its own iron and steel works, limestone quarries, and chemical and cement factories. The city is linked to Wuhu and Nanjing by rail.

A touching story is told of the city's name, which means Horse Saddle Hill. When the Kingdoms of Chu and Shu were at war in the third century, General Xiang Yu of Chu was defeated by Liu Bei and attempted to retreat to Wujiang on the north bank of the Yangzi. Finding only a small boat, he had his precious mount ferried across first. At this moment Liu Bei's pursuing soldiers arrived and Xiang Yu, knowing he was trapped, cut his throat with his own sword. Seeing his master's courageous suicide, the horse leapt into the river and drowned. The boatman buried its saddle on the nearby hill.

Buildings on **Coloured Stone Cliff (Caishi Ji)**, west of the city, commemorate the Tang poet, Li Bai (701–62). The three-storeyed Taibai Lou houses two Chinese boxwood statues of the poet, one depicting his immortal gesture of inviting the moon to join him in a cup of wine. Here too is the 'Tomb of Li Bai's Clothes and Official Hat'. According to the local legend, Li Bai's clothing was buried on Caishi Ji when he drowned after falling drunkenly from a boat one evening while attempting to embrace the moon's reflection in the river.

The **Three Scholars Grotto (Sanyuan Dong)** was allegedly built by three grateful gentlemen who, on their way to the capital to take the imperial examinations, found safety and shelter under the cliff when their boat was caught in a sudden and violent storm. After all three had gained first-class honours and promotions, they recalled their close shave and donated funds for the building of this grotto.

Nanjing

Nanjing—'Southern Capital'—along with Luoyang, Xi'an and Beijing, is one of the historical capitals of China, and the many imperial tombs and architectural remains in the city and its environs reflect its grandiose past. Today, the city is the capital of Jiangsu Province. Its industries include machine-building, automobile assembly, electronics, petroleum, iron and steel, textiles, shipbuilding and foodstuffs. A double-tiered road and rail bridge, completed in 1968, spans the Yangzi at Nanjing.

There is a visible military presence in Nanjing. Soldiers may approach you and gesture to not take photographs of that location. Many buildings and compounds in Nanjing are military areas and are not open to the public.

HISTORY OF NANJING
With the Yangzi on one side, and surrounded on the other three sides by hills, Nanjing was thought to be auspicious as well as strategically important. First historical records date from the Spring and Autumn period (770–476 BC) when the area was divided between the Kingdoms of Wu, Yue and Chu. A walled town was built during the Eastern Han period (AD 25–220), known as 'Stone City'.

Between the third and 14th centuries, eight dynasties established their capitals in the city, some of them building magnificent palaces and forts. Though many of these minor dynasties had incompetent rulers and regimes weakened by intrigue and debauchery, Nanjing emerged as a cultural centre of painting, philosophy and Buddhism. In the sixth century, the Sui dynasty established its capital at Xi'an, and ordered the complete destruction of earlier dynastic buildings in Nanjing.

The city flourished again during the Tang dynasty (618–907), when the great poets Li Bai, Bai Juyi and Liu Yuxi lived here for a while. For a brief period, Nanjing

(then called Jinling) became the capital of the Southern Song, but the dynastic base had to be moved to Hangzhou as the pursuing Nuzhen Tartar armies advanced. Marco Polo may have visited the city in 1275.

The founder of the Ming dynasty, Hongwu (Zhu Yuan Zhang), captured Nanjing in 1356 and set up his capital here, building palaces, temples and pagodas. (The famous green- and white-glazed-tile Porcelain Pagoda of the Bao'en Temple, so often praised as one of the seven wonders of the world by earlier travellers, belonged to this period, though it was totally destroyed during the Taiping Rebellion (1850–64). Some of its tiles are on exhibition at the Chaotian Gong.) He also enlarged the city wall to make it the longest in the world. Earlier Tang-dynasty poets had written lyrically of being entertained on 'singsong boats'—sort of floating bordellos—along the Qinhuai (a ten-kilometre, or six-mile, man-made river, said to have been dug during the second century BC, skirting the western and southern edges of Nanjing). A picture of more innocent pleasures is conjured up by a passage from *The Scholars*, an early 18th-century novel by Wu Ching-tzu:

> After the middle of the fourth month in Nanking, the Chin-huai River becomes quite lovely. The barges from other tributaries of the Yangtze dismantle their cabins, set up awnings, and paddle into the river. Each vessel carries a small, square, gilt-lacquered table, set with an Yihsing stoneware pot, cups of the finest Cheng Hua or Hsuan Te porcelain, and the choicest tea brewed with rain water. Boating parties bring wine, dishes and sweetmeats with them to the canal, and even people travelling by boat order a few cents' worth of good tea to drink on board as they proceed slowly on their way. At dusk two bright horn lanterns on each vessel are reflected in the water as the barges ply to and fro, so that above and below are bright. Fluting and singing are heard all night and every night from Literary Virtue Bridge to Lucky Crossing Bridge and East Water Guardhouse. The pleasure-goers buy water-rat fireworks too, which project from the water and look like pear trees in blossom when let off. The fun goes on till the fourth watch each night.

Translated by Yang Hsien-yi and Gladys Yang

During the Ming dynasty (1368–1644), an imperial decree established a special government department to oversee brothels which catered to the 200,000 garrisoned troops in the city. The capital was moved to Beijing in 1420, but Nanjing remained a subsidiary capital and financial centre. In the Qing dynasty (1644–1911) also troops were garrisoned in the city.

The Treaty of Nanking (Nanjing) ending the Opium War of (1839–1842) was signed aboard *HMS Cornwallis* between the British and the Chinese. It ceded the territory of Hong Kong to Britain, opened five Chinese ports to foreign trade, and exacted a payment of 21 million Mexican dollars as indemnity from the Chinese. It was the first of what became known as the Unequal Treaties. The pseudo-Christian Taiping Rebellion made its headquarters in Nanjing in 1853 and occupied it for 11 years (*see* page 112). Its leader, Hong Xiuquan, adopted the title 'Heavenly King' and appointed other leaders as Princes of the East, West, North and South'. The 'Heavenly King' built a large palace of which little now remains. The city was almost completely destroyed in the devastation and killings that followed the overthrow of this rebellion. Nanjing became a treaty port under the terms of the 1876 Chefoo (Yantai) Convention.

Following the revolution of 1911, Nanjing was declared the capital of the Republic of China in 1912. (Dr Sun Yat-sen, founder of the Nationalist Republic, was buried here in 1929.) The Nationalists regained control over Nanjing from the local warlord in 1926, and it remained the capital until just before the Japanese occupation of the city in 1937, when an estimated 400,000 residents perished in what became known as the 'Rape of Nanjing'. In early 1949 the People's Liberation Army entered Nanjing, driving the Nationalist government, the Guomindang, before it, first to Guangzhou and then to Taiwan.

What to See in Nanjing
Nanjing's streets are lined with poplars and sycamore trees—some of which came from France—that provide some relief from the oppressive summer temperatures. Gardens and parks add grace and a sense of spaciousness to the city. Two lakes, **Xuan Wu Lake** and **Mochou Lake**, are surrounded by parkland. Many of the historical relics—tombs, stelae and sculptures dating from the sixth century—are to be found in the hills and fields around Nanjing, the best known in the vicinity of Zijin Shan (Purple and Gold Mountain).

Xuan Wu Hu was originally a private retreat for the royal family. The 472-hectare park consists of a lake-shore path and five islands—Ling Zhou, Huan Zhou, Ying Zhou, Liang Zhou and Cui Zhou. Ling Zhou has an aviary. Ying Zhou sits inside Huan Zhou, separated by a lotus-filled moat. Huan Zhou has a man-made waterfall and a Tibetan Buddhist Temple built in 1937. The statues were installed in a 1993 restoration. Liang Zhou is the only island to feature some pre-republican artefacts—four Qing-dynasty pavilions. Cui Zhou has some new gardens.

Mochou Hu is graced by several Ming-Qing pavilions. One is located on the island and can be reached by hire boat. Local legend says that the Ming General, Xu Da, received the park as a gift from the Emperor, when he beat him at chess. One pavilion is called Sheng Qi Ting (Winning at Chess Pavilion). Next to the Sheng Qi Pavilion is a walled garden containing a statue of the mythical heroine Mochou.

Sights Within the City
■ MING DYNASTY CITY WALL (MINGGU CHENG QIANG)
Built by the first Ming emperor, Hongwu (Zhu Yuan Zhang), this wall of clay bricks took 20 years to construct (1366–86), and included remains of an earlier Eastern Han city wall (Stone City). It encloses an area of 41 square kilometres (16 square miles),

(following pages) *The Yangzi River Bridge, Nanjing*

making it the longest city wall in the world. Its highest point is 18 metres (60 feet), and it varies in width from seven to 12 metres (30 to 40 feet). Some 200,000 workers cemented the bricks—each stamped with details of the brickmaker and overseer—with a mortar mixture of glutinous rice, tung oil and lime.

Some long sections of the Ming city wall had no entry or exit points. There were no gates at all along the shore of Xuan Wu Hu stretching from Tai Ping Men to He Ping Men. Zhong Hua Men was the only gate south of the city and there was one gate in the east between Tai Ping Men and Guang Hua Men. The Republican government added gates after the 1911 Revolution. By then there were 24 gates.

Still, in 1927 when the Guomindang attacked, the city wall was so impregnable that the resident foreign community became trapped inside the city. In order to escape they had to climb down the wall from Ding Shan using 'ropes' made from sheets. The wall was further extended in 1929 in order for the funeral procession of Sun Zhongshan to cross from west to east and in 1930, the Guomindang drafted a plan for the wall to become a ring road for traffic. From 1949 until the end of the Cultural Revolution, much of the city wall was destroyed. But original sections of the Ming wall are still so strong today that modern buildings have been constructed on top of them. In some places, people have made their home in chambers inside the walls.

Since 1981, the Nanjing government has taken steps to restore and reconstruct the ancient monuments. In 1994, a section of wall (1.7 km) was restored along the Xuan Wu Hu shore from Jiefang Men to Taiping Men. Restoration is currently underway around the base of Lion Peak, near Jing Hai Si.

Many areas of the city are still known by the Ming City gates which once stood there. Tai Ping Men is the local name for the neighbourhood but the gate is no longer standing. Recent accounts state that there are nine city gates still standing. Five gates are original Ming-dynasty gates and four gates date from the Republican era.

The five surviving Ming-dynasty gates are: **Wu Chao Men** (Meridian gate)—located in the grounds of the old Ming Palace where Zhu Yuan Zhang, or Taizu, lived in the 14th century. All the original palace buildings were destroyed between 1853–1864 during the Taiping rebellion. **Zhong Hua Men** (formerly Treasure gate) is located in the middle of a traffic circle on Zhong Hua Lu, near the Qin Huai River. It served as a fortress housing 3000 soldiers inside its 27 caves. **Han Zhong Men** sits in a park at the intersecton of Huju Nan Lu, Huju Lu and Hanzhong Lu. This gate is disconnected from the city wall. It forms a long tunnel through the base of a fortress. **Qing Liang Men**, built in 1368, sits beside Shitou Cheng Lu near Qing Liang Shan. **He Ping Men** is located on top of a small promontory hill overlooking the northwest corner of Xuan Wu Hu. It can only be viewed by appointment as it is within a military area. Tai Ping Men and Zhong Yang Men are no longer standing but are the names of local areas. Some tour guides may claim that Zhong Yang Men is still standing because they refer to He Ping Men by this name.

The four surviving Republican era gates are: **Xuan Wu Men**–built in the final year of the Qing Dynasty just before the 1911 revolution. It provided access to five islands and the Xuan Wu Hu park. This area was a private retreat for the imperial family. **Yi Jiang Men**, alongside Zhongshan Bei Lu, was built in 1921. There is a pavilion on top of the gate with a photographic exhibition of the Communist Party victory in 1949. From this spot, below you can see the wooded winding bends of the former city moat and to your west is Lion Peak. The second small hill seen to your right is Ding Shan where a community of foreigners from the treaty ports lived during the Guomindang occupation of Nanjing in 1927. **Zhong Shan Men** was built in 1929 to facilitate the movement of Sun Zhongshan's funeral procession towards Zijin Shan. It replaced the Ming-dynasty gate (Chao Yeng Men). This gate is the main access to Ming Ling Lu, the road to the Ming Tomb. If you climb to the top of this gate, the view (on a clear day) of Zijin Shan and tree-lined Zhongshan Dong Lu is excellent. Facing west, to your right, you can see the remains of the old city moat, Yue Ya Hu Chen He. The Nanjing Museum is next to the gate; **Jie Fang Men**, built in 1952, allows access to Xuan Wu Hu Park. The city gates are focal points for entertainment on weekends and holidays. The locals gather there to watch videos, listen to music and sing. Zhong-shan Men is the main spot for this free fun.

Santai Xiang is a narrow alley which branches off Zhongshan Dong Lu. If you sit here in the evening at one of the sidewalk cafes, local musicians (mostly ladies) who walk up and down the path will be happy to play their guitar and sing a Chinese song for you for a small fee.

■ CITY WALL MUSEUM (CHENG QIANG BOWUGUAN)
This museum is found on top of Jiefang Men and has photographs of long-gone city gates, maps of the walled city and a full-scale model of the walled city. Captions are only in Chinese.

■ THE DRUM TOWER (GU LOU) AND BELL PAVILION (DAZHONG TING)
The Drum Tower marks the centre of Nanjing. It was built in 1382, and was followed in 1388 by the Bell Pavilion, to the northeast. Both were used to sound out the two-hourly night watches over the city. The Drum Tower is a Qing-dynasty (1644–1911) reconstruction built over the 14th-century Ming foundations. A tea-room at the top offers a fine view of the city. The hexagonal Bell Pavilion, also originally erected in the Ming dynasty, houses a huge one-ton bronze bell and a memorial hall. The hall is dedicated to the two daughters of the artisan who was ordered by the emperor to cast the bell. Legend tells how, after the craftsman had made several unsuccessful attempts to produce a correct blend of metals for the bronze, the two girls threw themselves into the smelter, whereupon the composition of the alloy was miracu-lously perfected. As a result of this filial sacrifice, he was literally saved by the bell from certain execution, but the same story is told of two other bells in Beijing. The existing two-storey pavilion dates from 1889.

(following pages) *Golden Island (Jin Shan) with its temple situated on a bend in the Yangzi River at Zhenjiang. Sketched by William Alexander in 1793.*

W. Alexander delt.

VIEW of the *TCHIN-SHAN, or GOLDEN ISLA*

Lond.

YG-TSE-KIANG, or *GREAT RIVER of CHINA.*

Wilson sculp.

Nicol.

■ YANGZI RIVER BRIDGE (CHANGJIANG DAQIAO)
The waters of the Yangzi become tidal at Nanjing. Astride the swirling current stands the Great Changjiang Bridge. The visitor is proudly shown this city landmark, which provides a vital link between the north of China and the fertile fields of Jiangnan. Before the bridge was completed in 1968, all traffic had to cross the river by ferry.

Initially the bridge was to be constructed with the help of the Russians, who agreed to supply the design, technical expertise and steel. When deteriorating Sino-Soviet relations led to the Russians' withdrawal in 1960, the Chinese not only constructed the bridge themselves but revamped the domestic steel industry to produce the necessary tonnage. The project took them eight years.

At either end of the bridge stand four towers. In one of these is housed the visitors' briefing room and a fine model of the Yangzi Bridge. The bridge, 1.6 kilometres (one mile) long, is two-tiered, with the top level for vehicles and the lower one for trains. A visit to the railway deck to look along the great grey tunnel of steel is awe-inspiring, especially if a train thunders past.

■ NANJING MUSEUM (NANJING BOWUGUAN)
This museum was founded by Cai Yuan Pei in 1933 and constructed in the style of a traditional Chinese temple. It is located right next to the city gate, Zhongshan Men. The 400,000 cultural relics here date from around the 11th century BC up to the founding of the People's Republic. Exhibits include jade, pottery and stone implements from Jiangsu's prehistoric period; artefacts from the Longshan and associated cultures from 4000 to 2500 BC; and a wide range of porcelain, paintings and bronzes, as well as maps and displays of traditional handicrafts. The famous jade burial suit, exhibited abroad in the 1970s, belongs to this museum. It is thought to be 1,800 years old and is made of 2,600 rectangles of jade sewn together with silver thread. The jade suit was made to totally encapsulate the body with the object of preserving it, but when archaeologists dug it up in Xuzhou in 1970 all they discovered inside were bones.

One of the most fascinating exhibits is the large wooden copy of a statue of a man showing all the body's acupuncture points. The original bronze statue is believed to date from the Warring States period (480–221 BC). Another reminder of China's superiority in early medical pioneering is a portrait of Hua Tuo (141–203), who practised acupuncture and surgery and reputedly employed anaesthetics 1,000 years before they were discovered in the West. It is located at 321 East Zhongshan Lu.

■ RUINS OF THE MING IMPERIAL PALACE (MING GU GONG)
Nearby, on Yudao Jie near Wuchao Gate, is the site of the palace built by the first Ming emperor, Hongwu (reigned 1368–98). It was destroyed in 1645 and all that remains are some foundation stones, stone lions and the stone screen wall facing the former palace.

■ TAIPING BOWUGUAN

Housed in the remains of the former palace of the Eastern Prince of the Heavenly Kingdom is a detailed exhibition of maps, paintings, documents and other relics of the Taiping Rebellion (*see* pages 112–113). Many of the documents are copies, as the originals are held in Beijing. Linked to the museum is the charming **Zhan Yuan**, a traditional Chinese garden which originated in the early Ming dynasty and eventually became incorporated into the palace of the Eastern Prince, Yang Xiuqing, in the 19th century. Although this museum is located at 128 Zhan Yuan Lu, many of the Taiping exhibits and relics have been moved to **Tushuo Zongtongfu** at 292 Changjiang Lu. This includes military weapons, the imperial jade seal and the imperial robes of Hong Xiuquan.

■ NORTH POLE TOWER (BEI JI GE)

Built by the Guomindang in 1929 as a meteorological research institute, this site offers excellent views of Jiming Si and Xuan Wu Hu. A long winding road makes a steep climb to the top. The tower stands in a walled compound on the peak. Although it is not open to the public, staff may allow escorted visits.

■ PLUM GARDEN VILLAGE (MEIYUAN XINCUN)

At the end of the Sino-Japanese War, abortive peace talks took place between the Guomindang and the Communist Party of China. During this period—May 1946 to March 1947—the Communists made their headquarters at 17, 30 and 31 Meiyuan Xincun, a suburb close to the centre of Nanjing.

The Communist delegation was led by Zhou Enlai and Dong Biwu. Zhou Enlai and his wife, Deng Yingchao, lived at No.30, and the charming house and garden remain just as the couple left them, with jackets hanging from a hatstand and a battered leather briefcase on the chest of drawers in the spartan bedroom. A doorway knocked into the eastern garden wall connects No.30 to No.31. This short cut enabled the Communists to evade constant surveillance by Guomindang secret agents posted in the streets outside. At No.17 is a small conference room where Zhou Enlai met the press during negotiations. Upstairs is the secret radio equipment used for communicating directly with Mao Zedong in Yan'an.

The houses, now museums, still exude the cloak-and-dagger flavour of the period and the austerity and dedication of their occupants.

■ CONFUCIUS TEMPLE (FUZI MIAO)

In the south of the city, near a stretch of the Qinhuai River, is an area where Qing-style buildings house shops and restaurants. The city fathers have recreated the bustling bazaar that clustered round the Song-dynasty Confucius Temple (Fuzi Miao) that stood here. The temple, destroyed at the time of the Japanese invasion in 1937, has been reconstructed.

Every morning at seven o'clock people gather in this small park in Nanjing to enjoy an hour of dancing before going to work.

■ MING EXAMINATION HALL, GONGYUAN JIE

Imperial examinations were held at the capital every three years during the early Ming dynasty (1368–1644); even when the capital was moved to Beijing, candidates for high office travelled to Nanjing from nearby provinces. The Examination Hall comprised 20,600 tiny cubicles in which candidates were locked and kept guarded during the lengthy examinations. They had to write essays to achieve official rank in the imperial bureaucracy. Food was passed in daily to sustain the candidates through the trying ordeal which often lasted one month.

A stone bridge and a square tower are all that remain of this huge establishment. Inside the tower are stelae inscribed with the rules of conduct for the examinations and the history of the hall itself.

■ SITE OF THE FORMER PRESIDENT PALACE (TUSHUO ZONGTONGFU)

Xu Yuan Garden, a lake, and a large marble boat are all that remain and pre-date the large palace built by Hong Xiuquan (1813–64), instigator of the Taiping Rebellion and self-styled 'Heavenly King' (*see* page 112). His palace was destroyed by the Qing troops after the defeat of the rebellion in 1864. During the Qing dynasty, officials used the site as a *yamen* (offices) and as the residence of the Liang Jiang Viceroy, an official who governed the three provinces of Jiangsu, Anhui and Jiangsi.

In 1912, Sun Zhongshan was inaugurated provisional President of the new Republic in **Xi Hua Dian**, the hall in the west of this garden. He lived in a two-storey wooden house near the north-east corner of the garden.

The Guomindang government buildings erected on this site were the country's administrative headquarters between 1927 and 1937 (when the Japanese entered the city). The late Generalissimo Chiang Kai-shek's (Jiang Jie shi) office was in this complex during that period. You can visit the auditorium where he was inaugurated President in 1948 and his personal air raid shelter used during the war with Japan.

The buildings were the headquarters of the Jiangsu Provincial Communist Party until the museum opened in 2000. The site, at 292 Changjiang Lu, is now open to the public.

■ ROOSTER CROW TEMPLE (JIMING SI)

The original halls dated from the late Qing-dynasty, but housed Ming sculpture. The first Ming emperor, Hongwu, decreed the construction of this temple. It was a nunnery until destroyed by fire in 1973. The main temple buildings were rebuilt in 1981, after which new bronze statues of Buddha and Guanyin were contributed by Thailand. It was not until eight years later when the landmark seven-storey Yao Shi Ta pagoda was reconstructed in 1989. The entrance is on Jiming Si Lu.

■ QUIET SEA TEMPLE (JING HAI SI)

This temple was built in honour of Admiral Zheng He, during the reign of the Ming Emperor Cheng Zu. Jing Hai means 'quiet sea', conveying the wish that Zheng He's fleet would have safe journeys. This temple, at the base of Lion Peak, was also the site of the 1842 Sino-British negotiations which resulted in the Treaty of Nanking ending the Opium War of 1839–42. The treaty was signed on board HMS Cornwallis anchored in the Yangzi River. The original temple was burned down by the Japanese in 1937 but rebuilt in 1987. It houses a museum about the Treaty of Nanking. There are also three Ming-style exhibition halls but all captions are in Chinese.

■ MOSQUE

This is a functioning mosque inside a series of Qing-dynasty buildings with courtyards surrounded by a wall. Services are held on Fridays. On a separate site at **Zheng He Park** and Museum, may be found memorials dedicated to the famous Chinese Muslim, Ming-dynasty Admiral, Zheng He.

■ HEAVEN WORSHIPPING PALACE (CHAOTIAN GONG)

This site consists of four courtyards and three main buildings within a walled compound. Several of the buildings house exhibits of the Nanjing Municipal Museum. The first two courtyards are free to enter and contain a lively bazaar, alongside the Crescent Pool (first courtyard) and a statue of Confucius (second courtyard). Da Cheng Palace, in the third courtyard, is a museum of the Six Dynasties period in Nanjing's history. Costume performances of Ming court ceremonies are held in this courtyard. In the fourth courtyard, facing Chong Sheng Palace, is a new building housing relics from the Ming-dynasty era in Nanjing.

■ XIAO BAI LOU (LITTLE WHITE HOUSE)
This former British consulate is now a luxurious banquet facility. Built in 1919, it was the British Consulate where the British Consul was assassinated by Guomindang troops in 1927. His assassination triggered the exodus by the foreigners over the city wall. The building, located at 185 Huju Bei Lu, is kept in pristine condition. Visitors are welcome to look around inside. Brochures describing the building's history in English are available on request.

■ THE WATERFRONT AND THE BUND
This area lies in the Xia Guan district of the city outside the northwestern city wall. Almost all the shipping industry is now located across the river on the Pukuo side. Jian Bian Lu has an old waterfront breakwater with a raised pedestrian promenade that allows you to see over the top and look at the river. After several blocks, turn left onto Da Ma Lu and see three impressive pre-1937 European-style buildings which survived the wars, revolutions and economic development of the city. This was the old pre-war business and finance centre. The area now seems abandoned. Continue down Jian Bian Lu along the waterfront and at its intersection with Zhongshan Bei Lu you reach Zhongshan Wharf, the arrival and departure point for passenger ships travelling the Yangzi River.

SIGHTS OUTSIDE THE CITY CENTRE
■ YUHUATAI (TERRACE OF THE RAIN OF FLOWERS)
A monument to 100,000 Communist revolutionaries killed on this site—used by the Guomindang as an execution ground—was erected in 1950. In the sixth century, the legend goes, a Buddhist monk, Yun Guang, lived and preached here. So eloquent was he that the heavens showered flowers upon him, and these turned into beautiful little agate stones. These rain-flower pebbles are sold to visitors in containers of water to enhance their coloration.

■ SIGHTS ON ZIJINSHAN (PURPLE AND GOLD MOUNTAIN)
The three peaks of Zijinshan (the highest is 448 metres, or 1,470 feet) form this evergreen scenic area east of Nanjing. Some of the city's most famous sights are to be seen in this region.

■ THE MING TOMB (MINGXIAO LING)
The first emperor of the Ming dynasty, Hongwu, was buried here in 1398, alongside his empress, Ma Hou, who died in 1382. The tomb, begun in 1381, is recorded as having taken 100,000 labourers 32 years to complete. Most of the buildings of the

mausoleum have been destroyed; the Taiping rebels plundered the vicinity and in the 1800s. The tomb is in poor condition compared with those of Hongwu's descendants, who were buried outside Beijing after the capital was moved there. The wall around the tomb is 22.5 km long. The former approach to the tomb formed a long, winding s-shaped path. But now visitors miss much of the Sacred Way because Ming Ling Lu leads directly to the tomb. Along the Sacred Way are pairs of stone animals and, at the far end, statues of warriors and civil servants. The style of carving is typical of the early Ming period.

The original Sacred Way started near the town of Weigang. The **Xiama Men** in the town is engraved with instructions "get down from your horses". At this point, all horseriders were to dismount, in respect for the Emperor, and walk the rest of the distance to the tomb. The second gate, **Da Jing Men**, is on Zhongshan Ling Lu. Opposite is **Sifangcheng** Pavilion which is near **Shi Xiang Lu**, the section of the Sacred Way with the twelve pairs of animal statues. A further section of the Sacred Way is found in the middle of a traffic strip on Weng Zhong Lu. Here there are stone statues of four civil officials and four generals.

Continuing on Weng Zhong Lu, you reach the **Ling Xing Men** and the **Jing Shi Qiao** (three parallel stone-arched bridges) at the entrance of the tomb. Following the brick avenue lined with cedar trees you reach **Weng Wu Men** (the first outer wall and the five gates). Passing through the Weng Wu Men, you reach the Stele Pavilion (Bei Dian) containing five stone stele, including one engraved by Qing Emperor Kang Xi in 1699. You can also see a plaque posted on the outside of the building by the Qing government in 1909 commanding the preservation of the tomb.

Next comes the **Xiaoling Dian** (Sacrificial Hall). The original was constructed in 1383, but was destroyed during the Taiping Rebellion of 1850-1864. This Qing reconstruction was built in 1873, and is a much smaller one than the original. It sits on top of a raised rectangular flat platform with several tiers. The stone base of this platform and its tiers are decorated with the remains of protruding stone animal heads resembling alligators. In fact they represent a legendary animal, the *lishou*, which was a Ming symbol.

Continuing on up the long tree-lined avenue, you reach the Inner Wall, which is painted red and has a single gate. Passing through this inner Red Gate, the long tree-lined avenue continues until you cross a stone arched bridge (Da Shi Qiao) and reach the giant rectangular Ming tower. A tunnel cuts through the centre of the building at an inclined angle and emerges at the back, from where a flight of steps ascends to the top of the tower. Four walls are all that remain of a building that once stood there. From the top you have a view of the whole approach.

Behind the Ming tower sits the **Bao Cheng** or treasure mound. Inside this circular mound are the unexcavated tombs of the first Ming Emperor and his wife. To reach the Ming tombs either take Ming Ling Lu and Weng Zhong Lu from Zhongshan Men to the main gate of the mausoleum, or take Zhongshan Ling Yuan Lu from

Ling Hang Gong Lu, near Weigang village, to see the whole Sacred Way from its starting point.

■ DR SUN YATSEN'S MAUSOLEUM (ZHONGSHAN LING)
Nanjing's most famous landmark is the elegant blue and white mausoleum of Dr Sun Yat-sen (1866–1925), father of the Chinese Republic. Dr Sun's body was kept at the Bai Yun Guan Temple in the Western Hills of Beijing until this mausoleum was completed in 1929. 'Universal Love' are the characters above the triple-arched centre gate, through which an avenue of tall trees leads to the main gate, with four Chinese characters inscribed saying "All for the nation", "Serving the public under heaven" and "The world belongs to everyone". A flight of 392 marble steps leads to the memorial hall in which is a gypsum statue of a seated Dr Sun (sculpted in France by a Polish friend, Landowski). Dr Sun's remains are beneath a recumbent marble statue of him (executed by Japanese associates) in the circular crypt behind the hall. His wish had always been to be buried on Zijin Shan in Nanjing. The site for his tomb was selected by his wife, Song Qing Ling, on April 21, 1925. The mausoleum was designed by Lu Yanzhi and the colours are those of the Guomindang flag. The perimeter of the entire site was originally meant to take the shape of a giant bell, symbolic of Sun himself as the human alarm bell, but the growth of trees has now obscured this.

The full distance from the Gate of Universal Love to the Ceremonial Hall is 700 metres. There are a total of 14 flights of stone steps. Although the view from the top is spectacular in the daytime, a visit at night is worthwhile because the mausoleum is floodlit, the crowds are gone and admission is free.

After passing through the Mausoleum Gate, you ascend two more flights of steps and reach the second terrace with its **Bei Ting** (Tablet Pavilion), inside which is a stone stele engraved with the words, "The Guomindang party buried its Prime Minister Sun Zhongshan here on June 1, 1929."

From the Tablet Pavilion you ascend eight more flights of steep steps to the third terrace and its **Ji Tang** (Ceremonial Hall), behind which is the tomb chamber itself. Above the three arched doorways of the Ceremonial Hall are engraved the characters for the Three People's Principles (San Ming Zhu Yi) of Nationalism (min zu), Democracy (min zhu) and People's Livelihood (min sheng), which were the core of Sun Zhongshan's ideology. Ascend the final short flight of steps leading into the Cermemonial Hall and you will see a white marble statue of a seated Sun Zhongshan. On the east and west walls of the hall is engraved the complete text of Sun Zhongshan's book, "Outline of National Reconstruction" (Jian Guo Da Gong).

Ge Ben-ling, a 55-year-old retired car mechanic, rises at 4:30 each morning before going to teach tai-chi at a playground near his home in Nanjing. This slow-motion exercise is said to have been developed by a monk who lived during the 13th or 14th century.

At the back of the room is a small doorway which leads into the **Mu Shi Li Ceng** (Tomb Chamber). This is a circular room with a dome over the top. In the centre of the room lies a white marble statue of Sun Zhongshan in a reclining position. Below this lies his coffin.

Exit the Ceremonial Hall and walk around the outside of the building to your right and you can visit the back of the domed Tomb Chamber which is known as the **Mu Shi Wai Ceng** (Tomb Fort). Here there is usually an outdoor display of photographs showing the construction of the tomb.

■ DR SUN YATSEN'S MUSEUM (SUN ZHONGSHAN JI LIAN GUAN)

This is located inside the Buddhist Scripture Hall (Cang Jing Lou) and is an important museum devoted to Sun Zhongshan. The building was first constructed in 1935–1936, and completely renovated in 1982. It sits in between Zhongshan Ling and Ling Gu Si on a separate narrow mountain road which forms a loop off Ling Gu Si Lu. The museum has a photographic exhibition depicting the construction of Zhongshan Ling, as well as famous visitors to the mausoleum over the years. A film of Sun Zhongshan's elaborate 1929 funeral ceremony is shown continuously.

■ YONG MU LOU

This is the house where Sun Ke and Song Qing Ling stayed during their 1929 period of mourning immediately after Sun Zhongshan's funeral. Sun Ke Lou and Yong Mu Lou can both be reached by a stone paved road from Ling Gu Ta, or by a steep stone-paved trail that ascends the hillside, starting from the road to Zhongshan Bowuguan, across the road from a small restaurant. The trail is unmarked.

■ ZHENG QI TING

This is the site Jiang Jie-shi (Chiang Kai-shek) chose for his tomb in November 1946 before his flight to Taiwan. It sits at the end of a long, steep walking trail which climbs up from behind Zi Xia Hu. The Pavilion is inscribed both by him and Sun Ke. A single Guomindang symbol adorns the centre of the ceiling.

■ ZIJINSHAN OBSERVATORY

Situated on one peak of Zijin Shan, this third largest of China's observatories was built in 1934. There is a small but fascinating collection on display of magnificent Ming (1368–1644) reproductions of early astrological instruments: a celestial globe, an armillary sphere for detecting solar bodies, a gnomon (a sun and seasons dial) and an earthquake detector first made over 2,000 years ago. The last two instruments have had a disturbed history. In 1900, Germans absconded with the earthquake detector (which was then in the Beijing Observatory) but it was returned, along with the other instruments taken as spoils of war, in 1919. In the early 1930s the Japanese tried unsuccessfully to remove the gnomon; they even cut the base in half.

If you climb onto the platform of one of the observatory domes you will find yourself above the tree line, and, unfurling below you, a marvellous view of Nanjing and the Yangzi.

■ VALLEY OF THE SOUL's RETREAT (LING GU GONGYUAN)
This park, and the admission ticket for it, includes Ling Gu Tower (Ling Gu Ta), Ling Gu Temple (Ling Gu Si), Beamless Hall (Wu Liang Hall), Zhi Gong Hall, Bao Gong Stupa, and the Gui Lin Stone House. The memorial archway at the entrance to the park is remarkable for its blue and white Guomindang symbols mounted over the top of each of its five gates.

In order to build his grand mausoleum on an auspicious site, the Ming emperor Hongwu (reigned 1368–98) had first to remove an existing temple, the Ling Gu Si, to its present wooded peak. All that remains of that Ming temple is the 46-metre (150-foot) long Beamless Hall (Wu Liang Dian).

The current **Ling Gu Si** buildings are a Qing-dynasty reconstruction completed by Zeng Guo Fan in 1867. It has a special chapel devoted to the famous travelling Buddhist monk Xuan Zang (596–664) who went to India in the 7th century on a long journey which lasted 16 years. In 645 he returned to the Tang-dynasty capital city of Chang An (Xian) bringing with him over 650 Buddhist manuscripts which he later translated into Chinese. This chapel devoted to him holds what is purported to be a piece of his skull, which is kept on public display in a clear wine glass sitting inside a small model pagoda. A community of monks live here.

Wu Liang Dian (**Beamless Hall**) was originally a Buddhist temple which in 1929 was turned into a memorial to Guomindang military officers and soldiers who perished in the Northern Expedition of 1925–1927. The names and ranks of all 33,224 martyrs are still listed on a stone tablet inside. The structure itself is remarkable for having been built with no nails and no wooden beams. The ceiling is made of bricks forming a rounded vault over the walls. Today it contains an exhibit of mannequins acting out scenes from China's revolutions.

To the north of the Beamless Hall stands the nine-storeyed **Linggu Pagoda**, which was built by the Guomindang in 1929. The walls are inscribed with the text of two speeches given by Sun Zhongshan at the Whampoa Military Academy in Guangzhou. For the energetic, the long climb to the top of the circular staircase is rewarded with a fine view over wooded countryside.

Zhi Gong Hall (Zhi Gong Dian) and **Bao Gong Stupa** (Bao Gong Ta) are both dedicated to the memory of the Liang Dynasty Buddhist monk Bao Zhi (436–514). Bao Zhi was originally buried on the site of Ming Xiao Ling, but his grave was moved to near Ling Gu Ta in 1379, when the first Ming emperor's tomb was being built. The stupa was destroyed three different times, until finally the grave site itself was lost. The current stupa is a new construction dating from 1981. It no longer marks the actual grave site, which is now unknown. A few yards in front of the stupa sits Zhi Gong Hall, which was first built in 1934 and renovated in 1941. This hall contains stone tablets dated 1382 recording the moving of Bao Zhi's grave to the new site.

Gui Lin Stone House was the home of Ling Seng, chairman of the Guomindang party during the 1930s. The house was built completely out of stone in 1932, and sits on top of a high promontory on the southern slope of Zijin Shan. A steep, narrow, stone-paved road approaches it from two directions, either Ling Gu Ta or Zhongshan Bowuguan. This site descends downward sharply in three directions and upward sharply in the fourth. The house was destroyed by the Japanese during their occupation, leaving behind the foundation and some ruined walls, including a staircase that now ascends into the air. The walls are still scarred black from the fire. You can still see some of the Ming-style stone statues Ling Seng used to decorate his house, including copies of some at the Ming Xiao Ling.

■ FORMER HOME OF CHIANG KAI SHEK (MEI LING BIESHU)
Song Mei Ling Villa (Mei Ling Bieshu) is the former home of Jiang Jie shi (Chiang Kai-shek) and his third wife Song Mei Ling. It was built in 1931 and served as the official presidential residence (Xiao Hong Shan) until 1949. The three-storey house is decorated with period furnishings meant to show how it looked when Jiang lived there. Photos of its famous former residents grace the walls. A map room displays the military situation in 1949. Jiang's original car, a black Buick, is parked outside the house. It sits on Zijin Shan at No.9 Zhongshan Ling Yuan Lu.

■ AIR FORCE MEMORIAL (HANG KONG LIE SHI GONG MU)
Built by the Guomindang in 1932, it was badly damaged during the Japanese occupation. Restored and expanded in 1994, it now includes the names of both Chinese and foreign pilots who died in the air battles with Japan from 1932 to 1945. The memorial sits just off Jiang Wang Miao Lu, on the North slope of Zijin Shan.

■ ZIJIN SHAN CABLE CAR (SHAN DING GONGYUAN)
A cable car takes passengers up to Shan Ding Gongyuan—the highest central peak of Zijin Shan's three peaks. The top of this peak can also be reached via a stone paved road that begins from behind Ling Gu Ta and ascends the ridge, traversing the third peak and then ascending the second peak. This is a very long walk . You can also hire a taxi driver to take you there.

SIGHTS SOUTH OF NANJING
■ NIUSHOU SHAN
The tomb of famous Chinese Muslim Ming-dynasty Admiral, **Zheng He** (1371–1435), whose ships sailed the seven seas in the 15th century, is here. Take Zhongshan Nan

Lu to Yu Hua Xi Lu travelling out of the city heading south. When Yu Hua Xi Lu forks into two directions, take the left fork onto Ning Dan Lu and follow this across hills to Niu Shou Shan.

The 12th-century **fortifications of Yue Fei** stretch from Hanfu Shan to Niushou Shan, south of the city. Yue Fei (1103–1141) was a famous Southern Song general who wanted to recapture the north after the Song had been driven south to their new capital in Hangzhou. In 1129 he recaptured the Nanjing area and held a front line along the Yangzi. In 1136 he advanced to the Yellow River. By 1139–1140 he raided Henan Province and the old Song capital at Kaifeng. However, at that point he was ordered to withdraw from North China by the Song Emperor Qin Gui who preferred reaching a diplomatic solution with the Jin invaders. Yue Fei was recalled to the capital at Hangzhou and imprisoned, dying a mysterious death in 1141. A popular temple is devoted to him in Hangzhou on West Lake.

■ ZUTANG SHAN

Located on the southern slope of Zutang Shan are the tombs (**Nan Tang Er Ling**) of two Southern Tang-dynasty emperors, Li Bian (Li Sheng) (937-943), and Li Jing (943-961). The two underground tombs are well lit and can be entered on foot without a guide. This place is nearly deserted as it is well off the tourist track. Located to the right of Li Jing's tomb, the tomb of Li Sheng is more impressive. Inside you will find three main rooms with domed ceilings, marble columns, detailed bas relief rock carvings of warrior guardians armed with swords, and other decorations such as dragons and stone tripod roof brackets just like those used on traditional wooden Chinese buildings today. Notice the ten side chambers where his wives and retainers were buried alive with him.

Near the entrance gate, there is a small museum displaying (with Chinese captions) some of the 640 artefacts discovered in the tombs when they were first opened in 1950. Over the wall behind the museum, you can see three stone statues overgrown with vines—two soldiers are facing each other and one scholar. This is the remains of the Sacred Way leading to these tombs.

SIGHTS EAST OF NANJING (QIXIA MOUNTAIN)

For visitors spending more than a few days in Nanjing, a visit to these sites on Qixia Hill are strongly recommended. Seventeen kilometres (10.5 miles) east of Nanjing, the drive to the Buddhist grottoes and temple of Qixia takes the visitor through an area rich in tomb sites of the nobility of the Liang dynasty (502–57). In particular there are stone figures from the tombs of three of Emperor Wudi's brothers, Xiao Dan, Xiao Hui and Xiao Xiu. Xiao Dan's tomb includes a well-preserved stele on the back of a stone tortoise and two large stone winged lions. Xiao Xiu's tomb figures include wonderfully carved winged lions, tortoises and columns.

■ QIXIA TEMPLE (QIXIA SI)
First built in the fifth century, this temple has repeatedly been destroyed and restored thereafter. The present temple buildings date from the early 20th century. Serving as headquarters of the Jiangsu Branch of the Buddhist Association of China, the temple is an active centre of worship where the monks hold regular services. The temple also boasts an exceptional library of 7,200 volumes of Buddhist scriptures. Behind the temple is the **Sheli Pagoda**, one of the oldest stone pagodas south of the Yangzi River. This 15-metre (50-foot) high, five-storeyed pagoda was built in 601, and is embellished with detailed carvings of Buddha's life.

■ QIXIA THOUSAND BUDDHA CLIFF (QIAN FO YAN)
There are 294 shrines and 515 rock carvings in niches and grottoes in the cliff-face near the temple. The earliest date from the fifth century, and they continued to be carved until the Ming dynasty (1368–1644). Many of their heads were defaced or lopped off during the Cultural Revolution (1966–76). One figure is a 13-metre (43-foot) high Buddha, said to have been carved by Zhongzhang, son of the magistrate-turned-hermit, Ming Sengshao, who donated his home as the original Qixia Temple.

Zhenjiang

Zhenjiang, on the south bank, is situated in the middle of Jiangsu Province, at the junction of the Yangzi and the Grand Canal, 63 kilometres (40 miles) from Nanjing. It was the capital of the province during the Republican period (1911–49) when Nanjing was the national capital. Earlier Chinese travellers classified Zhenjiang's scenery as 'The Best Landscape under Heaven', and indeed the area known as the Southern Suburbs was often used as a theme in landscapes by famous Chinese painters. Marco Polo may have visited the city in the 13th century, commenting: 'The people of Zhenjiang live by industry and commerce; they produce much silk and brocade and the rustic flavour of the place is suitable for the production of many things.'

The American Nobel Prize-winning writer, Pearl S Buck (1892–1973), author of *The Good Earth* and other novels about China, lived in Zhenjiang for 15 years before attending boarding school in Shanghai. Her missionary parents' house still stands in the northern part of the city, incorporated into a radio factory. Handicrafts include jade carvings, palace lanterns and screens of natural stone. Zhenjiang is also known for its black vinegar and pickled vegetables.

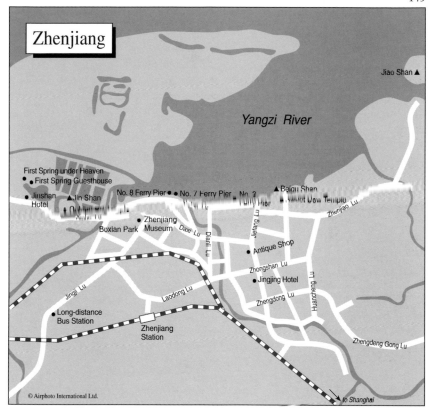

HISTORY OF ZHENJIANG

Zhenjiang, under various names, has existed for 2,500 years. In 213 BC, its importance as a ferry crossing led Emperor Qin Shihuangdi to conclude that Zhenjiang's *fengshui* (geomantic) powers were too strong. He ordered 3,000 prisoners to dig a tunnel through one of the hills to divert the influences.

During the convoluted politics of the Three Kingdoms period (220–265, *see* page 42), Sun Quan, ruler of the kingdom of Wu, made his capital here and Zhenjiang was the site of many 'mini-summits' on military strategy between the warring kingdoms. Thereafter the settlement grew steadily, benefiting greatly from the construction of the Grand Canal under the Sui dynasty (581–618). Its key location at the intersection of the Grand Canal and the Yangzi made it the hub of water transportation from the seventh century onwards.

Under the Song dynasty (960–1279) the city's development reached its height, producing fine silks, satins and silverware as tribute to the imperial court. Troops were stationed here to defend the river (*Zhenjiang* means 'guard the river')—a wise

THE GRAND CANAL —Judy Bonavia

The Grand Canal zigzags some 2,500 kilometres (1,554 miles) down the length of eastern China and remains the longest man-made waterway in the world. In ancient times it was crucial in the transportation of grain from the fertile Yangzi delta to the relatively barren north, and in developing communications across the vast territory that the waterway system served. From the Yellow River valley, from which Chinese civilization sprang, culture and learning spread southwards along the canal, until by the Tang dynasty (618–907) such cities as Yangzhou and Hangzhou had themselves become centres of art and philosophy.

The first link in this canal system was constructed in the fifth century BC by the King of Wu to facilitate his invasion of the Kingdom of Ji to the north. Other canals were constructed as political and economic demands arose. It was the Sui emperor Yangdi who, in the seventh century, set about creating an inter-communicating system linking his capital of Luoyang with the rice lands of the Yangzi River plains. The network was extended to the northern city, later called Beijing, to supply his armies, then fighting the Koreans. Tens of thousands of men and women were conscripted to labour on these projects, and to plant trees along the banks.

Ma Shumou, the emperor's cruel overseer, was known as Mahu—'Ma the Barbarous'. Yangzhou mothers to this day chastise their children by threatening 'Mahu will get you'. It was reputed that during the building of the Grand Canal he demanded a daily meal of a steamed two-year old child.

During the Tang dynasty (618–907) over 300,000 tons of grain were shipped northwards annually under the escort of 120,000 soldiers.

When the Mongol Yuan dynasty (1279–1368) established its capital in present-day Beijing, the need for a rapid supply of grain, unimpeded by pirates along the sea route, led to the digging of a direct canal northwards, which shortened the route by some 700 to 800 kilometres (435 to 500 miles). The reduced length of 1,782 kilometres (1,108 miles) was bordered by a paved highway allowing travellers to cover the distance in 40 days.

Throughout its history the canal supplied not only the essentials of life but also the luxuries. Scholars and officials travelled on it to and from the capital for imperial examinations or affairs of state. Emperor Yangdi's retinue, in magnificent boats styled as dragons, tigers and birds, was pulled by 80,000 trackers along it.

During the Qing dynasty (1644–1911) official corruption, flooding and silting caused the gradual decline of the Grand Canal. Twelve thousand bridges span the canal, which in recent years has been dredged and repaired. Water from the Yangzi is being diverted along this age-old channel for irrigation of the northern plains and the cities of Beijing and Tianjin. Stretches of it are now open to tourism.

precaution, as it turned out, when they had to take on invading Jin troops in a naval battle near Jin Shan in 1130.

During the Opium War of 1842, Zhenjiang was bombarded by British men-of-war. Seven thousand British troops stormed the walled city, which was defended by only about 3,000 courageous Chinese soldiers. The governor of the city and his family committed suicide. On the British side, 105 soldiers were killed or wounded. This battle was a turning point, as it led to the signing of the Treaty of Nanking only a month later. The treaty provided for the surrender of Hong Kong to Britain and for the payment of 21 million Mexican dollars by the Chinese as indemnity.

The city was again captured in 1853 by the Taiping rebels (see page 112) and held by them for four years, which left it crippled for some time. A small foreign concession was established in 1861. A H Rasmussen, a Scandinavian trader who lived in Zhenjiang for many years, wrote:

> Then I went into the silent street for a breath of fresh air and walked up and down the bund, three hundred paces one way and three hundred paces back. To get a little change I walked up and down the only cross street to the south gate of the Concession, two hundred paces one way and two hundred paces back.

Life was very restricted, and the hunting of wild boar in the surrounding hills became the main pastime for the resident foreigners.

Trade recovered, however. Customs house records show that in the first decade of the 20th century the value of goods trans-shipped in one year through Zhenjiang exceeded a staggering 35 million taels of silver (one tael is roughly 50 grammes or 1.8 ounces).

But the coming of the railway put an end to this spate of merchandise; by the 1920s, much of it was being conveyed by freight trains. Yet Zhenjiang is still a busy transportation hub. A new port at nearby Dagang has enhanced its importance and it is on the Shanghai-Nanjing railroad line. Industries include metallurgy, electronics and vehicle and ship construction.

WHAT TO SEE IN ZHENJIANG

With some 300 factories employing well over a third of its population of 390,000, Zhenjiang is now indisputably industrial. Yet it still enjoys the appellation 'City of Forests and Hills', which was coined by the celebrated landscape painter Mi Fu (1051–1107) because it is flanked on three sides by tree-clad mountains.

The busiest area of the city is within the confines of Zhengdong Lu, Jiefang Lu and Renmin Lu. The old city is further west, near Boxian Park. The foreign concession was there; its British consulate is now the **Zhenjiang Museum**. On Boxian Lu an old American church still retains the stone plaque set into a wall which reads, though not clearly:

First Baptist Church
Organized
... D 1885
Rebuilt 1921

■ **XIAO MATOU JIE (SMALL JETTY STREET)**

Take this charming little cobbled street through the oldest part of town. The rows of Qing-dynasty (1644–1911) buildings are intersected by stone arches at regular intervals. One of these is the **Zhaoguan Stupa**—five metres (16 feet) high rising behind a stone archway—which dates from the Yuan dynasty (1279–1368). The names engraved on either side commemorate those who were officials of the prefecture when the *stupa* was restored in 1583.

The cobbled pathway was once lined with shops selling incense to devotees at Jin Shan Temple. West of the *stupa* is the **Western Ferry Crossing (Xi Jindu Jie)**. Its stone steps once led straight down to the riverside, where there was a ferry service to Jin Shan and the other side of the Yangzi. Marco Polo is said to have come ashore at this very spot.

■ **JIN SHAN (GOLDEN HILL)**

The 44-metre (144-foot) Golden Hill, with its famous temple, was an island in the centre of the Yangzi until it merged with the river bank in the middle of the last century. Visitors used to take a ferry from the Western Ferry Crossing, and then rode mules to the top. Jin Shan Temple was first built over 1,500 years ago. In its heyday, the temple was looked after by 3,000 Buddhist monks.

Visitors may be shown the most interesting of the several sights and relics on Jin Shan. **Jin Shan Pagoda** was first built 1,400 years ago and rebuilt many times: in the Song dynasty as two pagodas, in the Ming as a single tower and three times in the Qing period. **Fa Hai** or **Pei Gong Cave** is identified by a statue of the monk Fa Hai, son of a Tang-dynasty prime minister. Fa Hai lived here when he came to the temple, having first studied at Lushan. It is said that when the monk discovered a pot of gold, he gave it to the local officials. The emperor ordered that the gold be returned to Fai Hai, to rebuild the temple, thereafter named Golden Hill Temple.

The extraordinary folk tale of the White Snake is connected to Fa Hai. The story tells of a 1,000-year old white snake, Bai Suzhen, who, longing for a life among mortals, changed herself into a beautiful maiden. She married a young herbalist, Xu Xian, whom she first met on the famous Broken Bridge on the West Lake in Hangzhou. The happy couple set up business dispensing medicines, but Suzhen's magical cures aroused the anger of the powerful Buddhist monk, Fa Hai. His machinations put the couple through many trials and tribulations, including imprisonment of Xu Xian, before he was eventually defeated. At one point Xu Xian escaped through the **Bai Long Dong (White Dragon Cave)** on Jin Shan, for though narrow it is said to lead to Hangzhou, where the herbalist and Suzhen were reunited.

In the temple, a bronze drum, presented in the Qing dynasty (1644–1911), is one of the treasures of the **Four Precious Rooms (Sibao Shi)**. It is believed to have belonged to Zhuge Liang (181–234, *see* page 42) and to have doubled as a cooking pot when not being beaten in war. Another is Su Dongpo's official mandarin belt of 20 jade pieces. Su apparently had to forfeit his belt when he lost a debate on Buddhism with his friend, the monk Fo Yin.

The scroll-adorned **Fo Dian (Buddha Hall)**, with its 18 *luohan* (disciples of Buddha) statues, is where the monks hold their services.

West of Jin Shan, along the road that runs beside an artificial lake, is **Zhongling Spring**, the 'Foremost Spring under Heaven'. It was graded by the Tang scholar, Lu Yu, whose *Book of Teas* listed and classified seven springs in China according to the water's compatibility with tea. Zhongling's water was judged the sweetest for brewing tea. The bubbling spring trickles into a small pool enclosed by bamboo groves, but today its water is anything but sweet.

■ BEIGU SHAN

Rising from the Yangzi the steep cliff face of the 53-metre (174-foot) high Beigu Shan was a natural fortification and was chosen by the King of Wu, Sun Quan, as the site of his capital, Tiewangcheng, in the third century. The Martyr's Monument now stands where the great Wu general, Zhou Yu, made his headquarters. The novel *Romance of the Three Kingdoms* (*see* page 42) contains many stories concerning Beigu Shan.

The exquisite **Iron Pagoda** dates from the Song dynasty (960–1279) and has an extraordinary history of survival. Erected in the 11th century on the site of an earlier pagoda, it had nine tiers. In the Ming dynasty (1368–1644), a tidal wave destroyed seven tiers, which were later replaced. In the Qing (1644–1911), the upper tiers were again destroyed, this time by lightning. Several Ming tiers were discovered nearby during restoration in 1961 and replaced in position above the only two remaining original Tang tiers. Over 2,000 Tang (618–907) relics were also found at that time. The **Ganlu (Sweet Dew) Temple** buildings now house painting exhibits.

The **Hen Stone** was carved into the shape of a ram at the end of the last century. It is believed that the King of Wu sat on this stone when planning his strategy for the great Battle of the Red Cliff (*see* page 89).

The pretty **Duojing Lou (Tower of Many Views)** is said to have been the dressing room of Liu Bei's wife, the sister of Sun Quan. Song-dynasty literati frequently held banquets in it.

Liu Bei's wife is said to have committed suicide from the **Jijiang Ting (Sacrificing to the River Pavilion)**. She threw herself into the river upon hearing of the death of her husband at Baidi Cheng (*see* pages 42 and 54), after his defeat by her brother, the treacherous Sun Quan.

The two **Shijian Shi (Sword Testing Stones)**, each split neatly in two, were reputedly cloven by the swords of Liu Bei and Sun Quan, who were at that time

outwardly in alliance over regaining the city of Jiangling (present-day Jingzhou, *see* page 86) but each secretly plotting to betray the other.

The three characters *liu ma jian*—'Hold back the horse from the cliff'—on the face below the hill, are associated with a story that also involves Liu and Sun. At a banquet together, Liu, who being from the northwest was an expert cavalryman but was less adept at naval warfare, said to Sun, 'Now I know why southerners can row boats so well, and northerners manage their horses.' Sun took offence at what he considered a backhanded compliment, and challenged Liu to a race. In a drunken state they leapt on to their horses. As they reached the cliff edge Liu reined in his horse, but Sun could not and was saved from death only at the last moment by Liu.

■ JIAO SHAN

Four kilometres (2.5 miles) northeast of Zhenjiang, the tiny island of Jiao Shan can be reached by a local ferry. It was named after a hermit scholar-monk, Jiao Guang, of the Eastern Han period (25–220), who is said to have lived in what is known as the **Three Summons Cave**.

Thrice Jiao was invited by the emperor to take an official post, and thrice he refused. He lived to be 120 years old, treating and healing the local fisherfolk.

At the foot of the hill is **Dinghui Temple (Temple of Stability and Wisdom)**, built on the site of an earlier temple in the Tang dynasty (618–907). It was burnt down and rebuilt in the Ming (1368–1644). Old ginkgo trees stand in front

(above) Jinshan Temple in Zhenjiang has been an important Buddhist temple for centuries.

(left) *Two hundred years ago Jinshan Temple stood on an island in the Yangzi River; now, due to silting, it has become part of the southern bank near Zhenjiang. The river can just be seen running along the horizon.*

of the main hall which contains some fine bronze *luohan* (disciples of Buddha) statues, presented by temples at Wutai Shan in Shanxi Province.

The chief attraction of the **Jiao Shan Forest of Tablets (Bei Lin)**, a collection of over 260 inscribed stones classified into literary, artistic and historic works, the earliest of which date from the Eastern Jin dynasty (317–420), is the White Crane Tablet cut with the calligraphy of Wang Yizhe (321–79). Wang was fond of white cranes (which symbolize longevity) and on seeing one on Jiao Shan asked if he could have it. The monk refused at first, but on learning Wang's identity agreed that he could collect the crane on his next visit.

Returning a year later, Wang discovered that the crane had died and had been buried, wrapped in yellow silk, on the hillside. His text of the sad story of the crane was preserved on a tablet on the hill. Later, during an earthquake, part of the inscription broke off and fell into the river. A thousand years later, in 1713, five pieces were recovered upstream, and were restored to their rightful place.

The **Cannon Platform** dates from the first Anglo-Chinese Opium War. (Another lies on Elephant Hill on the south bank of the Yangzi.) In the course of the war, British naval ships sailed up the river and, in a two-pronged attack, captured the stronghold, killing 500 Chinese troops. The walls, pockmarked with cannon shell, are made of rammed earth and sticky-rice water.

Near the top of the hill are viewing pavilions and the **Bie Feng Yan** cottage in which Zheng Banqiao (1693–1765), one of the Eight Eccentric Painters of the Yangzhou school, lived for five years.

■ ZHENJIANG MUSEUM

A fascinating survivor of the foreign concession in Zhenjiang is the former British Consulate at the foot of a knoll overlooking the port. The compound consists of seven buildings, a couple of which now form the city's museum. They house a collection of ancient bronzeware, celadon, porcelain, fabrics and a cache of Tang-dynasty silverware (618–907) unearthed in the Danyang area in 1983. Outside in the overgrown garden lies the abandoned anchor of *HMS Amethyst*, trapped and nearly sunk by Communist shell-fire in 1949. Cannons brought back from Jiaoshan recall Zhenjiang's involvement in the first Opium War.

Yangzhou

There is a little verse, much quoted in reference to Yangzhou, which goes something like this:

> Brilliant moonlight, orioles, flowers and pavilions of jade,
> All attest to the past and present glories of Yangzhou.

To these glories might also be added Yangzhou's tradition of producing beautiful women.

Yangzhou was one of the most important cities on the Grand Canal and is a delightful place to visit, retaining to some degree the feeling of its rich cultural and historical traditions. A vehicular ferry from Zhenjiang crosses the Yangzi and from the north bank the drive to Yangzhou takes half an hour. Many traditional arts and crafts are still practised: lacquerware, paper-cuts, lanterns, embroidery, *penjing* (miniature gardens) and seal carving.

Yangzhou has one of the great cuisines of China and every foreigner knows— indirectly—about it, for Yangzhou is the home of the worldwide favourite Chinese dish of fried rice (*Yangzhou chaofan*).

HISTORY OF YANGZHOU

The city's history began over 2,400 years ago in the Spring and Autumn period (722– 481 BC); one of the early nine provincial areas of China was called after it. The Sui

Sailing the Yangzi

I sailed 1,500 miles downstream, from Chungking to Shanghai. Every mile of it was different; but there were 1,200 miles I did not see. It crosses ten provinces, 700 rivers are joined to it—all Yangtze statistics are hopeless, huge and ungraspable; they obscure rather than clarify. And since words have a greater precision than numbers, one day I asked a Chinese ship captain if he thought the river had a distinct personality.

He said, 'The mood of the river changes according to the season. It changes every day. It is not easy. Navigating the river is always a struggle against nature. And there is only one way to pilot a ship well.' He explained—he was smiling and blowing smoke out of his nostrils—'It is necessary to see the river as an enemy.'

Later a man told me that in the course of one afternoon he had counted nine human corpses bobbing hideously down the river.

The Yangtze is China's main artery, its major waterway, the source of many of its myths, the scene of much of its history. On its banks are some of its greatest cities. It is the fountainhead of superstition; it provides income and food to half the population. It is one of the most dangerous rivers in the world, in some places one of the dirtiest, in others one of the most spectacular. The Chinese drink it and bathe in it and wash clothes in it and shit in it. It represents both life and death. It is a wellspring, a sewer and a tomb; depthless in the gorges, puddle-shallow at its rapids. The Chinese say if you haven't been up the Great River, you haven't been anywhere.

They also say that in the winter, on the river, the days are so dark that when the sun comes out the dogs bark at it. Chungking was dark at nine in the morning, when I took the rattling tin tram on the cog railway that leads down the black crags which are Chungking's ramparts, down the sooty cliffs, past the tenements and billboards ('Flying Pigeon Bicycles', 'Seagull Watches', 'Parrot Accordions') to the landing stage. A thick, sulphurous fog lay over the city, a Coketown of six million . . . Doctor Ringrose, who was from Leeds, sniffed and said, 'That is the smell of my childhood.'

Paul Theroux, Sailing Through China, 1984

emperor, Yangdi, initiated the construction of the Grand Canal here in 605, which eventually made Yangzhou the hub of land and water transportation. Emperor Yangdi visited the city three times in grand dragon-boats. He built a palace, retired and was buried here, after being assassinated in 618. Yangzhou was also a centre of classical learning and religion. Emperors, prime ministers and men of letters through the ages visited Yangzhou and many held official positions, including the great traveller Marco Polo, who was supposedly governor general of the city for three years, although no contemporary documents support this.

By the Tang dynasty (618–907) Yangzhou's trading links with Arab merchants were well established. A foreign community numbering about a thousand lived in the city. It was said that 'at night a thousand lamps lit up the clouds'. The economy was based on the salt monopoly and on grain shipments to the capital.

Yangzhou, along with so many other middle and lower Yangzi cities, suffered badly during the Taiping Rebellion in the mid-19th century (see page 112). In addition, the silting of the Yangzi and the flooding of the Grand Canal gradually undermined its entrepôt role, as grain shipments were increasingly transported by sea via Shanghai, rather than along the Grand Canal. Changes in the salt administration and the arrival of the railways were the coup de grâce in Yangzhou's decline.

During the late 18th century an individualistic school of painters sprang up, known as the Eight Eccentrics of Yangzhou, whose bold style has a strong following today.

WHAT TO SEE IN YANGZHOU

The streets of Yangzhou reveal much that is charming and interesting. Stroll down Guoqing Lu past craftsmen painting mirrors and making bamboo steamers and cloth shoes, then along Dujiang Lu where wooden-fronted shops, partitioned with rattan matting, sell household goods, basketware and fireworks, and itinerant sugarcane vendors hawk their wares. The road eventually reaches the Grand Canal, where, from the bridge, boat life can be observed as it passes by. The courtyards of the small, grey-tiled houses are cluttered with pots of flowers and miniature penjing plants—a speciality of the region. Rows of white cabbage and strips of turnip hang out to dry. One may also walk along the small canals.

The Imperial Jetty, where the Qing emperors disembarked, is situated on the canal in front of Xiyuan Hotel. Visit also **Yechun Yuan**, where a poetry club used to meet in the Qing dynasty (1644–1911). It is now a tea-house and specializes in Yellow Bridge Buns, which were first created to supply the troops during the Sino-Japanese War. Further on is the **Luyang Cun**, a garden filled with miniature plants, goldfish and birds.

■ SLENDER WEST LAKE (SHOUXI HU)

This is a beautiful man-made lake dating from the Tang dynasty (618–907) and surrounded by weeping willows and pavilions. The Fishing Platform at the end of the

Dyke of Spring Willows was reputedly used by Emperor Qianlong (reigned 1736–96). Through its arches different views of the beautiful **Five Pavilion Bridge (Wuting Qiao)**, built in 1757, are presented. The red pillars of the pavilions with their yellow-tiled roofs rest on 15 stone arches; extravagant claims are made about the splendid moonlit scene at the bridge at the Mid-autumn Festival—in a particularly auspicious year the moon is said to be reflected in the water under each arch. Near the bridge is a white *stupa*, whose origin is attributed to Emperor Qianlong. It seems that he remarked on a visit that though this scenic spot reminded him of Beihai Park in Beijing, it was a pity that there was no white *stupa* to complete the resemblance. The zealous local officials worked through the night to carve a full-sized *stupa* from salt. The emperor was duly impressed and, when he returned north, the permanent version that stands today was built. **The Friendship Hall** contains a stone tablet with a description of Marco Polo's three-year governorship in Yangzhou, and his portrait. The lovely Yu Garden was built in 1915 as the residence of the local warlord, Yu Baoshan.

■ WENFENG PAGODA

This seven-tiered wooden and brick pagoda stands beside a busy stretch of the Grand Canal south of the city, where boats load and unload goods—bamboo matting, soya beans, rice and cotton. Most of the boats are made of concrete; very few are of wood. Men beating gongs parade up and down with carts; they do the shopping for the boat-people who are too busy to go ashore and do their own. The pagoda offers a good overview of the town.

■ XIANHE MOSQUE (FAIRY CRANE MOSQUE)

This ancient mosque was first built in 1275 to serve the needs of the Arab traders and was rebuilt twice in the Ming dynasty (1368–1644). Its ancient pine and ginkgo trees are believed to be around 800 years old. The mosque is supposed to resemble a crane in shape: the main entrance is the head; the wells on either side, the eyes; the left-hand path, the neck; the prayer hall, the body; the north and south halls, the wings.

Arabic scrolls executed in Chinese calligraphic style hang in one of the halls. There are some 3,600 Hui (Muslims) in Yangzhou.

■ TOMB OF PUHADDIN

Puhaddin was a 16th-generation descendant of the Prophet Mohammed, founder of Islam. He came to China in the second half of the 13th century and was in Yangzhou between 1265 and 1275, helping to build the Fairy Crane Mosque. He travelled to Shandong Province to spread the word of Islam, but became ill and died there. He was buried, according to his wish, in Yangzhou.

A fine, carved white marble stairway leads to the cemetery. The majority of the 25 tombs here are those of Chinese Muslims but a few are the tombs of early Arab traders; the architectural style of the tombs is completely Arabian.

■ YANGZHOU MUSEUM

This building was originally erected in 1772 around the tomb of Shi Kefa (1601–45) who was in command of Yangzhou when the Qing armies moved south to consolidate their power. A supporter of the Ming dynasty, Shi and his 4,000 troops held out against the Qing army for ten days, five times refusing to surrender and fighting to the death. The museum's most prized possession is its collection of 18th-century paintings and calligraphy by the Eight Eccentrics of Yangzhou, whose rejection of the orthodox style of the day was a major breakthrough in Chinese painting.

■ GARDENS

The rich salt merchants of Yangzhou left a legacy of many exquisite gardens. The delightful Ge Garden north of Dongguan Jie was the home of a rich 19th-century salt merchant, Huang Yingtai. Its architecture, bamboo groves and landscaping are typical of the famous private gardens of Suzhou. The garden got its name from its bamboo leaves, shaped like the Chinese character for ge (see index page 206). On Xuningmen Jie is the popular **He Garden**, built by He Zhidao. It once belonged to the Qing Court's ambassador to France, and some Western architectural influences can be seen.

■ WENCHANG GE (PAVILION OF FLOURISHING CULTURE)

This 'mini' Temple of Heaven, dedicated to the god of literary success, is three storeys high and took ten years to build; just before completion it burnt down, only to be immediately rebuilt in 1585. Originally situated on a bridge across a canal, the area was transformed into a wide roadway, so Wenchang Ge now stands at the intersection of Wenhe Jie and Shita Jie. Nearby is the **Stone Pagoda** (Shi Ta), a highly valued Tang-dynasty relic. Its six sides are decorated with floral patterns.

■ TIANNING TEMPLE (TEMPLE OF HEAVENLY TRANQUILLITY)

The present buildings date from the Ming dynasty (1368–1644), though a temple existed here in the Song dynasty (960 1279). The Qing emperor, Qianlong, had a travel lodge built on one of his inspection tours. The temple is next to the Xiyuan Hotel.

■ DAMING TEMPLE

Daming Temple is part of a complex of buildings. The temple was built in the fifth century. Large incense burners with bells stand in front of the main hall in which services are held daily at 4pm.

The temple has strong ties with Japan. The Buddhist abbot, Jian Zhen (688–763), was invited to teach in Japan, and made five attempts to go there, but failed each time. It was on his sixth attempt, at the age of 66 and by then blind, that he succeeded in reaching the Japanese capital of Nara, where he set up a study centre at one of the temples. His contribution in bringing understanding of Chinese literature and arts, architecture, medicine and printing to Japan was commemorated in 1963, when a number of Chinese and Japanese Buddhists decided to build the **Jian Zhen Memorial Hall**. The walls are decorated with murals depicting his journeys. In 1980 the Japanese donated a wooden statue of Jian Zhen, a copy of the beautiful lacquer statue of the monk in the Nara Temple in Japan. In front of the wooden statue is an incense burner presented by Emperor Hirohito of Japan.

Pingshan Hall was built by the great Song-dynasty scholar, statesman and poet, Ouyang Xiu, in 1048 to entertain his guests when he was prefect of Yangzhou. A statue of him now stands in the hall. A student of his, Su Dongpo, also an official in Yangzhou, wrote a commemorative poem about Ouyang, which is engraved in stone on the walls.

In the gardens of the temple is another of the seven great springs of China, mentioned in the Tang-dynasty *Book of Teas*. This one is known as the 'Fifth Spring under Heaven' (*see* page 149).

Parts of the Tang (618–907) city walls can be seen in the vicinity of Daming Temple and on **Guanyin Hill**, the site of the Sui Emperor Yangdi's palace.

Nantong

Nantong is one of the 14 port cities opened to foreign investment projects under China's current policies of modernization. The city is an integral part of the Shanghai Economic Zone. The population of 7.4 million is engaged in industrial production, especially textiles. It is hoped that textile, precision machinery and communications industries will be established either as joint ventures or entirely foreign enterprises. Ten thousand-ton vessels berth at its deep-water harbour.

One of the city's heroes was Cao Gong, who in 1557 successfully defended the town against Japanese pirates roaming the coast of China. His heroic exploits earned him a high official position which he refused to accept. Cao was killed in another pirate raid shortly after. The **Cao Gong Zhu Memorial Temple** was built in his honour.

East of the city is **Lang Shan (Wolf Hill)**, said to be haunted by the spirit of a white wolf. The temple on top is dedicated to a Song-dynasty Buddhist monk, whom legend endowed with magical powers over water demons. Boat people prayed to him for safe journeys. The main hall contains models of different types of river craft. At the base of Lang Shan is the **Five Hills Park**.

■ BAOSHAN
The giant Baoshan Steel Works on the south bank, near the mouth of the Huangpu River, is one of the largest in China. Japanese and West German technology and plant are being used. In the early stages the project ran into difficulties, not the least of which was the choice of site—marshy ground that caused subsidence. Moreover, the

estuary was found to be too shallow to allow 100,000-ton freighters bearing imported iron ore to unload. The mill began operation in 1985.

■ HUANGPU RIVER

Just below Baoshan, boats pass by a large lighthouse and between buoys to turn south into the Huangpu River, on the last stage of the journey from Chongqing to Shanghai. The 25-kilometre (13-mile) cruise today takes one through the heart of Shanghai's port; on either side of the muddy river stretch wharf installations with facilities to handle ocean-going ships of 25,000 tons, and an annual shipping volume of about 100 million tons. This is China's largest port and its busiest. Apart from the hundreds of foreign and Chinese registered ships, the river is busy all day long with ferries, naval and police craft, lighters and dredgers.

The Huangpu is 114 kilometres (70 miles) in length, rising from Dianshan Lake southwest of Shanghai. Its banks were once simply mud flats. The river is subject to heavy silting from the Yangzi and requires constant dredging to keep the channels free.

Soon after entering the river, on the western bank is the area known as **Wusong**, where in 1842, during the Opium War, a fleet of British warships and support vessels opened fire on the ill-defended Chinese fort and its miles of earthworks. After a two-hour bombardment they forced their way up to Suzhou Creek and on to Shanghai. The fort was heroically defended but the Chinese were no match for the British fleet. Among the many Chinese casualties was a highly respected 76-year-old admiral who had been at sea for 50 years and who, it was said, wrapped himself in cotton wool before his battles to make himself invulnerable. This was a decisive battle, for it enabled the fleet to occupy Shanghai and move on up the Yangzi; later in the year, the Treaty of Nanking was signed, opening many Chinese cities to foreign trade.

Before the opium trade was legitimized in 1860, opium clippers and steamers unloaded their cargo on to hulks permanently moored at Wusong, Shanghai's outer anchorage, before they were smuggled into the hinterland.

Gradually Shanghai's imposing skyline appears as boats sidle up to the berth alongside Zhongshan Lu, once known as the Bund, and lined with impressive European-style buildings from a bygone era.

Shanghai

A conurbation of over 18 million people, Shanghai is China's second-largest city and is one of the four centrally administered cities in the country, the other three being Beijing, Tianjin and Chongqing. It is also one of China's most important industrial and cultural centres.

To most foreigners, Shanghai conjures up stories of adventure and intrigue, of vice and pleasure. Many of these were probably no exaggeration, for it was a dynamic,

River Rites   —by Madeleine Lynn

Life on board a junk was hard and dangerous work. Cornell Plant, River Inspector for the Chinese Imperial Maritime Service in the 1900s, wrote about the risks of travelling through the Three Gorges: Chinese say that one junk in ten is badly damaged, and one in 20 totally wrecked each trip. Probably not 20 per cent reach Chungking unscathed, and never one without experiencing some hair's-breadth escape.

It was common for trackers to fall from the tow-paths to their deaths or to break a limb and be left behind by their junk. Thus Yangzi boatmen had a wealth of rites and taboos that had to be observed to ensure a safe passage.

At the beginning of a voyage and also before entering the Three Gorges, the most dangerous stretch of the river, it was the cook's task to light incense, set off firecrackers and, most importantly, to kill a rooster and sprinkle the blood on the bows of the junk. Writing in 1880, Captain Gill described how to get through the Xintan Rapids safely. The junk could hire a shaman who would come on board with a yellow flag inscribed 'Power of the Water! A happy star for the whole journey'. As the boat ploughed through the waves dragged by the straining trackers, the shaman would stand at the bow, waving the flag in a regular motion to appease the powers of the water. It was also essential to sprinkle rice on the water all the way through the rapids.

Like fishermen everywhere in China, many Yangzi boatmen still believe that it is very bad luck to turn over a fish at table: 'capsize fish, capsize boat'. Another taboo is resting chopsticks on top of a rice bowl in a position that suggests a junk ran aground. Unlike Western sailors, however, there is no taboo against women aboard ship and junk owners usually brought their wives along.

Sometimes fish swimming upstream used to jump onto the decks. They were considered demons and had to be taken ashore and buried. Boatmen also had to contend with the ghosts of the drowned, who would string themselves in a line behind a boat, preparing to board the vessel and cause trouble. The way to shake them loose was to cut quickly in front of another boat, so that the ghosts would lose their grip and attach themselves to the boat behind. Not a very neighbourly thing to do! Describing this to explorer Wong How Man in 1986, a boat captain recounted that, 'In the past, it was a game that often left the trailing boat's owner jumping, cursing and shooting off firecrackers to pacify his increased string of ghosts.'

Meanwhile those living on shore had floods to contend with. The lovely pagodas all along the river were built for flood prevention. It was believed that floods were often caused by dragons (since they have the power to control the waters), or by evil demons. A pagoda built on top of the hill inhabited by one of these creatures could prevent him from coming out and causing trouble. A pagoda could also prevent the wealth of the nearby town from being swept away by the current.

After the disastrous flood of 1788, which inundated over 30 counties in Hubei Province, the Emperor ordered nine iron oxen to be placed along the banks of the river. According to the court record: 'The Sea Dragon submits to Iron and the Ox belongs to Earth, Earth controls Water, the Iron Ox can suppress the flood.' This was following Chinese theories of the properties of the elements: fire, metal, earth, water and air.

violent and colourful city. Most of the European-style quarters of the old International Settlement and the French Concession areas can still be seen, though they are much in need of repair. One can still clearly imagine the extraordinary life of pre-1949 Shanghai.

HISTORY OF SHANGHAI

The name Shanghai, which means 'on the sea', was first used in AD 960 when the settlement was a backward fishing village. In 1554, the town was surrounded by a seven-metre (23-foot) high crenellated city wall and a moat to protect it against the frequent incursions of Japanese pirates. By the 17th century there were signs of growing wealth, but when the British troops stormed its undefended walls in 1842, Shanghai was still only a county town of no great importance.

The first foreign settlement was established in 1843, when the newly-appointed British Consul arrived to negotiate for a 138-acre (just over 0.5 square kilometres) site north of the existing city. This site was joined with the American Settlement, founded in 1848 north of Suzhou Creek, to form the International Settlement in 1863. Subsequent negotiations with the Chinese increased the area of the International Settlement to more than 5,500 acres (about 22 square kilometres). The French Concession was established on 164 acres (about 0.6 square kilometres) in 1849 and was finally extended to about 2,500 acres (about 10 square kilometres). The Japanese, also, had secured a concession by the end of the last century, which became a centre for cotton-spinning factories. These settlements were self-administered and were outside Chinese government jurisdiction.

The old Chinese City, occupied by one group of the Taiping rebels—the Small Sword Society—between 1853 and 1855, became the scene of lawlessness and fighting. The foreign community, concerned for its own safety, formed the Shanghai Volunteer Corps, recruited from local traders and diplomats. They were even prepared to take on the imperial troops: backed by British and American officers and

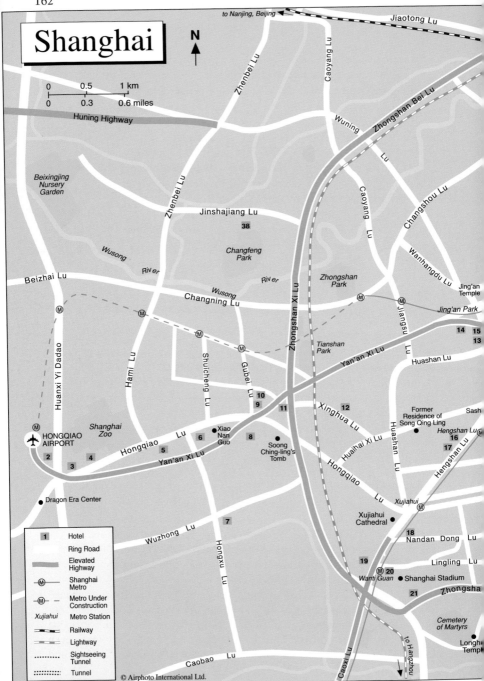

Shanghai

N

0	0.5	1 km
0	0.3	0.6 miles

to Nanjing, Beijing

Jiaotong Lu

Huning Highway

Zhenbei Lu

Caoyang Lu

Zhongshan Bei Lu

Wuning

Changshou Lu

Caoyang Lu

Wanhangdu Lu

Beixingjing Nursery Garden

Zhenbei Lu

Jinshajiang Lu

38

Changfeng Park

Wusong

River

River

Zhongshan Park

Jing'an Temple

Beizhai Lu

Wusong

Changning Lu

Zhongshan Xi Lu

Jiangsu Lu

Jing'an Park

Huanxi Yi Dadao

Hami Lu

Shuicheng Lu

Gubei Lu

Tianshan Park

Yan'an Xi Lu

Huashan Lu

14 **15**

13

HONGQIAO AIRPORT

Shanghai Zoo

Hongqiao Lu

10

9

11

Xinghua Lu

12

Former Residence of Song Qing Ling

Sash

Hengshan Lu

16

2

4

6

Xiao Nan Guo

8

Soong Ching-ling's Tomb

Huaihai Xi Lu

Huashan Lu

17

3

5

Yan'an Xi Lu

Hongqiao Lu

Xujiahui

Xujiahui

Hengshan Lu

Dragon Era Center

7

Wuzhong Lu

Hongxu Lu

Xujiahui Cathedral

18

Nandan Dong Lu

Lingling Lu

19

20

Wanti Guan

Shanghai Stadium

Zhongsha

21

Cemetery of Martyrs

Caobao Lu

Caoxi Lu

to Hangzhou

Longhu Templ

1	Hotel
	Ring Road
	Elevated Highway
Ⓜ	Shanghai Metro
Ⓜ ---	Metro Under Construction
Xujiahui	Metro Station
	Railway
	Lightway
....	Sightseeing Tunnel
::::::::	Tunnel

© Airphoto International Ltd.

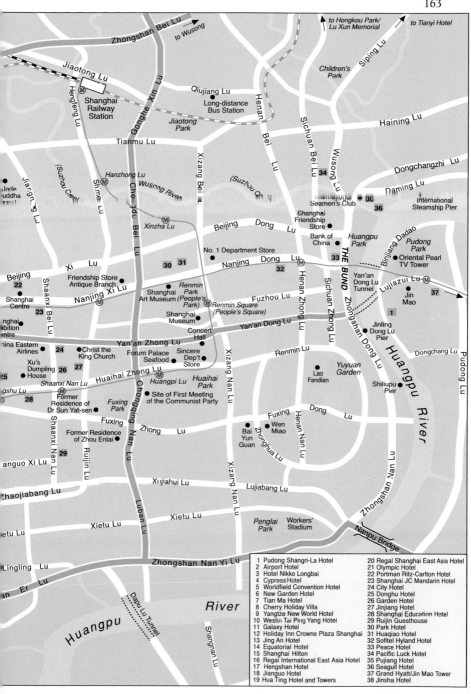

to Wusong

Zhongshan Bei Lu

to Hongkou Park/
Lu Xun Memorial

to Tianyi Hotel

Siping Lu

Jiaotong Lu

Children's
Park

Haining Lu

Qiujiang Lu

Shanghai
Railway
Station

Long-distance
Bus Station

Dongchangzhi Lu

Jiaotong
Park

Tianmu Lu

Daming Lu

Hanzhong Lu

Wusong River

Seamen's Club

International
Steamship Pier

Xinzha Lu

Beijing   Dong   Lu

Shanghai
Friendship
Store

Pudong
Park

Oriental Pearl
TV Tower

Xi   Lu

No. 1 Department Store

Nanjing   Dong   Lu

Bank of
China

Huangpu
Park

Beijing
22

Friendship Store
Antique Branch

Nanjing Xi Lu

Renmin
Park
(People's
Park)

30 **31**

33

32

Yan'an
Dong Lu
Tunnel

Jin
Mao

37

Shanghai Centre

Shanghai
Art Museum

Fuzhou   Lu

23

Shanghai
Museum

Renmin Square
(People's Square)

1

China Eastern
Airlines

Concert
Hall

Yan'an Dong Lu

Jinling
Dong Lu
Pier

24

Christ the
King Church

Yan'an Zhong Lu

Renmin Lu

Xu's
Dumpling
House

Forum Palace
Seafood

Sincere
Dep't
Store

Yuyuan
Garden

Shiliupu
Pier

26 **27**

Lao
Fandian

Shaanxi Nan Lu

Huaihai Zhong Lu

Huangpi Lu

Huaihai
Park

Dongchang Lu

28

Former
Residence of
Dr Sun Yat-sen

Site of First Meeting
of the Communist Party

Fuxing
Park

Fuxing   Dong   Lu

Former Residence
of Zhou Enlai

Fuxing

Zhong   Lu

Wen
Miao

Bai
Yun
Guan

29

Xujiahui Lu

Lujiabang Lu

Huangpu River

Xietu Lu

Penglai
Park

Workers'
Stadium

Nanpu Bridge

Xietu Lu

Xizang Nan Lu

Lingling Lu

Zhongshan Nan Yi Lu

Er Lu

1 Pudong Shangri-La Hotel	20 Regal Shanghai East Asia Hotel
2 Airport Hotel	21 Olympic Hotel
3 Hotel Nikko Longbai	22 Portman Ritz-Carlton Hotel
4 Cypress Hotel	23 Shanghai JC Mandarin Hotel
5 Worldfield Convention Hotel	24 City Hotel
6 New Garden Hotel	25 Donghu Hotel
7 Tian Ma Hotel	26 Garden Hotel
8 Cherry Holiday Villa	27 Jinjiang Hotel
9 Yangtze New World Hotel	28 Shanghai Education Hotel
10 Westin Tai Ping Yang Hotel	29 Ruijin Guesthouse
11 Galaxy Hotel	30 Park Hotel
12 Holiday Inn Crowne Plaza Shanghai	31 Huaqiao Hotel
13 Jing An Hotel	32 Sofitel Hyland Hotel
14 Equatorial Hotel	33 Peace Hotel
15 Shanghai Hilton	34 Pacific Luck Hotel
16 Regal International East Asia Hotel	35 Pujiang Hotel
17 Hengshan Hotel	36 Seagull Hotel
18 Jianguo Hotel	37 Grand Hyatt/Jin Mao Tower
19 Hua Ting Hotel and Towers	38 Jinsha Hotel

Huangpu   River

Dapu Lu Tunnel

Shangnan Lu

men from visiting warships, the volunteers issued an ultimatum for the troops' removal, an action which precipitated the Battle of Muddy Flat in 1854. The imperial troops were duly driven away from their encampment, which was the site of the old racecourse, now the People's Park.

Shanghai was again threatened by the Taiping rebels in the 1860s, but they were quelled by the Ever Victorious Army made up of foreigners and Chinese, established for this very purpose. An American, Frederick Townsend Ward, a Frenchman, Henri A Burgevine, and a Briton, Charles George Gordon ('Chinese Gordon', later of Khartoum fame), took successive command and were all made officers of the Qing Imperial Army (*see* page 113).

The nationwide upheavals in the 20th century—the 1900 Boxer Rebellion, the 1911 Revolution, the Sino-Japanese War—took their toll on Shanghai's millions. Hundreds of thousands of Chinese poured into the foreign settlements for protection and then stayed on. Nevertheless, Shanghai continued to flourish as an entrepôt with its staple exports of tea and silk, and imports of piece goods and opium. Banking played an important part in this great trading city, which had its own stock exchange.

The foreigners' lifestyle was grand and lavish for those who could afford to participate in clubs, race meetings, paper chases and nightclubs. The arrival in the 1930s of some 25,000 White Russian refugees enlivened the nightlife of cabarets and dance halls in 'Frenchtown', as the French Concession was called by the Anglo-Saxons. Chinese secret societies controlled the seamy side of Shanghai life, and the city was the Hollywood of China with a thriving movie industry.

But the Shanghai workers were subjected to appalling working conditions, overcrowding and exploitation, a situation leading inevitably to industrial unrest and revolutionary activity. The Communist Party of China was founded in Shanghai in 1921 at a secret meeting in the French Concession. The Party fomented strikes and uprisings—some of them actually planned by Zhou Enlai, later Premier—but these activities were violently suppressed by the Nationalist government. This was a period of debate among Chinese intellectuals, who were influenced by the philosophies and experience of the more industrialized West. Many of these Chinese had studied abroad or at missionary institutions of higher learning in Shanghai.

The beginning of the Sino-Japanese War saw bombing and fierce fighting in and around Shanghai, but the foreign concessions were not occupied by the Japanese until after the bombing of Pearl Harbour, when Allied nationals were interned. In 1943 extra-territoriality came to an end by common consent, but the Chinese only regained control of Shanghai after the defeat of the Japanese.

When a People's Republic was proclaimed in China at the end of the civil war, foreigners and Chinese industrialists, fleeing Communism, left Shanghai, many re-establishing themselves in Hong Kong.

Because of the city's long history of foreign capitalist exploitation and 'bourgeois attitudes', adherents of the Cultural Revolution in the 1960s and '70s were particularly vociferous in Shanghai, which became the headquarters of the so-called Gang of Four, the ultra-leftist elements of this chaotic period.

When China began to reform her economic system and opened her doors to the outside world, one imagined that there would be a resurgence of the entrepreneurial spirit in Shanghai. But it took some while for today's momentum to build. Until recently, Shanghai has been starved of investment, Beijing having siphoned off much of its huge earnings. As the population continued to grow, the problems of housing and traffic congestion grew ever more acute.

However, in 1988, Beijing and Shanghai entered a new revenue agreement. Instead of surrendering more than three-quarters of its annual revenues, Shanghai began contributing a fixed amount to the central government and keeping any surpluses for its own use. The revitalizing of Shanghai could scarcely be more ambitious: bridges; tunnels; an urban subway system; suburban housing; the technical upgrading and expansion of its textile industry; the building of a microelectronics industry in Caohejing, a would-be Silicon Valley; and the establishment of a new port and free trade and export processing zone in Pudong.

What to See in Shanghai

While Shanghai's historical monuments may not compare with China's older cities, the city's appeal lies in its vitality, its 1930s European architecture in a medley of styles, and its bustling, tree-lined streets, crammed with shops. Above all, Shanghai still has a style and flair quite different from any other Chinese city.

■ THE BUND (WAI TAN)

Walking along Zhongshan Lu, you can enjoy the faded grandeur of old Shanghai, for this was the Bund, where the great trading houses and banks had their headquarters. On one side is a line of imposing 1930s European buildings, while on the other is the Huangpu River. The Bund has undergone a face-lift, which included raising the level of the breakwater to prevent flooding. The raised pedestrian promenade gives a good view of the Huangpu River with the futuristic-looking buildings of the new Pudong area on the other side. As before, the improved riverside promenade of the Bund continually throngs with Shanghai residents, who stroll about in the hot summer evenings and in the mornings practise *taijiquan* and martial arts.

The **Bank of China** is in one of the few buildings still run by its original occupants. The former **Shanghai Club** at 2 Zhongshan Dong Yi Lu was the **Dongfeng Hotel** until it closed in 1998. The Long Bar was, in its heyday, the longest in the world. Built in 1910, this was a bastion for the elite classes. Padlocked iron gates now stop visitors from entering the building site but the facade has been repainted recently making it now the most outstanding building on the Bund.

A branch of the Pudong Development Bank is now housed in the columned building that was the **Hongkong and Shanghai Bank headquarters**, built in 1923. Visit the coffee shop there to read, relax and absorb the atmosphere of the Bund. The green-roofed **Peace Hotel** was the handsome Cathay Hotel, where Noel Coward wrote his play *Private Lives* in 1928. The **Palace Hotel**, opposite, now the south

SHANGHAI'S HISTORY THROUGH ITS NAMES

When the Chinese want to be literary, or brief, they call Shanghai 'Hu'. The name bespeaks Shanghai's origins as a fishing village, for *hu* is a bamboo fishing device, used in the third century by the people who lived around the Songjiang River (which was subsequently renamed Wusong River, and which forms the upper reaches of the Suzhou Creek). Shanghai is also sometimes known as Chunshen—or Shen for short—because in the third century BC, at the time of the Warring States (475–221 BC), the site on which the city now stands was a fief of the Lord Chunshen, prime minister to the King of the State of Chu. Another name with which Shanghai is associated is Huating. This was a county established in 751, over an area which covers part of present-day Shanghai.

Shanghai took its name from the Shanghai River, a tributary, long since gone, of the Songjiang. A township sprang into being on the west bank of the river, as, recognising its natural advantages as a port, junks and ships came to berth there. This was Shanghai, which presently became the largest town in Huating County. In 1292, Shanghai and four other towns in Huating were brought together to form the County of Shanghai. It was at about this time that the Songjiang was renamed the Wusong River.

But today when most Chinese think of Shanghai, they think not so much of the Wusong as of the Huangpu River. Shanghai's qualifications as a deep water port were greatly improved when a canal—forming that part of the Huangpu downstream of Waibaidu Bridge—was dredged and widened in the fourteenth century. Ships crowded the wharves of Shanghai, and the port itself grew in size and importance, thriving off the trade in cotton and other goods between the coast and the inland provinces on the Yangzi (Yangtse) River.

These were the foundations upon which the Western powers built when, with the opening of Shanghai as a Treaty Port, they came and carved out their enclaves there. The first of the foreign settlements, the British Concession, was bounded on the east along the Huangpu River by the Bund (today's Zhongshan Dong Yi Lu), on the west by Yu Ya Ching Road (today's Xizang Zhonglu), and on the south by the Yangjingbang Creek (which, after it was filled, was named Avenue Edward VII and which is now called Yan'an Donglu). The creek separated the British from the French Concession; the latter started from a wedge between the British Concession and the old Chinese city, and then ballooned out to a large area to the southwest of the city. To the north of the Suzhou Creek, in the district known then and now as Hongkou, lay the American Concession. This was later merged with the British Concession to form the International Settlement.

In the British Concession, the streets spread out behind the Bund in a grid. The main thoroughfare, Nanking Road (Nanjing Lu), ran eastwards from the Bund. The streets parallel to it were named after China's other cities (such as Canton, Fuzhou and Ningbo), while those which ran perpendicular to it (i.e. north-south) were named after the provinces (such as Henan, Sichuan and Zhejiang). There was no mistaking the French Concession, because most of the streets there had French names: Rue Lafayette, Avenue Foch, to name but two. The smartest was Avenue Joffre (today's Huaihai Lu), which was to the French Concession what Nanking Road was to the British. Needless to say, these were all renamed when the communists took over.

THE CUSTOM HOUSE, SHANGHAI.

The Custom House, Shanghai

building of the Peace Hotel, was Sassoon House (named after one of Shanghai's Jewish tycoons). It was built in 1906.

At the end of the Bund, where Suzhou Creek meets the Huangpu, is **Huangpu Park**. It was first laid out by the British, who called it the Public Gardens. In the old days British residents held Sunday afternoon concerts and promenaded there. Though the regulations of the International Settlement did indeed forbid Chinese (other than servants and nannies) as well as dogs from the gardens, the infamous sign 'No Dogs or Chinese Allowed' never existed. The waterfront building with the clock tower is the old Customs House built in 1927.

With the multitude of choices for crossing the Huangpu River from Puxi to Pudong, still none can surpass the ferry ride. Get on at Shiliupu Wharf on Zhong-shang Dong Er Lu. This short trip offers the best view of the Bund.

■ WAI TAN BOWUGUAN (THE BUND MUSEUM)
Start your tour of the waterfront here. The museum is in the old Signal Tower on the Bund at 1 Zhongshan Dong Er Lu and has many old black and white photographs of Shanghai's waterfront dating from treaty port days. The Signal Tower was built in 1865 and was originally located a few yards away before being moved to its current location in 1993. In 1999 it was restored as a museum. Climb the circular staircase inside the tower for a wonderful view of the present-day Bund.

■ SOME POPULAR SHOPPING STREETS
Nanjing Lu, the main shopping street of Shanghai, is a pedestrian mall between Xizang Lu and Henan Lu. East and West of the mall, it stretches for nearly ten kilometres (six miles) from the Bund to Jiangsu Lu. Few of the original pre-war department stores buildings have changed since the 1930s except in name. For the Chinese, Shanghai offers the best shopping in the country, so this street is constantly jammed with out-of-towners as well as local shoppers. Nanjing Lu passes People's Park and the Shanghai Art Museum, formerly the Municipal Library and before that the Shanghai Race Course Club. English-speaking Shanghainese gather here, especially on Sunday mornings, to practise among themselves.

Another important shopping street was **Huaihai Lu**, which was the main street of the French Concession, then called Avenue Joffre. The famous Huating Street Market was closed down in 2000 and moved to a new location at Xianyang Lu and Huaihai Lu, near the Shanxi Nan Lu metro station. It is a popular place but not quite as colourful as the old one.

Just one block away from Xizang Nan Lu and bisecting Fuxing Lu, is **Dongtai Lu Antique Market**—still the main antique market in the city, lined with three blocks of shops and stalls. Beware cheap fakes but a few remarkable genuine items can be found, including original posters of Sun Zhongshan flanked by the Guomindang state and party flags or stone Buddha heads.

Book stores—antiquarian and modern—are a speciality of **Fuzhou Lu**, as well as stationery and calligraphy accoutrements, though in earlier times it was a red-light district.

As a word of caution, protect your wallet and avoid the male and female touts who hover around the main streets travelled by visiting foreigners (Lao Wei) such as Ruijin Lu where it runs beside the Garden Hotel, Huai Hai Zhong Lu in front of Isetan Department Store, Nanjing Lu near the Peace Hotel, and Hengshan Lu. They will approach foreign men in particular and chant "Shanghai Ladies, Shanghai Ladies. " They may physically grab your arm and try to steer you in their chosen direction. If you go with them, you will be 'entertained' at your expense but not with your prior consent. You will have to pay the bill

■ THE OLD TOWN (NAN SHI CHU) AND HUXINTING TEAHOUSE
Renmin Lu and Zhonghua Lu form the perimeters of the old city wall (destroyed in 1912) that enclosed the Chinese City. Still within this area, which includes the famous **Yu Garden**, visitors jostle in the ever-crowded alleys of the bazaar, whose small shops, restaurants and teahouses provide local specialities of all descriptions. The narrow streets nearby reveal an intimate and fascinating picture of daily life. In the old town is Fuyu Lu— formely the flea market, this role has been lost now due to urban development.

Should you get tired of walking around the Old Town you can always rest in the beautiful old Huxinting (mid-lake) Teahouse. This five-sided pavilion stands in the middle of a rectangular pool near the entrance to the Yu Garden, connected to land by the Bridge of Nine Turnings (zigzagged, it is said, because evil spirits cannot go round corners).

■ OLD SHANGHAI TEAHOUSE
This teahouse has an admirable collection of genuine Shanghai historical artefacts such as old maps, a gramophone which plays records, copies of 'Shanghai Volunteers Corps' publications, and a wall poster of Sun Zhongshan. Although the food and drinks prices are high, the atmosphere is delightful. It is to be found at 385 Fangbang Zhong Lu.

■ YU GARDEN (YU YUAN)
This Garden of Leisurely Repose on the northeast side of the old Chinese Town was first established in 1559 by a mandarin named Pan. Laid out by a landscape artist, Zhang Nanyang, it has become one of the most renowned gardens in southern China. As the Pan family fortunes declined, the garden was neglected and overgrown until it was restored in 1760 by the local gentry. It became the headquarters of the Dagger Society in 1853, during the early part of the Taiping Rebellion, and was badly damaged. Part of the garden became the bazaar and local guildhalls, but over 20,000 square metres (24,000 square yards) remain of tall rockeries, halls, ponds and pavilions linked by zigzag corridors. The **Spring Hall**, used by the Dagger Society,

(above) *View across the Huangpu River towards Pudong;* (below) *The Bund, Shanghai*

houses exhibits of coins and weapons from that period. The five-ton porous **Exquisite Jade Rock** is one of the attractions: legend claims that when it was discovered some 900 years ago, it joined Emperor Huizong's collection of weird and grotesque rocks before finding a resting place in Yu Garden.

■ JADE BUDDHA TEMPLE (YU FO SI)

The yellow-walled temple buildings were constructed between 1911 and 1918. The two jade Buddhas (out of five brought back from Burma in 1882 by the priest Hui Gen) were first kept in a suburb of Shanghai. They are carved entirely from single blocks of jade and were a gift from Burma. Three halls make up the temple complex. In the Jade Buddha Hall is the tranquil two-metre (6.5-foot) high seated statue of Sakyamuni, while downstairs in the Reclining Buddha Hall is the white jade image of Sakyamuni in repose. Precious statues of the Northern Wei (386–534) and Tang (618-907) dynasties are on display in the temple's exhibition hall, along with hand-copied Tang-dynasty Buddhist scriptures and paintings. Over 70 monks hold daily services. The temple runs a vegetarian restaurant whose menu boasts 'meat' dishes such as pickled duck, sliced eel and chicken, all made of beancurd and vegetables. Crackling rice and mushroom soup is recommended. It is located at 170 An Yuan Lu.

■ SHANGHAI MUSEUM (SHANGHAI BOWUGUAN)

This museum is without doubt the finest in all of China and must rank among the great museums of the world. The modern display, with sound and even a holographic movie kiosk, opened in 1995. The artefacts of Shanghai's commercial past are revealing and nostalgic. While the city rapidly tears down its heritage, this museum is a great look back. It is located at 201 Renmin Da Dao.

■ SHANGHAI ART MUSEUM (SHANGHAI MEISHUGUAN)

This museum is located in the former Shanghai Race Club at 325 Nanjing Xi Lu. The race track is now Renmin Gongyuan (People's Park) and the Renmin Dad Dao (People's Square). It is immediately noticeable for its trademark clock tower. The building is marked with the insignia SRC, standing for Shanghai Race Club—the main staircase is decorated with iron railings in the shape of horse's heads. In the front stairwell on the third floor there is a European war monument devoted to the people of Shanghai who died in World War I, probably the only monument of its type still remaining. The one which stood on the Waitan was destroyed. It is possible to go up on the roof for an excellent view of the city.

■ SHANGHAI HISTORY MUSEUM (SHANGHAI LISHI BOWUGUAN)

Formerly situated at Hongqiao Lu, this museum is now located at 1 Shi Da Dao, Pudong within the Oriental Television Tower.

■ LONG HUA PAGODA AND TEMPLE (LONG HUA SI)

Situated in Shanghai's southwest area, the pagoda and temple were originally built between the 10th and the 13th centuries—historical records vary as to the exact dates. The temple belongs to the Chan (Zen) sect. The present seven-storeyed pagoda is just over 40 metres (130 feet) high and dates from the early Song dynasty, but was restored at the end of the Qing (1644–1911). The Longhua Temple nearby is a complex of five halls flanked by bell and drum towers; the sound of the evening bell of Longhua was known as one of the old traditions of Shanghai. On New Year's Eve, this bell is rung 108 times at midnight. To hear this event is considered good luck. A flower terrace overlooked from a tea room, is also one of the attractions of the temple, for in its peony gardens there is a 100-year-old peony said to have been planted first in a Hangzhou temple during the reign of Emperor Xianfeng and later transplanted here. Engravings on a boundary stone indicate that the stone was placed at the southwest corner of this temple during the Five Dynasties period (907–960). West of the temple is **Martyrs' Cemetery**, once part of the temple's peach orchard, and now replanted and expanded.

■ WAR GOD TEMPLE (DAJING GUAN GONG)

This authentic temple was originally connected on two sides with the Ming-dynasty city wall built in 1553. As late as the mid-1930s, it was full of carved statues of various gods, including the Taoist immortals, but sadly those have now all disappeared. Today it is no longer a functioning temple, and is rarely visited by tourists, but still offers plenty to see.

A fake replica of a small piece of the city wall stands on its grounds. Ironically, directly outside this fake wall stands the only original Qing-dynasty city gate still standing, the Small North Gate (Xiao Bei Men). You can still read some of the inscriptions on it which were covered up with plaster during the Cultural Revolution. Sadly, it is used by the neighbourhood people to hang their wet laundry and is in disrepair. This gate was left standing when the rest of the wall was torn down in 1911 because it was connected with what was then a functioning temple.

Inside Dajing Miao is a city wall museum which includes a scale model of Shanghai's old city wall complete with models of the entire Nanshi District as it looked in Qing times. There is also an exhibit of old photographs. Be sure to look upward at the roof of the original temple buildings and you will find many roof ornament figurines in the shape of various historic warriors, gods and animals. It is located at 259 Da Jing Ge Lu.

■ CITY GOD TEMPLE (CHENG HUANG MIAO)

Located within the Yu Yuan Bazaar shopping complex, unlike the surrounding faux Ming-Qing style buildings constructed in 1994, this is an authentic temple first constructed during the reign of Ming Emperor Yong Le (1403-1424). It was renovated

Cool Depths

Stars and Moon on the Yangtse

After sudden rain, a clear autumn night.
On golden waves the sparkle of the Jewelled Cord.
The River of Heaven white from eternity,
The Yangtse's shallows limpid since just now.
Reflections, pearls from a snapped string:
High in the sky one mirror rises.
Afterlight which fades as the clock drips,
Still fainter as the dewdrops settle on the flowers.

Du Fu (712–770),
translated by A C Graham

Sadness of the Gorges

Above the gorges, one thread of sky:
Cascades in the gorges twine a thousand cords.
High up, the slant of splintered sunlight, moonlight:
Beneath, curbs to the wild heave of the waves.
The shock of a gleam, and then another,
In depths of shadow frozen for centuries:
The rays between the gorges do not halt at noon;
Where the straits are perilous, more hungry spittle.
Trees lock their roots in rotted coffins
And the twisted skeletons hang tilted upright:
Branches weep as the frost perches
Mournful cadences, remote and clear.
A spurned exile's shrivelled guts
Scald and seethe in the water and fire he walks through.
A lifetime's like a fine-spun thread,
The road goes up by the rope at the edge.
When he pours his libation of tears to the ghosts in the stream
The ghosts gather, a shimmer on the waves.

Meng Jiao (751–814),
translated by A C Graham

Aerial view from Pudong across the Huangpu River, with the Oriental TV Tower in the foreground and the entrance to Suzhou Creek beyond.

in 1926 and again in 1994. During the Cultural Revolution it was a factory, but reopened as a temple after the 1994 renovations of the Yu Yuan Bazaar. This Taoist temple is dedicated to the City God Qin Yu Bo, but also serves as a place of Taoist worship.

■ CHEN XIANG GE SI

A functioning Buddhist nunnery housed in authentic Ming-dynasty buildings dating from the year 1600. It is near the more famous Cheng Huang Miao, but down a side alley off of the main street at 29 Chen Xiang Ge Lu. It was closed during the Cultural Revolution and reopened in 1994.

■ WHITE CLOUD TAOIST TEMPLE (BAI YUN GUAN)

This is a functioning Taoist temple built in 1882. Each day you can see worshippers and monks performing authentic ceremonies including playing various musical instruments, chanting long hymns, burning incense and paper money. There is a training school for new Taoist monks. Despite its fascinating nature, this temple is seldom visited by foreign tourists, probably due its location. Located down a long narrow alleyway which begins near the Lao Xi Men (Old West Gate) police station just off Xizang Nan Lu. Look for the decorative gate over the alleyway's entrance, read the English language sign on the wall, then follow the long alleyway to its end. Plain looking walls on the outside disguise the beautiful courtyard structure within. Look upward at the rooftop ornaments of historical figures brandishing weapons and wearing traditional clothes, as well as nature scenes of sacred animals. This is also the headquarters of the Shanghai Taoist Association. It is located at 8 Xilin Hou Lu, Lane 100, Lao Ximen District.

■ FA ZANG JIANG SI

A Buddhist Temple located at the corner of Fuxing Lu and Ji An Lu, within walking distance from Huaihai Zhong Lu and Huangpi Nan Lu metro station. It is an impressive pre-revolutionary temple. During the Cultural Revolution it was a factory, much like Chenghuang Miao was. A community of resident monks live here. The worshippers and monks are friendly and welcome the chance to explain their faith to visitors. They belong to the Pure Land Sect which worships Amitabha Pusa or Om-i-to-fu. This sect has an almost Christian belief in an after-death rebirth in a Western Land or Pure Land similar to heaven.

■ XIAO TAO YUAN MOSQUE

First established in 1917, and renovated in 1925, today this is a functioning mosque which also serves as the headquarters of the Shanghai Islamic Association. It is situated at 52 Xiao Tao Yuan Lu in the Nanshi District.

Dancers practise their tango, one of many early morning activities on Shanghai's Bund

■ SHANGHAI BOTANICAL GARDENS (SHANGHAI ZHIWUYUAN)
South of the Longhua Pagoda at 111 Long Wu Lu, the gardens' greenhouses, bamboo groves and flower gardens cover some 67 hectares (165 acres) of land. Among the gardens' miniature *penjing* trees is a pomegranate over 240 years old.

■ GUI LIN PARK (GU LIN GONG YUAN)
This traditional Chinese garden is full of wooden pavilions, lakes, trees, flowers, and a tea house. It was built in 1931 by a famous Shanghai gangster, Huang Jin Rong, who dreamt of living the life of a Confucian mandarin. While sitting within its walls you can forget that you are in a city. It is located on the corner of Gui Lin Lu and Cao Bao Lu.

■ SHANGHAI ZOO (SHANGHAI DONG WU YUAN)
Across 70 hectares, the zoo houses over 600 species of animals including giant pandas from Sichuan, golden-haired monkeys—which once frequented the Yangzi gorges—and rare Yangzi River alligators. It is situated at 2381 Hong Qiao Lu, near the airport.

■ SHANGHAI WILD ANIMAL PARK (SHANGHAI YESHEN DONG WU YUAN)
This park is populated with lions, tigers and bears. Visitors have been confined to tour buses after a man was killed by a lion several years ago. It is located in Pudong.

Revolutionary Sites

Several buildings reflect the city's revolutionary history. In a two-storeyed building at 76 Xingye Lu, the Communist Party of China was founded in 1921; it is proudly shown to visitors as the site of the First National Congress of the Communist Party of China. The former residence of the late premier Zhou Enlai is situated at 73 Sinan Lu.

■ FORMER HOME OF SUN ZHONGSHAN (SUN ZHONGSHAN GU JU)

This house was owned and lived in by Sun Zhongshan and his wife Song Qing Ling from 1918 to 1924. After Sun's death in 1925, Song Qing Ling continued to stay there periodically until the Sino-Japanese War broke out in 1937. The house has been decorated with period furnishings, photographs of former occupants and some original household items. The library contains a variety of titles read by Dr Sun such as books on the US constitution and the multinational Habsburg Empire. It is located at 7 Xiang Shan Lu (a cul de sac) at the intersection of Sinan Lu and Xiang Shan Lu near Fuxing Park. In treaty port days the address was 29 Molière Road.

■ FORMER HOME OF SONG QING LING (SONG QING LING GU JU)

When the Sino Japanese War ended in 1945, the Guomindang government gave Song Qing Ling this house to live in. After 1949 the Communist government allowed her to keep it until her death in 1981. Sitting on Huai Hai Zhong Lu, the house is surrounded by a garden estate. The two-storey house is decorated with original furnishings and gifts she received from foreign heads of state during the time she was the honorary President of the People's Republic of China. The automobile from Stalin is parked in the garage.

A museum is located next to the house and contains English correspondence Song Qing Ling exchanged with world leaders during the period before 1949, a time when she was campaigning for a third way political compromise between the two extremes of the Guomindang on the right and the Communists on the left.

■ FORMER HOME OF CHIANG KAI SHEK (JIANG JIE SHI GU JU)

Jiang Jie Shi's former Shanghai residence is located at 9 Dong Ping Lu, and is part of the former Song family walled compound which included a home for each of the members of this most influential and wealthy family of pre-1949 China. Jiang's house is part of the Shanghai Conservatory of Music. The home of his brother-in-law, T.V. Song (Song Zi Wen), is nearby on the corner of Hengshan Lu and Dongping Lu. Jiang began staying at this house during his short visits to Shanghai from the Guomindang capital in Nanjing after he married T.V. Song's sister, Song Mei Ling, in 1927. T.V. Song's house has become the fashionable Sasha's Restaurant.

■ LU XUN MUSEUM (LU XUN BOWUGUAN)
This museum is dedicated to China's great revolutionary writer, Lu Xun (1881-1936) who spent the last ten years of his life in Shanghai. It is located in the Honkou district inside Lu Xun Park. Lu is buried in Hongkou Park. He lived in a three-storeyed house at 9 Dalu New Village, Shanyin Lu, from 1933 until his death.

■ MARTYRS' CEMETERY (LONGHUA LEISHI LINGYUAN)
Also known as Martyrs Cemetery, this site is located on Longhua Lu next to Longhua Si. The museum is dedicated to the Chinese Revolution. In addition to Communist Party members, the museum now honours some Qing-dynasty and Guomindang individuals as national heroes who resisted foreign invasions. Outside the building are rows of graves of Communist martyrs.

In another corner of the park are the buildings of the 1927 Guomindang headquarters used at the end of the Northern Expedition from Guangzhou. Later it became a detention camp for opponents of the Guomindang regime. This is where the famous five Chinese writers were executed in 1931.

Green Belts

The site where the Communist Party was founded in July 1921 at 76 Xingye Lu is now part of a large new development project known as **Xintiandi**. This project aimed to preserve and restore old Shikumen houses (old Guomindang-era Stone Gate houses) but in reality it has become a shopping centre built in Shikumen style.

Across Huangpi Nan Lu from Xintiandi, Shikumen were destroyed on New Year's Day 2001 in order to make room for a huge new park, **Taiping Qiao**, which will include a man-made lake. The area affected covers about six square city blocks between Huangpi Nan Lu, Zizhong Lu and Dongtai Lu and was formerly bisected by Shunchang Lu, Xingye Lu, Jinan Lu and Zhaozhou Lu. More than 3,800 homes were lost as a result of the destruction of this historic residential neighbourhood. Gone now are the chamber pots, communal cooking and washing areas, courtyard games of chess (wei qi), the click-clack sound of the Mahjong dice and the music of Heng Lou Meng drifting from windows.

The development of the green belts has raised the issue of historical preservation. The green belt on Huangpi Nan Lu also threatened the hundred-year-old stone house built by the family of world famous architect I.M. Pei. Although distant relatives of his had continued to occupy the house and the architect had written personal appeals to national leaders, this building, **IM Pei House**, was due for demolition in 2001.

Excursions from Shanghai

SUZHOU AND HANGZHOU

'In heaven there is paradise; on earth there are Suzhou and Hangzhou' is a proverb known to every Chinese. While today both of these earthly paradises have been invaded to some extent by industries and modern buildings, they still have considerable charm.

■ SUZHOU

Suzhou is the nearer of the two (two hours by car, 90 minutes by train) and makes a pleasant day trip. Known as the Venice of the East, the old part of town is still a city of canals, hump-backed bridges, and low, white-washed houses. Above all, Suzhou is famous for its exquisite gardens, over 100 of which survive. The **Garden of the Master of the Fishing Nets** (part of which has been reproduced in the Metropolitan Museum in New York), the **Humble Administrator's Garden** and the **Lingering Garden** are some fine examples. The city is also notable for its silk production, silk embroidery and other handicrafts such as sandalwood fans.

■ HANGZHOU

Hangzhou's fabled **West Lake** was formerly perhaps China's best-known beauty spot. With its willow trees, lotus blossoms in July and arched stone bridges, it conforms to everyone's idea of what Chinese scenery should look like. Many Chinese come here for their honeymoon. The huge lake has four landscaped islands and the whole area is dotted with pavilions and temples.

In addition to enjoying the scenery, you may visit silk factories (as in Suzhou) and also one of the tea plantations producing the famous Hangzhou Longjing (Dragon Well) tea.

Hangzhou is three to four hours by train from Shanghai or 30 minutes by plane. It can be visited in a day, but an overnight stay is recommended to relax and enjoy the atmosphere.

SHANGHAI'S OUTLYING COUNTIES

Those with more time who have seen Shanghai's major sights and visited Suzhou and Hangzhou might be interested in visiting some of the outlying counties, which are part of Shanghai Municipality.

Qingpu County, with its canals and whitewashed cottages, reflects the surrounding countryside of Jiangsu Province

■ SONGJIANG COUNTY

In Songjiang, a county seat for over 2,500 years and situated 19 kilometres (12 miles) southwest of Shanghai, is the beautiful **Square Pagoda** (Si Fang Ta), which is 900 years old. Although renovated in 1975, much of the 11th-century brick and wood structure is original. It is over 48 metres (157 feet) high with nine storeys and was once part of Xingshengjiao Temple, of which one hall remains. There is also a Tang-dynasty stele, engraved with Buddhist scriptures, lions' heads, lotus petals and cloud patterns. It is said that the stele was erected to redeem the souls of criminals who were executed here. The **Hu Zhu Pagoda** (Hu Zhu Ta), an octagonal seven-storey leaning brick tower was built in 1079 during the Northern Song dynasty (960–1127). The Xilin Pagoda (Xi Lin Ta) was built during the Southern Song dynasty during 1127–1279.

A lovely example of a classical Chinese garden, with bizarre rocks, ponds and miniature landscaping, can be seen on a visit to **Zhuibaichi Park**. This once-private garden probably dates from the late Ming dynasty and became the villa of a painter, Gu Dashen, in the mid-17th century.

The local speciality is Four-grilled Perch, which is now rather rare and has been known for centuries as 'the number one dish south of the Yangzi'. Emperor Yang of the Sui dynasty (581–618) praised the fish, saying it was 'as precious as gold and jade', while the Qing emperor Qianlong (reigned 1736–96) had it sent to him annually.

■ JIADING COUNTY

Twenty-five kilometres (15.5 miles) northwest of Shanghai is Jiading County, where a **Confucian temple** has existed since the 13th century. In the courtyard, stelae set into plinths of stone turtles record the temple restorations and meritorious deeds of various officials. Three old cypress trees are all that are left of 60 planted in the Yuan dynasty (1279–1368). Memorial tablets of Confucius' disciples and records of the achievements of local scholars line two corridors, which are part of the county museum.

Five streams converge at the site of the **Huilong Tan (Pool of Convergent Dragons)**, and adorning the surrounding stone railings are 72 different lions (Confucius had 72 disciples). During the Taiping Rebellion (*see* pages 112–113), the soldiers of the Dagger Society were bound to the trees beside the pool and executed. **Yingkui Hill** in the centre of the pool dates from the Ming dynasty, while the **Literary God Tower**, on the eastern bank, was restored recently after being bombed in the Sino-Japanese War.

The **Garden of Autumn Clouds (Qiuxia Pu)**, near Huilong Pool, is another example of private garden architecture. This was laid out by Minister of Defence, Gong Hong, in around 1520. Another garden, **Guyi Yuan (Garden of Ancient Splendour)**, built by a high official of the Ming dynasty, can be seen at the town of **Nanxiang** in Jiading County.

Nanxiang dumplings are famous in the area, their skin being especially thin.

Chen He set up his dumpling shop 100 years ago and his recipe was so successful that the dumplings took on the name of the town, rather than of his shop.

■ QINGPU COUNTY

Qingpu County is 22.5 kilometres (14 miles) west of Shanghai, is the city's main supplier of freshwater fish. **Zhujiajiao** is a delightful old town criss-crossed by canals, spanned by 16th-century stone-arched foot bridges, with traditional wooden boats moored alongside ancient stone houses. You can spend a day walking along the narrow stone-paved lanes, riding in the boats or sitting beside the canals at sidewalk cafes. There is an active 18th-century City God Temple (Cheng Huang Miao) and an active Christian church dating from the 19th century. The town is one hour away from Shanghai by bus or taxi, and about 15 minutes' drive from Dianshan Hu. This town is similar in style to Zhouzhuang but less crowded.

DIANSHAN LAKE (DIANSHAN HU)

This huge lake covers 6,300 hectares (15,570 acres), some 12 times larger than Hangzhou's West Lake, and teems with fish, freshwater shrimp and crabs. A holiday resort popular with Shanghainese has been developed near Yangshe Village on the southeastern stretch of the lake.

The landscaped garden, **Daguanyuan** (Grand View Garden), is on the shores of **Dianshan Hu**. Constructed in 1984, it represents authentic Song-Qing-Ming architecture. It is presented as a 'Heng Lou Meng' theme park, with music, costumed characters, and exhibits all based upon the stories from that most famous of Chinese novels, *The Dream of the Red Chamber*. Look for the 'wishing trees' onto which people have tossed written wishes tied to bright red ribbons. You can only see the lake if you exit the walled enclosure. An expansive free garden area stretches along the water's edge. Across the road from Daguanyuan sits a **Nationalities Village** with examples of traditional architecture from each of China's 43 ethnic minorities.

DAYING LAKE

The Meandering Stream Garden (Qushui Yuan), on the banks of the lake, is also a popular excursion for Shanghainese. It was built with funds donated by local townsfolk in 1745 and redeveloped in 1927.

CHONGMING ISLAND

This is a delightful piece of rural countryside, incorporating several National Parks, situated in the middle of the Yangzi (Changjiang) River's mouth. It is a part of the Shanghai municipality although the environment is light years away from the urban centre. You can take a relaxing hour-long ferry boat ride from Wusong Port up the Huangpu and into the Changjiang to this island. Many former residents of the Three Gorges have been resettled on Chongming Island. It is also the place where the transatlantic telecommunications cable connects China with the U.S.A. It is home to the Dongping National Forest Park (Dongping Guojia Senlin Gongyuan).

(following pages) *GEOPIC™ photograph of the Yangzi River entering the East China Sea just north of Shanghai, taken in 1978*

Chongming Island

Shanghai

Huangpu River

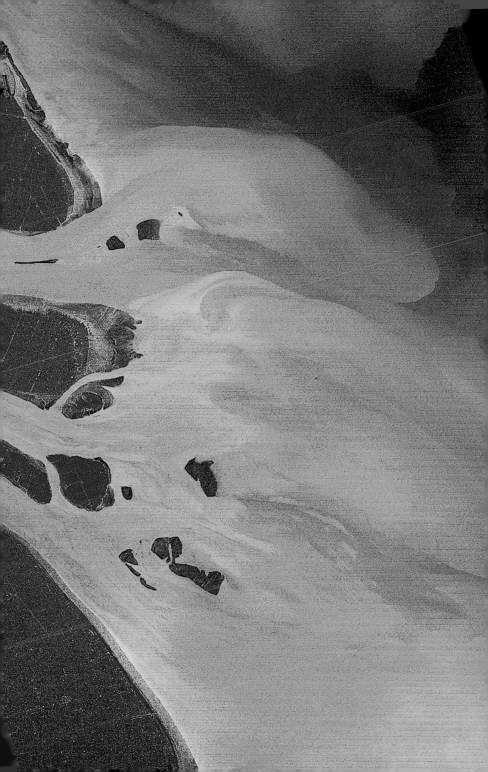

Practical Information

Tour Operators

The following are a selection of the many companies which can arrange Yangzi Tours, listed in alphabetical order.

■ **ABERCROMBIE AND KENT INTERNATIONAL, INC.**
ENGLAND:
    Abercrombie & Kent Travel
    Sloane Square House
    Holbein Place, London SW1W 8NS, England
    Tel (0207) 730-9600, Fax (0207) 730-9376
    Website: http://www.abercrombiekent.com
HONG KONG:
    19th Floor, Gitic Centre
    28 Queen's Road East, Wanchai, Hong Kong
    Tel (852) 2865-7818, Fax (852) 2866-0556
USA:
    1520 Kensington Road
    Oak Brook, Chicago, Il 60521, USA
    Tel (630) 954-2944, toll-free (800) 323-7308, Fax (630) 954-3324
    Website: http://www.abercrombiekent.com

■ **GEOGRAPHIC EXPEDITIONS**
    2627 Lombard Street
    San Francisco, California 94123, USA
    Tel (800) 777-8183, (415) 922-0448, Fax (415) 346-5535
    E-mail: info@geoex.com
    Website: http://www.geoex.com

■ **HELEN WONG'S TOURS**
    Level 18, 456 Kent Street, Sydney, Australia
    Tel (2) 9267-7833, Fax (2) 9267-7717
    Email: info@helenwongstours.com
    Website: http://helenwongstours.com

■ **ORIENT ROYAL CRUISER LTD**
CHINA:
    (Head Office)
    316 Xinhua Road, Suite E, Liang You Bldg.
    Hankou, Wuhan, 430012, China
    Tel (027) 857-722-20, Fax (027) 857-666-88
    E-mail: wuhan@orientroyalcruise.com
    Website: http://www.orientroyalcruise.com

USA:

2405 Vantage Court, Denville, NJ 07834, USA
Tel (Toll Free)(888) 565-4088/(973) 334-4080, Fax (973) 334-8819
E-mail: orc_usua@worldnet.att.net
Website: http://www.orientcruisetravel.com

■ PAGE & MOY LTD.

136–140 London Road
Leicester, LE2 1EN, England
Tel (0116) 250-7336, Fax (0116) 250-7199
Bookings: (44) 8700-10-6212
Website: http://www.go-nowtravel.com

■ REGAL CHINA CRUISES

CHINA:

(Head Office)
645 Zhongshan North Road
Nanjing 210011, Jiangsu Province, China
Tel (025) 881-6886, Fax (025) 881-6880

USA:

57 West 38th Street, New York, USA
Tel (toll-free)(800) 808-3388, (212) 768-3388, Fax (212) 768-4939

■ REGENT HOLIDAYS

15 John Street, Bristol, BS1 2HR, England
Tel (0117) 921-1711, Fax (0117) 925-4866
E-mail: regent@regent holidays.co.uk
Website: http://www.regent-holidays.co.uk

■ SAGA HOLIDAYS LIMITED

The Saga Building, Enbrook Park
Sandgate, Folkestone, Kent CT20 3SE, England
Tel (0800) 504-555, Website: http://www. saga.co.uk

■ VICTORIA CRUISES INC.

57–08 39th Ave
Woodside NY 11377, USA
Tel (212) 818-1698, Fax (212) 818-9889

■ VOYAGES JULES VERNE

Travel Promotions Ltd.
21 Dorset Square
London NW1 6QG, England
Tel (0207) 616-1000, Fax (0207) 723-8629
Website: http://www.vjv.co.uk

Chongqing (023)

■ HOTELS IN CHONGQING

Chongqing Guesthouse
235 Minsheng Lu. Tel 6384-5888, Fax 6383-0643
重庆宾馆　民生路235号
Not to be confused with the Chungking Hotel. Medium-range hotel in the heart of the city; restaurant, shop, bar and other usual services.

Chongqing Marriott Hotel
77 Qing Nian Lu, Yu Zhong District
Tel 6388-8888, Fax 6388-8777
重庆万豪酒店　渝中区青年路77号
A five-star facility.

Chungking Hotel (Chongqing Fandian)
41–43 Xinhua Lu. Tel 6384-9301, Fax 6384-3085
重庆饭店　新华路41–43号

Harbour Plaza Chongqing
WuYi Lu, Yu Zhong District
Tel 6370-0888, Fax 6370-0778, Email: chongqing@harbour-plaza.com
重庆海逸酒店　渝中区
A five-star facility.

Holiday Inn Yangtze Chongqing
15 Nanping Bei Lu,
Tel 6280-3380, toll-free from US 1-800 HOLIDAY, Fax 6280-0884
Web site http://holiday-inn.com
扬子江假日酒店　南坪北路 15 号

Mao Xiang Zhai
妙香斋　罗汉寺街7号
7 Luohan Si Street. Tel 6373-7144, Fax 6373-7162. Simple, clean and bright budget accommodation. Located above an excellent vegetarian restaurant inside the Luohan Temple.

Renmin Guesthouse
175 Renmin Lu. Tel 6385-1421, Fax 6385-2076
人民宾馆　人民路175号
The two older wings of this hotel abut the Chongqing People's Assembly Hall, a fake

Temple of Heaven built in the style of the original in Beijing. Dining rooms serve Sichuan food.

■ SICHUAN CUISINE
Sichuan food is one of the four principal styles of Chinese cooking (the others are Cantonese, Peking and Huaiyang). The cuisine is characterized by hot piquant dishes heavily laced with red chillies, ginger and other condiments. Favourite local dishes include 'mother-in-law' beancurd (*mapo doufu*), double-cooked pork, diced chicken with hot peppers, *dandan* noodles, sour and hot soup, deep-fried beef strips and camphor-smoked duck.

■ USEFUL ADDRESSES IN CHONGQING
Chongqing Changjiang Tourism Co.
Chaotianmen. Tel 6382-7108, ticket office 382-9592, Fax 6384-4984
重庆长江旅游公司　朝天门
Contact for arranging passage on tourist cruise ships and regular passenger boats.

Chongqing Yangzi Shipping Passenger Ticket Office
Chaotianmen. Tel (enquiries) 6384-1001
重庆长江航客运站售票处　朝天门

Jiujiang (0792)

■ HOTELS IN JIUJIANG
Jiujiang Binguan
30 Nan Hu Lu. Tel 856-0018, Fax 856-6677
九江宾馆　南湖路30号
One of the best hotels in town. On Nan Hu lake shore, next to the Nan Hu Binguan.

Jiu Long Binguan
75 Lushan Lu. Tel 823-6779, Fax 822-8634
九龙宾馆　庐山路75号
On the Gan Tang Hu lake shore.

White Deer Hotel (Bai Lu Binguan)
133 Xun Yang Lu. Tel 822-2818, Fax 822-1915
白鹿宾馆
Chinese style luxury hotel. Organized day trips costing to Lushan start from here. Located on the main street away from either the river or the lakes.

Lushan (0791)

■ HOTELS IN LUSHAN
Guling Fandian
104 He Dong Lu. Tel 828-2200, Fax 828-2209
谷岭饭店　河东路104号

Lushan Binguan
446 He Xi Lu. Tel 828-2060, Fax 828-2843
庐山宾馆　河西路446号

Lushan Da Sha
7506 He Xi Lu. Tel 828-2178
庐山大厦　河西路7506号
Former Guomindang officers' training school.

Nanjing (025)

■ HOTELS IN NANJING
Ge Plaza Hotel
89 Hanzhong Lu. Tel 471-8888, Fax 471-8727
南京金鹰大酒店　南京汉中路89号

Hilton Nanjing Hotel
319 Zhongshan Dong Lu. Tel 480-8888, Fax 480-9999
南京希尔顿国际大酒店　南京中山东路319号

Holiday Inn Yihua Nanjing
259 Zhongshan Bei Lu. Tel 343-8716, (US toll-free) 1-800 HOLIDAY,
Fax 342-6676; Website: http://holiday-inn.com
南京怡华假日酒店　南京中山北路259号

International Conference Hotel of Nanjing
2 Sifang Cheng Zhongshan Ling. Tel 443-0888, Fax 443-9255
南京国际会议大酒店　南京中山陵四方城2号

Jinling Hotel
2 Hanzhong Lu, Xinjiekou Sq. Tel 471-1888, Fax 471-1666;
Website: http://www.jinlinghotel.com
金陵饭店　南京新街口汉中路2号

Sheraton Nanjing Kingsley Hotel and Towers
169 Hanzhong Lu. Tel 666-8888, Fax 666-9999
喜来登南京金丝利酒店　南京汉中路169号

The Central Hotel (Zhongxin Da Jiudian)
75 Zhongshan Lu. Tel 473-3888, Fax 473-3999
中心大酒店　南京中山路75号
Good location and comprehensive facilities.

■ NANJING (JIANGSU) CUISINE

Food in Nanjing's major hotels is usually of a high standard. Regional specialities
iclude Nanjing pressed duck, mandarin fish stuffed with shrimp, and spare ribs in
a rich soybean sauce. Cooking styles from other parts of China may also be sampled
In Nanjing. The restaurants in the **Fuzi Miao** (**Confucius Temple**) area off Jiankang
Lu south of the city centre, are worth trying for the Jiangsu fare.

■ SHOPPING IN NANJING

Zhongshan Lu and **Xinjiekou** are the main shopping boulevards of the city, and the
People's Market (**Renmin Shangchang**) at 79 Zhongshan Nan Lu is worth a visit. A
vast emporium (**Nanjing Shangchang**) is in the north of the city; from this store you
can get an glimpse into the consumer side of contemporary Chinese life. Nanjing is
also the source of Yunjin brocade—one of three main types made in China. Woven
of fine gold and silver silk thread, it is decorative and ornate.

Xinjiekou Department Store
3 Zhongshan Nan Lu

Jinling Shopping Centre
2 Hanzhong Lu

Zhongyang Department Store
79 Zhongshan Nan Lu

Jinying International Shopping Centre
89 Hanzhong Lu

Taiping Department Store
279 Taiping Nan Lu

Jinling Flower Market
262 Yuhua Xi Lu

Jiangsu Foreign Languages Bookstore
165 Zhong Yang Lu at corner of Hunan Lu.

Foreign Langages Bookstore
Zhongshan Dong Lu

Xinhua Book Store
137 Zhongshan Dong Lu. Tel 451-8809

Nanjing Gu Ji Shu Dian
Taiping Nan Lu and Yang Gong Jin Lu

■ USEFUL ADDRESSES IN NANJING
Nanjing Tourist Bureau
4 Nan Dong Gua Shi. Tel 360-8901

Shanghai (021)

■ HOTELS IN SHANGHAI
Some years ago, Shanghai had a notorious shortage of hotel rooms. But the city has
many new hotels, many of which are of international class.

Cypress Hotel
2419 Hongqiao Lu. Tel 6268-8868, Fax 6268-1878, E-mail: sales@cypresshotel.com
龙柏饭店　虹桥路2419号
Numerous villas available for long let. The main building is a low-rise block set in
a pleasant garden. In the grounds can be found Sir Victor Sassoon's old villa, 'Eve's'—
a Tudor-style building set on a fine lawn—the scene of some of the wildest parties
in the 1930s.

Galaxy Hotel
888 Zhongshan Xi Lu. Shanghai 200051. Tel 6275-5888, Fax 6275-0201
银河宾馆　中山西路888号
Apartments also available. Located in the Hongqiao development zone seven kilometres from the airport. The Gallery Club, open until 4am, is a popular disco venue.

Garden Hotel Shanghai
58 Maoming Nan Lu. Shanghai 200020. Tel 6415-1111, Fax 6415-8866
E-mail: garden@online.sh.cn
上海花园酒店　茂名南路58号
Built on the site of the former Cercle Sportif Français, architects have ingeniously
incorporated some of the pre-1949 building into this high-rise hotel. The magnificent
oval ballroom, carefully restored to its former Art Deco splendour, is worth a visit.

Grand Hyatt
Jin Mao Tower, 2 Century Boulevard, Pudong, Shanghai 200121. Tel 5049-1234,
(US toll-free)(800) 233 1234, (UK toll-free)(0845) 758-1666, Fax 5049-1111
Website: http://www.hyatt.com
上海金茂凯悦大酒店　浦东世纪大道2号

Holiday Inn Crowne Plaza Shanghai
388 Panyu Lu. Shanghai 200052. Tel 6280-8888, Fax 6280-2788
E-mail: hicpsha@uninet.com.cn
上海银星皇冠假日酒店　番禺路388号
In the old French Concession, nine km from the airport.

Hotel Nikko Pudong Shanghai
969 Dongfang Lu, Pudong, Shanghai 200122. Tel 6875-8888, Fax 6875-8688
上海中浦日航大酒店　浦东东方路969号

Hotel Sofitel Hyland Shanghai
505 Nanjing Xi Lu. Shanghai 200001. Tel 6351-5888, Fax 6351-4088
E-mail: sohyland@prodigychina.com
海仑宾馆　南京西路505号

Jian'guo Hotel
439 Caoxi Bei Lu. Shanghai 200030 Tel 6439-9299, Fax 6439-9433
E-mail: shjgbc@online.sh.cn
上海建国宾馆　漕溪北路439号

Jinjiang Hotel
59 Maoming Nan Lu. Shanghai 200052. Tel 6258-2582, Fax 6472-5588
E-mail: jinjiang@public2.sta.net.cn
上海锦江饭店　茂名南路59号
Originally a residential hotel complex set in the heart of the French Concession, the hotel's oldest building—the north block—was known as the Cathay Mansions, dating from 1929.

JW Marriott Hotel
399 Nanjing Xi Lu. Shanghai 20003. Tel 3310-0703, Fax 3310-0702
E-mail: shanghaijwdom@marriott.com
上海明天广场JW万豪酒店　南京西路399号
A luxury hotel of advance design. Part of the Tomorrow Square. Close to the Peoples' Square, Shanghai Grand Theatre, the Shanghai Performance Arts Centre and the Shanghai Museum of Fine Arts. The Central Business District is within walking distance.

Peace Hotel
20 Nanjing Dong Lu. Tel 6321-6888, Fax 6329-0300,
E-mail: sales@shanghaipeacehotel.com
和平饭店　南京东路20号
The former Cathay Hotel—the most outstanding Art Deco hotel of the Far East. Opened in 1929, and now incorporating the old Palace Hotel which dates from 1906.

Portman Ritz-Carlton
1376 Nanjing Xi Lu. Tel 6279-8888, Fax 6279-8999
E-mail: portman@public.sta.net.cn
波特曼香格里拉酒店　南京西路1376号
Part of the impressive Shanghai Centre, this is one of Shanghai's most striking hotels. Conveniently located on Nanjing Xi Lu, the ambitious interior contains a range of impressive works of art.

Pudong Shangri-La
33 Fucheng Lu, Pudong, Shanghai 200120. Tel 6882-8888, Fax 6882-6688
E-mail: slpu@shangri-la.com
Website: http://www.shangri-la.com
浦东香格里拉大酒店　浦东富城路33号

Regal International East Asia Hotel
516 Hengshan Lu. Shanghai 200030. Tel 6415-5588, Fax 6445-8899
E-mail: rieah@regal-eastasia.com
上海富豪环球东亚大酒店　衡山路516号

Regal Shanghai East Asia Hotel
800 Ling Ling Lu, Xu Hui District. Shanghai 200030. Tel 6426-6888, Fax 6426-588
E-mail: rseah.rsvn@regal-eastasia.com
上海富豪东亚酒店　零陵路800号
Part of the 80,000-seat Shanghai Stadium with some rooms affording a view to events; conveniently located near the subway and Xujiahui.

Shanghai Hilton International
250 Huashan Lu. Shanghai 200040. Tel 6248-0000, Fax 6248-3848
E-mail: shhilton@public.sta.net.cn
上海静安希尔顿酒店　华山路250号
Conveniently situated between the city's established commercial districts and the Hongqiao development zone.

Shanghai International Equatorial Hotel
65 Yanan Xi Lu. Shanghai 200040. Tel 6248-1688, Fax 6248-1773
E-mail: equatsha@public.sta.net.cn
上海贵都酒店　延安西路65号

Shanghai JC Mandarin
1225 Nanjing Xi Lu. Tel 6279-1888, Fax 6279-1822
E-mail: shjcm@public.sta.net.cn

上海锦沧文华大酒店 南京西路1225号
A fine-looking hotel, well located on Nanjing Xi Lu, opposite the Shanghai Centre.

Shanghai Worldfield Convention Hotel
2106 Hongqiao Lu. Tel 6270-3388, Fax 6270-4554
E-mail: conventh@public.sta.net.cn
上海世博会议大酒店 虹桥路2106号
Conveniently located near Hongqiao Airport.

The Westin Tai Ping Yang
5 Zunyi Nan Lu. Shanghai 200036. Tel 6275-8888, Fax 6275 5120
E-mail: sales@westin-shanghai.com
上海威斯汀太平洋大饭店 遵义南路5号
An attractive hotel in the Hongqiao development zone. Situated 15 minutes from downtown.

Yangtze New World Hotel
2099 Yanan Xi Lu. Shanghai 200335. Tel 6275-0000, Fax 6275-0750
E-mail: yangtze@prodigychina.com
上海杨子江大酒店 延安西路2099号

■ SHANGHAI CUISINE

Shanghai cuisine is a variation of the Yangzhou style, which emphasizes presentation, fragrance and freshness. Full use is made of the products from this 'Land of Fish and Rice', such as prawns, crab, shad, mullet, duck, game, lotus seeds and roots. Yangzhou cooking does not use much heavy seasoning, apart from soya sauce and sugar. Famous Shanghai dishes include 'drunken' chicken, 'lion's head' (pork meatballs with cabbage), smoked fish, mock goose, braised eel and shrimps fried with egg white.

As one might expect from such a city, almost every style of Chinese regional cuisine is available as well as a variety of European food. Shanghai freshwater crabs—in season from October to December—are so popular that they are flown to Chinese and Japanese gourmets overseas. In the old city bazaar (near the Yu Garden), all kinds of local snacks may be tried: sesame cakes, egg rolls, glutinous rice in lotus leaves, noodles, deep-fried dough sticks (*youtiao*), steamed bread and dumplings.

■ SHOPPING IN SHANGHAI

The Shanghai area is famous for many arts and crafts—papercutting, jade carving, Jiading straw weaving, ivory carving, lacquerware, and needlepoint (introduced at the turn of this century by Western missionaries). The tradition of Gu silk embroidery is over 300 years old. It began with a local official, Gu Mingshi, who was fond of giving silk embroideries, made by his concubines, as presents.

■ ANTIQUES, ARTS AND CRAFTS
Chuangxin Old Wares Shop
1297 Huaihai Lu
创新古玩店　淮海路 1297 号

Guohua Porcelain Shop
550 Nanjing Dong Lu
国华瓷器商店　南京东路550号

Shanghai Antique and Curio Store
218 Guangdong Lu
上海文物商店　广东路218号

Shanghai Arts and Crafts Service Centre
190 Nanjing Xi Lu
上海工艺美术品服务部　南京西路190号

Shanghai Arts and Crafts Trade Centre, Shanghai Exhibition Centre
1000 Yan'an Zhong Lu
上海展览馆　延安中路1000号

Shanghai Changjiang Seal Carving Factory
722 Huaihai Zhong Lu
上海长江刻字厂　淮海中路722号

DEPARTMENT STORES
Friendship Store
33 Beijing Dong Lu
友谊商店　北京东路33号

Shanghai No 1 Department Store
830 Nanjing Dong Lu
上海第一百货公司　南京东路830号

Hualian Department Store
(previously the Shanghai No 10 Department Store) 635 Nanjing Dong Lu.
华联商厦　南京东路 635 号

THEATRES
Yi Fu Theater (Yi Fu Juyuan)
701 Fuzhou Lu. Tel 6351-4668
Traditional Peking Opera peformances nightly.

Shanghai Grand Theatre
300 Renmin Da Dao. Tel 6372-8701, 6372-8702, 6372-3833

Great World Entertainment Center (Da Shi Jie)
Xizang Nan Lu. Tel 6326-3760, 6374-6703
During the 1920s and 1930s this was a famous 'den'. Walk along its dusty corridors and look at some of the old photos on the walls you can still imagine how exciting it must have been then. Watch the daily performances of acrobatics on the outdoor stage in the courtyard and the Peking Opera on the indoor stage.

Wuhan (027)

■ **HOTELS IN WUHAN**
Holiday Inn Riverside
88 Ximachang Street, Hanyang. Tel 8471-6688
Website: http://www.china.basshotels.com
晴川饭店　汉阳洗马长街88号

Holiday Inn Tian An Wuhan (Wuhan tianan jiari jiudian)
868 Jiefang Dadao Avenue, Hankou. Tel 8586-7888
Website: http://www.china.basshotels.com
武汉天安假日酒店　汉口解放大道868号

Jianghan Hotel (Jianghan binguan)
245 Shengli Road, Hankou. Tel 8281-1600, Fax 8281-4342
江汉饭店　汉口胜利路245号
Built by the French in 1914 and originally known as the "Denim Hotel". One of the best examples of colonial architecture in Wuhan.

Shangri-la Hotel
700 Jianshen Dadao Avenue, Hankou. Tel 8580-6868, Fax 577-6868
香格里拉大酒店　汉口建设大道700号

Wuhan Asia Hotel (Yazhou dajiudian)
616 Wuhan Dadao Avenue, Hankou. Tel 8380-7777
武汉亚洲大酒店　汉口武汉大道616号
Revolving Western restaurant, Chinese restaurant, and nightclub.

Xuangong Hotel (Xuangong fandian)
57 Jianghan Yi Road, Hankou. Tel 8281-0365, Fax 8577-7825
Website: http://www.xunlinenhotel.phtml
璇宫饭店　汉口江汉一路57号
Treaty port-era European-style building dating from the 1920s.

Wuhu (0553)

■ HOTELS IN WUHU

Ying Ke Song Da Jiudian
2 Zhan Guangchang. Tel 311-7788, Fax 385-1799

Tie Shan Binguan
3 Gen Xin Lu. Tel 334-736

Yichang (0717)

■ HOTELS IN YICHANG

Peach Blossom Hotel (Tao Hua Ling Binguan)
29 Yunji Lu. Tel 643-6666, Fax 623-8888
桃花岭饭店　云集路29号
Luxury hotel in the city centre, with an expensive wing and cheaper old wing.
Near its intersection with Long Kang Lu.

Yichang International Hotel (Yichang Guo Ji Da Jiudian)
127 Yanjiang Dadao. Tel 622-2888, Fax 622-8186
宜昌国际大酒店　沿江大道127号
Luxury hotel with a revolving restaurant. Right on the waterfront.

Zhenjiang (0511)

■ HOTELS IN ZHENJIANG

Royal Hotel (Da Huang Jia)
35 Bo Xian Lu. Tel 527-1438
Dating from treaty port days, this old European-style hotel was where Jiang Jie Shi
stayed when he was in town.

Zhenjiang Binguan
92 Zhongshan Xi Lu. Tel 523-3888, Fax 523-1055
镇江宾馆　中山西路92号

Zhenjiang International Hotel (Guoji Fandian)
218 Jiefang Lu. Tel 502-1888, Fax 502-1777
镇江国际饭店　解放路218号
An upscale hotel in town.

A CHRONOLOGY OF PERIODS IN CHINESE HISTORY

Neolithic	7000–2200 BC
Ha	2200–1800 BC
Shang	1766–1122 BC
Western Zhou	1122–771 BC
Eastern Zhou	771–256 BC
Spring and Autumn Annals	722–481 BC
Warring States	480–221 BC
Qin	221–206 BC
Western (Former) Han	206 BC–AD 8
Xin	9–24
Eastern (Later) Han	25–220
Three Kingdoms	220–265
Western Jin	265–317
Eastern Jin	317–420
Northern and Southern Dynasties	386–589
Sixteen Kingdoms	317–439
Former Zhao	304–329
Former Qin	351–383
Later Qin	384–417
Northern Wei	386–534
Western Wei	535–556
Northern Zhou	557–581
Sui	581–618
Tang	618–907
Five Dynasties	907–960
Liao	916–1125
Northern Song	960–1127
Southern Song	1127–1279
Jin (Jurchen)	1115–1234
Yuan (Mongol)	1279–1368
Ming	1368–1644
Qing (Manchu)	1644–1911
Republic of China	1911–1949
People's Republic of China	1949–

A Guide to Pronouncing Chinese Names

The official system of romanization used in China, which the visitor will find on maps, road signs and city shopfronts, is known as *pinyin*. It is now almost universally adopted by the western media.

Some visitors may initially encounter some difficulty in pronouncing romanized Chinese words. In fact many of the sounds correspond to the usual pronunciation of the letters in English. The exceptions are:

Initials

c   is like the *ts* in 'i*ts*'

q   is like the *ch* in '*ch*eese'

x   has no English equivalent, and can best be described as a hissing consonant that lies somewhere between *sh* and *s*. The sound was rendered as *hs* under an earlier transcription system.

z   is like the *ds* in 'fa*ds*'

zh is unaspirated, and sounds like the *j* in 'jug'

a   sounds like '*ah*'

e   is pronounced as the *o* in 'm*o*ther'

i   is pronounced as in 'ski' (written as *yi* when not preceded by an initial consonant). However, in *ci, chi, ri, shi, zi* and *zhi*, the sound represented by the *i* final is quite different and is similar to the *ir* in 'si*r*', but without much stressing of the *r* sound.

o   sounds like the *aw* in 'l*aw*'

u   sounds like the *oo* in '*oo*ze'

ü   is pronounced as the German *ü* (written as *yu* when not preceded by an initial consonant). The last two finals are usually written simply as *e* and *u*.

Finals in Combination

When two or more finals are combined, such as in *hao, jiao* and *liu*, each letter retain its sound value as indicated in the list above, but note the following:

ai   is like the *ie* in 'tie'

ei   is like the *ay* in 'bay'

ian is like the *ien* in 'Vienna'
ie   similar to *ye* in '*yet*'
ou   is like the *o* in '*code*'
uai sounds like '*why*'
uan is like the *uan* in '*iguana*' (except when preceded by *j, q, x* and *y*; in these cases a *u* following any of these four consonants is in fact *ü* and *uan* is similar to *uen*).
ue   is like the *ue* in '*duet*'
ui   sounds like '*way*'

Examples
A few Chinese names are shown below with English phonetic spelling beside them:

Beijing	Bay-jing (*jing* sounds like *ging* in '*paging*')
Cixi	Tsi-shee
Guilin	Gway-lin
Hangzhou	Hahng-jo
Kangxi	Kahng-shee
Qianlong	Chien-loong
Tiantai	Tien-tie
Xi'an	Shee-ahn

An apostrophe is used to separate syllables in certain compound-character words to preclude confusion. For example, *Changan* (which can be *chang-an* or *chan-gan*) is sometimes written as *Chang'an*.

Tones
A Chinese syllable consists of not only an initial and a final or finals, but also a tone or pitch of the voice when the words are spoken. In *pinyin* the four basic tones are marked ‾ ´ ˇ ` . These marks are almost never shown in printed form except in language-learning texts.

Recommended Reading

General Background
Levathes, Louise, *When China Ruled the Seas....1405–1433*
(New York: Oxford University Press, 1996)
Spence, Jonathan D, *God's Chinese Son*
(W W Norton and Company, New York and London, 1996)
Van Slyke, Lyman P, *Yangtse: Nature, History and the River*
(Addison-Wesley Publishing Company Inc., Reading, Massachusetts, 1988)

Travel and Exploration Along the Yangzi
Bell, Dick, *To the Source of the Yangtse*
(Hodder & Stoughton, London 1991)
Earl, Lawrence, *Yangtse Incident: the Story of HMS Amethyst*
(New York, Knopf, 1951)
Elder Chris ed., *China's Treaty Ports*, Hong Kong
(Oxford University Press, 1999)
Gill, William, *The River of Golden Sand: The Narrative of a Journey through China
and Eastern Tibet to Burmah* (John Murray, London 1880,
Gregg International Publishers Ltd. Farnborough Hants, U.K., 1969)
Hessler, Peter, *River Town: Two Years on the Yangtze* (Harper Collins, 2001)
Little, Archibald, *Through the Yangtse Gorges*
(Sampson, Low, Marston & Co., London 1898, Ch'eng Wen Publishing
Co., Taipei, 1972)
Palmer, Martin, *Travel Through Sacred China: Guide to the Soul and Spiritual
Heritage of China* (Royal House, 1996)
Percival, William, *The Land of the Dragon: My Boating and Shooting Excursions
to the Gorges of the Upper Yangtse* (Hurst & Blackett Ltd., 1889)
McKenna, Richard, *The Sand Pebbles*, Annapolis (Naval Institute Press, 2000)
Meister, Cari, *The Yangtze* (Edina: Abdo, 2000)
Murphy, Rhoades, *Treaty Ports and China's Modernization*
(Ann Arbor: University of Michigan, 1970)
Farndale, Nigel, *Last Action Hero of the British Empire*
Cdr John Kerans 1915–1985 (Short Books, 2001)
Perry, Hamilton Darby, *The Panay Incident: Prelude to Pearl Harbor*
(New York, Macmillan, 1969)
Phillips, C.E. Lucas, *Escape of the Amethyst* (New York, Coward-McCann, 1958)

Pollard, Michael, *The Yangtze* (New York, Benchmark, 1998)

St. John, Jeffrey, *Voices from the Yangtze: Recollections of America's Maritime Frontier in China*, Napa (Western Maritime Press, 1993)

Stone, Albert H., & Reed, J. Hammond, editors
Historic Lushan, The Kuling Mountains
(Hankow, Arthington Press/Religious Tract Society, 1921)

Theroux, Paul, *Sailing Through China* (Houghton Mifflin Co., Boston, Massachusetts, 1984)

Wong, How Man, *Exploring the Yangtse, China's Longest River*
(Odyssey Productions Ltd., Hong Kong, 1989)

Winchester, Simon, *The River at the Centre of the World: A Journey Up the Yangtze and Back in Chinese Time* (Viking, London, 1997)

LITERATURE, AUTOBIOGRAPHY

Cooper, Arthur. Selected and translated with an introduction and notes *by Li Po and Tu Fu* (Penguin Books, Harmondsworth, 1973)

Espey, John J., *Tales Out of School*
More Delightful, Humorous Stories of a Boyhood in China
(New York: Knopf., 1947)

Han, Suyin, *Destination Chungking*
(Jonathan Cape, London 1942; Panther Books, London, 1973)

Hersey, John, *A Single Pebble* (Alfred A Knopf Inc., New York 1956;
Vintage Books Edition, Random House Inc., New York, 1989)

Luo, Guangzhong, *Romance of the Three Kingdoms*
(Charles E Tuttle Co. Inc., Tokyo 1973)
The classic 14th-century novel about the three warring states along
the Yangzi. In *Excerpts from Three Classical Novels* (Panda Books,
Beijing 1981)
there is an excerpt from the novel, entitled *The Battle of the Red Cliff*,
that vividly describes this event at a site just above Wuhan.

Lynn, Madeleine, *Yangzi River: The Wildest, Wickedest River on Earth*
(Oxford University Press, Hong Kong, 1997)
An anthology selection spanning 13 centuries, offers a literary history of
China's longest river, including classical poetry and Victorian memoirs.

Waley, Arthur, *The Poetry and Career of Li Po* (George Allen & Unwin, 1989)

Wu, Ching-tzu, *The Scholars* (Foreign Languages Press, Beijing, 1973)
Translated by Yang Hsien-yi and Gladys Yang

Xu, Xuanzhong, *100 Tang and Song Ci Poems*
(Commercial Press, Hong Kong, 1986)

TRAVEL AND EXPLORATION — SHANGHAI

Baker, Barbara ed., *Shanghai: Electric and Lurid City*
(Hong Kong, Oxford University Press, 1998, Anthology)
Johnston, Tess and Erh, Deke,
Frenchtown Shanghai: Western Architecture in Shanghai's Old French Concession (Shanghai, Old China Hand Press, 2000)
Lou, Rongmin ed., *The Bund: History and Vicissitudes*
(Shanghai, Shanghai Pictorial Publishing House, 1998)
Sergeant, Harriet, *Shanghai* (London, John Murray, 1991)
Wasserstein, Bernard, *Secret War in Shanghai*
(London, Profile Books, 1998)
Yatsko, Pamela, *New Shanghai: The Rocky Rebirth of China's Legendary City*
(New York, John Wiley & Sons, 2001)

TRAVEL AND EXPLORATION — NANJING

Administration Bureau of Dr. Sun Yat-sen's Mausoleum
The National Park of Dr. Sun Yat-sen
(Hong Kong, H.K. International Publishing House, 1998)
Bergere, Marie-Claire, *Sun Yat-sen* (Stanford, Stanford University Press, 1998)
Eastman, Lloyd E., et al, *The Nationalist Era in China, 1927–1949*
(New York, Cambridge University Press, 1991)
Epstein, Israel, *Woman in World History: Soong Ching Ling (Madame Sun Yat-sen)*
(Beijing, New World Press, 1995, Second Edition)
Hobart, Alice Tisdale, *Within the Walls of Nanking*
(New York, MacMillan Co., 1927)
Schiffrin, Harold Z., *Sun Yat-sen: Reluctant Revolutionary*
(Boston, Little, Brown, 1980)
Till, Barry and Swart, Paula, *In Search of Old Nanking*
(Hong Kong, H.K.S.H. Joint Publishing Company, 1982)
Wills, John E., *Mountain of Fame: Portraits in Chinese History*
(Princeton, Princeton University Press, 1994)
Wu, Wo-yao, *Vignettes from the Late Chi'ing: Bizarre Happenings Eyewitnessed Over Two Decades* (Hong Kong, Chinese University of Hong Kong, 1975)
Xu,Silin, *Yue Fei: Glory and Tragedy of China's Greatest War Hero*
(Singapore, Asiapac, 1995)

Index of Places

211

Practical information, such as telephone numbers and opening hours, is notoriously subject to change. We welcome corrections and suggestions from guidebook users; please write to:

Airphoto International Ltd.,
903 Seaview Commercial Building
21 Connaugh Road West
Sheung Wan, Hong Kong
Tel: (852) 2856 3896
Fax: (852) 2565 8004
E-mail: odyssey@asiaonline.net

Recommended Websites:
http://www.chinanow.com
http://www.han-yuan.com
http://www.sh-artmuseum.org.cn
http://www.culture.sh.cn
http://www.ismay.com